I0748516

MEMOIR

OF

WILLIAM DAVID STUART.

WITH COPIOUS EXTRACTS FROM HIS

DIARY AND LETTERS.

TOGETHER WITH

AN APPENDIX.

PHILADELPHIA:
PRINTED FOR PRIVATE CIRCULATION.

1865.

TO

THE BEREAVED ONE

WHO, WHILE BEARING HER GREAT SORROW WITH FORTITUDE,

IS FAITHFULLY DISCHARGING HER DUTIES AS

A CHRISTIAN,

This Volume

IS LOVINGLY DEDICATED.

TO THE READER.

N the preparation of this volume, my object has been, not so much to write a Memoir, as to make such a selection from William's papers as would clearly illustrate his life and character. I regret that the work has not fallen into abler hands; but it was the wish of the friends immediately interested that it should be prepared by some one intimately associated with the deceased, and I have yielded my wishes to theirs.

His Diary—from which copious extracts are given—was kept sacredly between God and his own soul; while on the portions of his Letters to M. now printed other eyes than hers were never expected to look; and neither would have been surrendered for publication had not their possessor believed that good would be accomplished by their perusal.

As the entire work of writing and editing has been performed since March last, in hours snatched from other employments, there will be found, almost necessarily, many defects; but I confidently rely on the indulgence of William's kindred and friends, for whom alone I have undertaken the unaccustomed avocation of authorship. If any who may peruse the volume shall be stimulated to a similar life of holiness and Christian activity, I shall feel abundantly rewarded for my labour of love.

J. M'M.

PHILADELPHIA, *July* 1864.

APPENDIX.

MEMOIR

OF

WILLIAM DAVID STUART.

MEMOIR.

WILLIAM DAVID STUART, son of George H. and Martha K. Stuart, was born on Monday, August 10, 1840, in the city of Philadelphia. On the day of his birth, the sad intelligence reached Mr. Stuart of the death of his much loved brother William. In memory of this brother, and of his deceased but honoured father, their first-born son was named WILLIAM DAVID. At the time of his birth, and for a few weeks after, there was much doubt whether his life or his mother's would be spared; which fact caused the mother to feel a peculiar tenderness for her child. This love was abundantly reciprocated in William's subsequent life.

When he had reached his third year, scarlet fever entered the household, and the eldest child, a little girl of five years, and an infant son, were laid in the grave within one week of each other. The stricken hearts of the parents clung yet closer to the little one that remained—for some time the only child—whose prattle broke the silence of the house where death had been. There was one other who had taken, on account of Mrs.

Stuart's feeble health, the principal charge of the little girl, and who mourned the loss of the dear children; and when little Fanny and the infant George were hidden from her sight, her affections centred on the remaining child—her very soul seemed knit to him, and she claimed him as her own. Mrs. Stuart rejoiced that she could brighten her mother's declining years by giving her son to be the special object of her care, and make her feel that there was still a precious child depending upon her. The love which sprang up between the pious grandmother and the boy was as rare as it was beautiful. By day and by night, in sickness and in health, she watched over him. For years they met every morning at an early hour, when she instructed him in the Word of God, and led him to the throne of grace. And well has this noble Christian woman been repaid for her faithful affection. Her desires were ever regarded; to her he went with his joys and sorrows; her chamber was usually the first sought when he entered his home; and even after he attained the years of manhood he might often be found seated on a stool by her side, as in his childish days. With the keenest anxiety he watched her health, and on seeing a slight change in her appearance, notes it in his journal: "Nanna*—oh, it pains me to say it—is not as I would wish to see her. She is looking very unwell, and it makes my heart bleed at the very thought of parting with her; and that, I was going to say, for ever; but no, blessed be God, 'the good shall meet above.'" Several times he feared he would be called upon to follow her to the tomb, and always spoke of it with dread.

* A name given by William to his grandmother Denison, when learning to talk, and by which she is known in the family to this day.

Little did he think that she would sit beside him in his last hours in perfect health, though advanced in life, having all her hopes in heaven, and longing to depart; while he, just in the dawn of manhood, with *everything* to render life desirable, was praying that if it were God's will his life might be spared. Truly, mysterious are the ways of the Almighty!

He grew into boyhood. At this period of his life his lovely disposition and personal beauty seem to have made a deep impression upon those who saw him. Impulsive and ardent in temperament, whatever he undertook, whether study, work, or play, was prosecuted with zeal and perseverance. He grew up to manhood retaining these characteristics, mentally and physically, a noble specimen of a young man. He possessed a fine figure; was over six feet in height, and was remarked by all for his manliness of bearing.

At a very early age he entered the infant class in the Sabbath School of the First Reformed Presbyterian Church. Passing rapidly up through the various gradations, he entered the Bible class as a pupil; and when less than fifteen years of age he became a teacher in the same school. On December 5, 1856, when a little over sixteen years of age, he was admitted a member of the Church on profession of his faith.

In childhood he had a severe attack of scarlet fever, which impaired his hearing to some degree ever after, the tympanum of one ear having been destroyed. At times, when entirely free from cold, this was scarcely noticeable, but often proved a serious inconvenience, and deprived him of much enjoyment. Twice during this period of his life he was taken to Europe, and placed under the treatment of a celebrated London aurist, who, however, gave him only temporary relief. The scenes and events of these visits made so deep an impression on him, that years afterwards, on going again to Europe, he recognized places, and inquired for people of whom he had since heard nothing, and would even refer to conversations remembered from that early period.

His powers of observation were remarkable, and enabled him, without being conscious of having paid any special attention, to take in everything before him at a glance; and much amusement did this faculty sometimes afford his friends. Often when something had been sportively said in his presence in an under-tone, which he was not supposed to hear, he would by a smile, or laughter, show that he had comprehended the whole, literally without catching a word. No doubt the defect in his hearing led him to observe manners and motions closely, and this atoned not a little for the loss of sounds.

In youth, as in manhood, he was a general favourite. While fond of boyish sports and games, in some of which he excelled, he did not neglect his studies; and in those branches in which he took a special interest he was always among the foremost of his class. His early education was directed by J. W. Faires, D.D., who has kindly furnished for this volume the following letter, indicating his character during his school-boy days:—

"J. M'M——. "PHILADELPHIA, *July* 18, 1864.

"DEAR SIR,—It might be supposed that having had charge of the education of William D. Stuart during so many years, I should be able to record many incidents illustrative of his character. But unfortunately this is not in my power. The daily routine of the school-room is seldom diversified by any occurrence sufficiently extraordinary to make a lasting impression upon the mind of the teacher. What follows is, therefore, only a very imperfect sketch of his general character.

"William D. Stuart was a boy of great liveliness of temperament, to whom it was impossible to continue quiet any long time. He was filled to overflowing with the spirit of fun. His sense of the ludicrous was keen. His transitions from one emotion to another were frequent and rapid, joy and laughter quickly succeeding sorrow and tears. He was kind-hearted, social, generous, and obliging, quick to resent, and equally quick to forgive an injury.

"His talents were of a superior order. His perceptive powers were quick. He acquired with great rapidity whatever he attempted to study. He had a memory both retentive and ready, and was gifted with uncommon fluency. It gave him no trouble to express his thoughts either by speech or writing. He had little taste for mathematics, but excelled in classics. His appreciation of the classic authors, the elegance of his translations, and the naturalness and correctness of his original compositions, indicated that he was well qualified to attain to excellence in literature. His morals were pure, and, no doubt, the religious character which he sustained before he left college was in process of formation while he was at school. I often thought what a bright Christian he would make, if his heart should be brought under the influence of divine grace. He was honourable, truthful, obedient, submissive to discipline, and affectionate toward his companions and instructors: while too many boys are disposed to treat their teachers as their natural enemies, he appeared while at school, and ever afterwards, to regard his teachers as his friends. It is hardly necessary to add, that his amiable qualities endeared him to myself, and that holding him in high esteem, viewing with deep interest the unfolding of his beautiful character, and entertaining high hopes of the usefulness and brilliance of his future career, I deplored most sincerely the early death which snatched him from the world.

"William D. Stuart entered my school August 30, 1847, when he was between seven and eight years of age, and continued under my care until he entered the University of Pennsylvania, June 28, 1855. —I remain yours very respectfully,

"J. W. FAIRES."

He was assisted in his preparation for college by Dr. Labberton, and after going regularly through the prescribed University curriculum, graduated creditably in the University of Pennsylvania, July 1, 1859.

In Dr. Labberton, to whom he became warmly attached, he enjoyed the instructions of a gentleman of remarkable gifts and accomplishments. Earnest and enthusiastic himself, he soon kindled in the mind of his pupil an eager love of knowledge, and stimulated him to exertion. William's proficiency in History and his love for the Microscope were greatly, if not entirely, owing to Dr. Labberton's instructions.

Though he was a hard student, with a genuine love for learning, yet in his college studies he cannot be said to have been wholly methodical and regular, being inclined sometimes to pursue, to the detriment of certain branches, others that especially interested him. Of these he would take up one at a time, reading all that he could find upon it, and then turn to something else. He was, too, very fond of general reading, and making experiments of various kinds, and would frequently amuse himself in this way until nine or ten o'clock in the evening, when he would take up his college studies, and work night after night until one, two, and even three in the morning. This impaired his health, and so injured his eyes that it was difficult for him to complete his last year at the University. Immediately after graduating, he took a trip to Minnesota for a little relaxation.

In all the natural sciences he took great delight. These seemed more accordant with the natural bent of his mind, and besides, had for him special attraction, as leading to the Creator. In astronomy, chemistry, botany, mineralogy, and particularly in entomology, he had made large attainments. Often has the writer, when strolling with him in the country, been charmed and instructed with his lucid discourse upon the beauties of the common flowers of the garden, dissecting them the while; or catching a tiny insect, he would with great enthusiasm show, with his pocket microscope, its beauties and perfections as coming from the hand of God. This love of nature and natural objects increased with his years, and manifested itself in his travels by his preference for Scotland and Switzerland above other countries. He read much concerning them, the latter particularly. The works of the Alpine Club, and accounts of all the expeditions he could find, together with various treatises on the formation of glaciers, he read with great avidity, and became familiar with the paths and passes even of those he had not seen.

He had collected a large and valuable cabinet of minerals, and a small but choice collection of coins. He had also a microscope, one of the best ever imported into this country, with a large number of exquisite preparations, collected chiefly in Europe. In the use of this instrument he would spend days together in prosecuting his favourite study of entomology. He prepared several lectures on "The Microscope and its Revelations," with other scientific subjects, which he delivered from time to time for the benefit of Sabbath schools and kindred objects. In a literary as well as scientific point of view, these lectures on the microscope are perhaps superior to anything he has written. Of the lectures, essays, tracts and speeches which he has left among his papers, Christianity and the God of nature form the substratum. As a specimen, we subjoin an extract from the introduction to one of his lectures on the microscope:—

"Do not despise small things, and turn jeeringly away, because, perhaps, a drop of muddy water may be our study.

"The perfection of this instrument is but recent, and we are yet, with all the grand discoveries, but in the outer court of this temple of nature, inhabited by Divinity himself. Forty years ago the microscope was a mere toy, and no one ever dreamed that it could be improved. Though for two centuries it had been in the hands of the most gifted students of nature, their progress had been but slow and unsatisfactory; while over the inner gate of the temple there seemed to be written, in undying and unchangeable characters, 'Hitherto shalt thou come, and no further.' But after a lapse of years, how changed the scene! Now we can behold the wisdom and goodness of the Creator displayed in the smallest objects of his workmanship. Here we are confronted with overwhelming evidence of the being and perfection of Him who is the omnipotent, omniscient, and omnipresent God, none of whose creatures are beneath his care. It has well been said by the infidel Rousseau, 'If the Author of nature is great in great things, he is *exceeding* great in small ones.'

"This world is a world of life—in the air we breathe, in the water we drink, in the ground on which we tread. Life is hurried on by the whirlwind, or borne on the wings of the summer breeze. It is in the blushing rose, or hid beneath the poison vine, lurking in the damp, dark shade of the wood. We see it in the mountain rivulet, the emblem of purity and joy, as it dances gaily along; and we find it in the stagnant pool, from whose turbid waters disease insidiously spreads. It is found on the banks of the noble river, and far down in ocean's dark and silent bed. Eternal snows and burning sun alike affect it not. All the forces of nature conspire to produce it. Every pore is bursting into life; every *death* is only a *new birth*—every grave a cradle. And of all this universal, all-pervading life we know but little, and think less. Why should we thus disregard this invisible creation? The same life that animates us animates them; we all come from the hand of the same Creator, and all are parts of one transcendent whole! Think of this, and I am sure you will look at nature with more interest and love, remembering, as we must, that they, as well as we, are links in that living chain whose beginning is God, whose end is the lowest of his creation."

While pursuing his college studies he was systematic, at home and abroad, in reading and studying the Scriptures, as well as other religious books, especially those on practical religion. His home training had indoctrinated him in the faith of Presbyterianism; and from his revered pastor, Dr. T. W. J. Wylie, a profound theologian, he had acquired a vast fund of sound biblical and doctrinal knowledge. During this period of college life he united with the Church, founded his mission school, and in many ways laboured earnestly in the cause of his Divine Master. Yet his Diary and Letters frequently exhibit him as mourning the hiding of God's countenance. When, however, the cloud lifted from between his Saviour's face and his own soul the rapture he experienced was beyond description.

Robert Hall says, that "The light and insinuations of the Divine Spirit so often accompany the conduct of a strictly religious education, that some of the most eminent Christians have acknowledged themselves at a loss to assign the precise era of their conversion." So it seems to have been with the subject of our Memoir. His early consecration to his Master's service may, without doubt, be traced to his surroundings and training. Made to feel from infancy, by the power of example, that religion is the chief concern of life—seeing always zeal and energetic action where Divine things were concerned, and enjoying companionship with godly men visiting almost constantly at his father's house;—under these influences, even as a boy, and prior to his connection with the Church, he "went about doing good" among his fellows.

He was eminently prayerful, and spent much time in the privacy of his chamber, pleading with God for himself and those he loved. Nor were his prayers confined to stated seasons or the quiet of his closet, but at all times, whether taking a solitary walk or in company surrounded by the gay and thoughtless, we have evidence that his spirit held frequent communion with the heavenly world.

While his joyous laugh, his fund of anecdote, his keen relish for wit and pleasantry, his readiness to participate in sport, his acute perception of the ridiculous, combined with excellent imitative powers, made him a most cheerful companion, there was a seriousness, a spirituality, the depth of which only one heart *fully* understood. All who knew him were impressed with the clearness of his views of truth, and the robustness of religious character so beautifully developed in one so young; all could testify to his goodness, his earnestness in the cause of his Master; and all felt that he had consecrated himself *wholly* to God. Yet there was an inner life, an almost constant soaring of the soul heavenward, a yearning for the fulness of Christ's spirit, which was totally unsuspected by those around him.

For the Sabbath his reverence, always profound, increased as his character developed. He once wrote to a friend,—

"I have often thought that if they who seek to do away with the Sabbath could enjoy it but once as I do, they would count it one of their choicest and dearest blessings."

Just one year after making a profession of religion, his preparations were completed for the realization of his darling plan—a mission school for the neglected and degraded coloured population of the city; and on Sabbath, December 6, 1857, with solemn religious services, it was formally opened for the reception of pupils. The first entry in his minute-book, made by this lad of but seventeen years, was in these words:—

"This morning, in the midst of a pouring rain, we opened our coloured mission school, with twenty children; which was highly gratifying. *May God bless and prosper us.*"

The school was in connection with the church of which he was a member, and still remains so. William had only two male teachers with him, pledged to the work, at the organization; but the subsequent history of the enterprise shows that God did abundantly bless and prosper his labours. He was its faithful and devoted superintendent until death took him from all his earthly cares.

In connection with the school a prayer-meeting was also established for adults, to be held on Sabbath and Wednesday evenings. On the first evening about forty persons were present; and on almost every occasion afterwards the attendance was limited only by the capacity of the apartment. The school was commenced in a little room near the corner of Thirteenth and Carpenter Streets, which soon proved too small, and it was then held in a larger one, over a tavern in the neighbourhood. This again becoming too strait, it was finally removed to the basement of a church in St. Mary's Street, between Sixth and Seventh, on the ground formerly occupied by the church in which the Rev. Samuel B. Wylie, D.D., first preached in Philadelphia.

In addition to superintending the school twice on the Sabbath and conducting his Sabbath and Wednesday evening prayer-meetings, he usually devoted two afternoons in the week to visiting the wretched inhabitants of the neighbourhood, to relieve their wants, to pray with the sick and dying, and to gather the children into the school. Sometimes one of his young Christian friends accompanied him, but in most cases he visited alone. In his record—for he kept a pocket-diary in which he noted nearly everything connected with this mission—there is an amazing amount of true Christian heroism displayed in overcoming the difficulties and removing the obstacles which constantly beset him, arising for the most part from the vice, the ignorance, and the squalid poverty of the population he wished to benefit. Amid all this misery and degradation, however, he was made happy by the consciousness of being assisted by Divine power in the discharge of duty. In thus feeding the hungry, clothing the naked, and ministering to their spiritual necessities, William became universally known and respected among the people, so that no insult or indignity was ever offered him by any of the desperadoes who inhabit a portion of this scene of his labours: not only so, when distress or disease came upon them, or death threatened, he was frequently sent for; and night or day, rain or sunshine, cheerfully responded. It is not improbable that the exposure to which he was thus subjected may have contributed not a little to hasten his death.

An extract or two from his Diary will illustrate the nature of his work. He was sent for to visit D—— P——, long a godless man, but now anxious about his soul—ill, perhaps on a dying bed, with a family around him. After a series of visits, the sick man is made to understand something of the nature of true repentance, and of the mercy of God in Christ Jesus in providing salvation for guilty sinners. William writes, April 8, 1860:—

"Visited P——. Found him in bed, and suffering much pain. Not so well as when I last saw him. Poor fellow, I fear he will not last long. He is suffering from the inhalation of the effluvia consequent on night work. He seems much happier, and is willing to die, if God sees fit to call him away, although he often exclaims, 'My poor family, what will become of them?' Read to him Christ's conversation with Nicodemus, and prayed. He was deeply interested, and when about to leave him he held my hand long and warmly. Gave him to think about the text, 'He that believeth on me shall not perish, but have everlasting life.' I trust, and confidently hope, that he has found Christ."

Again :—

"*April* 22.—As I feared, P——'s illness terminated fatally. He breathed his last on the morning of Tuesday, 17th, at half-past ten o'clock. All night long he was engaged in singing and prayer, even after the family had retired. His confidence in God remained firm and steadfast unto the end; and when he passed away from earth, it was but to enter heaven. This afternoon, at half-past five o'clock, I went to the house, and there being no clergyman present, took charge of the funeral services. We began by singing that beautiful hymn commencing, 'Why should we start and fear to die?' after which I read selected portions of Scripture, including those solemn and appropriate passages in Job iii., iv., xix.; Psalms xc. and ciii.; 1 Cor. xv.; and Rev. xxii. I then addressed those present at some length, endeavouring to point them beyond the grave, referring more particularly to the words, 'He, being dead, yet speaketh.' It was a solemn meeting, and all seemed deeply interested."

What but the grace of God could have moved to such severe and self-denying labours? He had no mean or selfish ends to subserve,—no earthly inducements to enter this trying and in some respects repulsive sphere of usefulness. Delicately nurtured, thoroughly educated, possessing fine conversational talents and an unusually attractive person, accustomed to all the amenities of cultivated and refined life, with a keen relish for the beautiful and the good, and with brilliant earthly prospects,—nothing but the constraining love of Jesus could have induced him to descend to these lowest places of the earth. But all these labours were only incidental to his great work of caring for the *young* of this degraded class, and gathering them into his school. On the perusal of his Diary and Letters, the reader will see how constantly this school was upon his heart, and how regularly he made it the subject of earnest prayer to God. When very sick, and prostrated by fatigue on his way to Santa Cruz, at an hour of the night when he should have been taking rest, he wrote a touching letter to his charge, which will be found in the Appendix, incorporated in Dr. Faires' Address to the Mission Schools.

After his return from Santa Cruz, while confined to his room, the following note—the last he ever penned—was written to the acting superintendent:—

"1313 SPRUCE STREET,
"*Saturday evening, March 21, 1863.*

"DEAR FRIEND W.—To-morrow afternoon the school will be visited by my father in company with a very particular friend of mine from Edinburgh—Mr. Thomas Nelson. I would like you to ask the teachers to visit a little, so as to ensure full classes and punctual attendance.

"Give my love to all the school: tell them they are ever in my thoughts by day, and through the waking hours of the night. My health is still very poor—my cough very painful at times; still I think I am improving. Should Mr. Nelson wish to visit any of the homes of the children, you might show him a few of the dens in Green's Court.

"This will greatly oblige yours truly,

"WILLIAM D. STUART."

In the religious life of his friends nothing seemed to escape him. If they were in a state of carelessness, he gently warned them, always praying for them. If awakened to their danger, he kindly showed them, and with remarkable clearness, the way of life. If they were rejoicing in a newly found Saviour, he rejoiced with them, thanking God that another soul had found its way through the labyrinths of sin to its Redeemer.

The following letter was addressed to a young lady of Philadelphia, one of his early friends:—

"1313 SPRUCE STREET,
"*Wednesday night, March* —, 1859.

"MY DEAR FRIEND C.—It was with feelings of no ordinary pleasure that I learned of your intention to devote yourself to God—giving yourself away to him in a solemn covenant engagement. My intention was to have spoken with you on the subject, but I have been prevented, and as I shall not probably see you until after the Sabbath, I will endeavour to express my thoughts in the form of a letter.

"The step which you are about to take is one of deep importance and solemnity. It is a step which, if properly taken, will decide your position and destiny, not for time only, but for eternity. Now is the time when Satan will attack your weakest points with his most subtile darts. His attacks will be desperate, and could you only look to yourself for succour, you might indeed be dismayed; but look above and hear your heavenly Father's voice saying, 'Fear not, for I am with thee.'

"You have done well in obeying your Saviour's summons to meet him at his table to commemorate his dying love: it is in remembrance of him; to testify to him that though absent from us in person, he is yet cherished in our minds. Who can ever forget such a Friend—one who laid down his life that we might be saved? Remember that in this solemn compact we bind our souls by a sacred bond; we surrender ourselves, soul and body, to be the Lord's for time and for eternity—striving ever to adorn our profession by a life and conversation becoming the gospel.

"But before we come to this ordinance we must first come to Christ himself. Alas! how many are there who, while they make a very near approach to God in their bodies, their souls are far from him, and who by their daily actions bring dishonour and shame upon the cross of Christ!

"Before partaking of this holy ordinance a strict self-examination is enjoined. 'Let a man examine himself,' said Paul to the Corinthians. Look into the deep recesses of your heart, and see what were the motives that prompted you to such a course. And you might with propriety ask me, 'What is the standard by which I shall examine myself?' The Word of God is the standard—just and true. Were we required to fulfil strictly all the requirements of that law, we might well shrink back; but the best coin is alloyed, and with us the great questions are, 'Is love to God and the interests of Christ's kingdom the predominant, prevailing interest in my soul? Do I love God, and hate sin with a perfect hatred? Is it the honest and sincere determination of my heart from this time henceforth to serve the Lord?' Examine yourself carefully, for conscience will not be deceived. This is no small matter. Upon it hangs the destiny of your immortal soul. The world may be deceived, but God cannot. The world calls many Christians of whom it shall be said, 'I never knew you.'

With what care and inquiry should we ask the question, 'Lord, is it I?' It is, then, necessary that our hearts and affections should be turned into a new channel. Is such your condition? Is Jesus to you 'the chief among ten thousand, and altogether lovely?' Does your heart burn within you as you think of his matchless love? And do you delight in the ordinances of his house? If so, then indeed it is well with you,—well for time, better for eternity.

"And now, C——, in reading over what I have told you as a few of the requisites to a proper performance of this solemn act, you might say, as I did, 'I can never come up to this standard of requirements, and therefore am not fit to approach the table of the Lord.' Not so. Of yourself you can do nothing, but in the strength of promised grace you can do all. Your heavenly Father met your necessity when he said, 'My grace is sufficient for thee.' And how is this grace to be obtained? By earnest, heartfelt prayer. Ah! there is the key that unlocks the treasure-house of Divine mercy. Who knows, who can estimate the power of prayer? The voice of Demosthenes opened the heart of the people of Athens; but the prayer of the humble believer opens the door of heaven, and brings down unnumbered mercies. He who is constant in prayer is like the tree whose roots are cooled by the running stream, and thus remain fresh and green while all around it has dried up and withered.

"If you would be a true follower of the meek and lowly Jesus, you must pray not only at stated times, but often. Prayer is the life-blood of the Christian: take it from him, and he dies. The reason why we of the present day have not the devotion and zeal, and do not receive the blessings that were bestowed upon those of former times, is simply because we do not pray as they did. Luther spent several hours daily in prayer. No wonder, then, that he possessed a faith unshaken by popish prelates or the fear of death.

"Spend, then, much of your time before going to the sanctuary in secret prayer, that God would show you the path of duty, and lead you in it. Make the Bible your daily study and guide-book. Let your soul be daily nourished with its precious truths. Let your thoughts dwell much on the things of eternity. Remember the solemnity of the step you are taking; and when at last you shall be seated at a communion table, and have received the emblems of a dying Saviour's love, then commit yourself to his keeping, trusting in him, and him only—feeling safe in him as a faithful Redeemer, who will present you in the great day pure and spotless before his Father's throne.

*   *   *   *   *

"May God's richest blessing descend upon you, guiding you now and ever in the path of duty. May you have grace given you to live a consistent Christian life, an honour to the Church, and a blessing to those with whom you are associated. May all earthly blessings be yours; and at last may you have a joyful entrance into those mansions of peace 'where the wicked cease from troubling and the weary are at rest.'

"That these may be yours is the prayer of yours truly,

"WM. D. STUART."

The large and well-selected library which he has left bears evidence of his good taste and judgment. In addition to a liberal supply of works on theology and science, the departments of history, poetry, Belles-lettres and the fine arts are fully and judiciously represented. He read rapidly, yet understandingly and with system, generally making notes as he progressed. He avoided, and indeed loathed, the pernicious "yellow-covered" literature of the day, but occasionally indulged in well-written works of fiction, by way of mental recreation. Possessing a discriminating mind and retentive memory, he was able to cull out all that was worth remembering; so that, in his intercourse with the world, he could avail himself of his rich stores of knowledge to adorn a conversation or fortify an argument. Naturally of a reserved and timid disposition, it was only where he felt himself well acquainted that his fine colloquial powers and well-stored mind were brought thoroughly into requisition.

As a writer, his style was free and dashing, often rising, when his feelings were interested, to eloquence and beauty. The journal written to his family while travelling in Europe abounds with such passages, and exhibits descriptive powers of a high order. With Scotland he was greatly pleased, and wrote enthusiastically of its rich and varied scenery. On bidding farewell to the island of Arran, and the warm friends who entertained him there, he thus apostrophizes :—

"Farewell Arran! with your lofty crags—your wild glens—your bleak, barren moors—your lovely valleys and heather-clad hills, among which I have wandered, and gathered many of nature's gems—your rocky shores and land-locked bays, which have yielded up to me many of ocean's hidden treasures; rich studies from whence lessons have been learned not soon to be forgotten. Farewell scenes of historic interest, haunts of the brave, where I have sat and been carried back to the days of Bruce, Scotland's guiding star! Farewell friends, who in no small degree have contributed to my enjoyment, and to whom I owe much of this pleasure! Farewell all!—and should my life be spared, many, many years after this, will I look back upon the days spent upon this island as a season of unmarred enjoyment."

Another extract, giving a description of a tiny shell-fish:—

"*August* 21, 1861.—About one o'clock went fishing with Mr. and Miss N——, but caught nothing. We then took to the dredge, and sailed up and down for about half an hour. The result of our haul was several star fish and goniasters, hermit crabs, ascidians, and, last of all, a lima—a creature for delicacy of form and beauty of colour unsurpassed in the treasures of the ocean. The fragile shell does not entirely cover this little mollusc; the most beautiful part, a delicate orange-coloured fringe, is entirely outside and unprotected; and were no means provided for its defence, it would be a most tempting morsel for some roving haddock or whiting. But the same wise and kind Creator who 'tempers the wind to the shorn lamb' has taught this little creature a wonderful art of self-preservation. It is not content with hiding itself amongst the loose coral, for it would soon be washed out by the storms: it becomes a marine mason, and builds for itself a nest—constructs a coral grotto; and proves that it is not only a mason, but a plasterer, a rope-spinner, and a weaver of most durable tapestry. In order that the little bits of coral composing its house may be firmly knit together, cordage is needed; and this cordage the lima spins. But how? We know not as yet. It has no spinnerets like the spider. The skill of the physiologist has as yet been unable to detect any organ set apart for this purpose. Yet the fact is the same; and it twines and intertwines its little ropes, with which it binds firmly together the walls of its habitation, and bids defiance to wind and wave and plunderer. When first you see this little house, you are inclined to throw it away as a mass of half-decayed sea-weed and blackened coral. But stop! look how wisely this is constructed. Externally it is hard enough, and thus better fitted to resist attack and keep secure its frail inhabitant. But look within, and see how it is lined with a curtain soft as silk. See how it has woven the little cords into a tapestry which protects its frail tentacles from being injured by the roughness of the outer walls! Removing the little creature from its nest, and putting it in a jar of sea water, what a beautiful object it is! Its mode of swimming is the same as that of the clam;—it suddenly opens the valves of the shell, and then as suddenly shuts them, and the water being forced out, impels the animal with great rapidity, and thus it swims by a succession of leaps. It is very delicate, and with the greatest care rarely lives in the aquarium longer than a fortnight. How prone we are to admire the creature and forget the Creator!—how apt to admire the dexterity and skill of these lower creatures, to wonder at them, without adoring Him who gave them these powers, and taught them to perform instinctively these things, which so loudly call forth our praise!"

Mr. Stuart's frequent absences from home, and his often recurring attacks of asthma, led William to feel a more than usual interest in all that concerned his mother, and to strive to relieve her from care as far as was in his power. He had the highest respect for her home management and discipline. His love for her was deep and quiet, manifesting itself in his uniformly affectionate manner of speaking of her; his unremitting attention to her when suffering from illness; and the pleasure with which he recalled scenes of his childish days in which she had borne a part—the songs she had then sung to him—and especially the happy evenings which, at a later time, he spent with her and his aunt, Mrs. R——, in showing them his minerals and other collections, or in talking over some book which they were reading. No doubt he owed much of his culture to their judgment and good taste, and to the encouragement given him by the interest they uniformly felt in his plans and pursuits.

While he had many acquaintances, his real friendships were few. With that keen discernment which seemed part of his nature, he sifted and weighed character before offering or accepting the slightest advances toward intimacy; but his confidence, once gained, was firm in every emergency. Never was a friend more noble, true, and disinterested.

On one occasion, when deceived in one whom he believed his friend, he writes:—

"I am sorry to say, that after fully weighing the matter, and even throwing all possibilities in his favour, my opinion is that he is guilty of all I have charged him with. I have fully forgiven him, nor will I ever cease to pray for him; yet I can never look upon him with the same degree of confidence again. I have learned a bitter but I trust profitable lesson by it. How few are our true friends, and how much should we love those who are really such! A friend is one of Heaven's choicest blessings."

Such magnanimity as this—such forgiveness of enemies and praying for them—could only be learned in the school of Christ. High-toned and chivalrous, manly and independent, he loathed everything vulgar, grovelling, or sycophantic. From persons who had nothing but money or dress to recommend them he instinctively shrank, and did not hesitate, in a becoming way, to express his contempt for their pretensions. There was nothing little or selfish about him. Generous to a fault, self-sacrificing even to his own injury, he lived for others. In a life of half a century we have known but *one* William David Stuart. From an intimacy of years, spending hours together almost daily, conversing on all subjects,—boating, riding, playing practical jokes, travelling, praying, and, in cases of emergency, sleeping together,—we knew the man in his inner as well as outer life, and can unhesitatingly affirm that never have we known one of his age possessed of so beautiful, so symmetrical a character. In William's death the writer lost his youngest, but his most valued friend.

With young men of his own age he had great influence; and when he could establish a bond of sympathy, in any way, he greatly enjoyed their society.

Kind and winning in his manners, he won the confidence of his associates; and, before they were aware of it, the great interests of eternity were, with a singularly happy tact, made the subject of discourse. Yet his tastes, pursuits, and enjoyments being different from those of the majority, and his mind more matured than usual, he naturally sought intercourse and companionship with older persons. The Letters at the close of this Memoir attest how highly he was valued by men of large experience and great learning. Well versed in theology, in several of the sciences, in history, in polite literature, and having kept pace with this rapid age, as its daily events transpired, he not only appeared to advantage among men of culture, but his society was sedulously sought for. On all the great national questions of the day, whether of home policy and politics or those of foreign nations, he was equally well informed, and all his views were broad and enlightened.

He loved his native land intensely, and would acknowledge no blot on her fair name, save the dark one of slavery;—of this he pleaded guilty before God and man. The genius and structure of her Institutions, her free and untrammelled constitutional liberty, her religion, her resources, her power, her population, were all thoroughly understood by him. In the great Rebellion all his sympathies were with the North; and often when travelling in Europe has he stood up nobly in defence of the right,—placing the subject in so clear a light as to turn the tide of sympathy in the true direction. In the circle in which he moved, America was the standing topic of conversation; and he has been known to forget, in the ardour of his zeal, his natural reserve, to explain at length, with great warmth, before crowded drawing-rooms, the nature and working of our Federal Government, insisting upon its superiority over their monarchical system—not unfrequently to the chagrin of some of his auditors, who were unable to reply to his arguments.

During the latter part of William's college life the choice of a profession gave him much anxiety. While his tastes would have led him to some scientific pursuit, duty, as usual with him, prevailed over inclination, and giving up the ministry, for which he feared his health would not be sufficiently strong, he decided on a business life. His Letters show how earnestly he prayed God to direct him to such a course as would best promote the cause of the Redeemer on earth.

On his return from a tour in the West, in 1859, his health seemed restored, and he entered his father's business house with the intention of applying himself with all his energy to its details, to qualify himself for active life as a merchant. Scarcely, however, had he commenced when his strength again began to give way, and he was able to give only partial attention to the department with which he had been entrusted.

In June 1860 he made a visit to Princeton, and was much benefited by his two weeks' recreation and outdoor exercise.

In January 1861, while visiting Milton, a distant town in his native State, to deliver a lecture on the microscope, he contracted a severe cold. The weather was intensely severe, the thermometer ranging from 10° to 20° below zero, and the winds high and piercing. Immense blocks of ice were heaped up like a wall on the banks of the Susquehanna. He was out in the air a great deal, wading through the snow to and from the Academy building to arrange the apparatus for exhibiting microscopic objects, as well as sleigh-riding, &c.; and it is probable that his exposure impaired his health for life, as from this time he was frequently troubled with a cough.

On his return to Philadelphia, though far from strong, he endeavoured to attend to his business duties and his mission school; but after leaving the latter on the Sabbath, he was often forced to return home, unable from exhaustion to remain at church.

Toward the close of February he was obliged to acknowledge himself an invalid. On the 21st of this month he writes from his sick-room:—

"Here I am, a prisoner again. I had hoped, although confined to the house all day yesterday, to have been able to go out in the evening; but at dark the doctor came in, and after looking at me gravely for several moments, feeling my pulse, and examining my tongue, strictly ordered me to stay in the house and undergo a course of treatment,—the first time he has prescribed for me since I was fourteen years old. Yesterday I was much alarmed at myself; but the doctor has quieted my fears. I had got the idea firmly fixed in my mind that my cold had settled on my lungs, and that I was beginning to waste away; which was strengthened by my entire loss of appetite—a thing unusual with me. However, after taking two or three doses of my medicine, I feel much better and brighter, and hope soon to be as strong and hearty as ever. It is so dull staying in the house: true, I have plenty of books and my microscope; but even these I sometimes do not care to use. Then I like to stretch myself on the lounge, and build beautiful hopes for the future.

"I have lately become impressed more than ever with the duty of self-examination,—looking very often, into our hearts, and seeing how they stand toward God. It is very important that we should know this. Just as the careful merchant often examines his books to see how his credit stands with those with whom he deals, so should we look very often to see how we stand with God. No one can do it for us—it must be a personal work; and if attended to in a Christian spirit and with prayer, will tend greatly to our growth in grace."

The spring weather being such that he could not often get out in the air to gain strength, he prepared in April for a trip to Savannah; but many of his friends objecting to this, he sailed for Europe, May 18, 1861. He remained abroad about six months, and, in accordance with the advice of Dr. Quain of London, spent some time at the sea side at Blackpool. He also made excursions in the Lake District in England; then went to Scotland, visited the Islands on the western coast, and passed through the Highlands. From Scotland he went up to London, thence to Paris and Switzerland, to Baden-Baden, and back to London *via* Paris.

During this visit, while he was hospitably entertained by the numerous relatives and friends of his father, he made many new and lasting friends of his own. The kind attentions he received—especially those of his kindred in Birkenhead and Manchester, and his friends in Edinburgh—will not soon be forgotten by his surviving family.

He returned home, October 25, 1861, looking remarkably well, and having gained some thirty pounds in weight. As cold weather approached, however, it was found that his health was not permanently established. During the winter and following spring he was much confined to the house, and it was thought advisable for him to make another voyage to Europe. He sailed, May 7, 1862, for Liverpool, but very reluctantly, being quite wearied with travelling and with being so much from home; and, indeed, he would not have consented but for the opportunity of obtaining a knowledge of business by accompanying his friend Mr. Caldwell, one of the partners in his father's house, to the manufacturing districts of England. He could not be prevailed upon to stay longer than was required for business, and for a little trip in Ireland, which he greatly enjoyed, in spite of the weather. He was very hospitably received by the warm-hearted Irish friends and kindred of his father and himself. He also spent a few days in Scotland, and made a hurried visit to Paris.

He reached home early in July, looking rather better than when he left, but in reality not much benefited by his trip. The weather during his absence was very unfavourable, there being scarcely a day without rain. His cold and cough became worse as autumn approached, and he gradually lost strength; yet he was ever hopeful with regard to himself, and the report of several physicians led his friends to dismiss all serious fears for his life, and believe that he would soon recover.

He would not, even at this time, acknowledge himself an invalid; for about the first of September he joined a military company whose services were expected to be speedily required at the capital of the State, to assist in repelling a threatened invasion by the rebels; but his failing strength soon forced him to give up the drill.

We now come to the second great event in his life—his marriage to Miss Mary Ella Johnson, a daughter of the late Laurence Johnson, Esq., of this city. To this young lady he had been several years engaged, and her personal attractions, intelligence, culture, and piety, rendered her in every respect worthy to be his companion for life. Her love had long been the sunshine of his existence. Even while yet children they seem to have been irresistibly attracted to each other, and an affection so pure and holy is rarely to be found on earth. As winter had approached, his health had steadily declined, and a voyage to Santa Cruz was recommended, with a short residence on that island. This decided the time of his marriage, for he could not bear to contemplate another separation from all he loved; while the true heart, on whom he was daily learning more and more to lean, rejoiced in the opportunity of nursing him in sickness, and being his solace and support while journeying far from home. They were united on the 4th of December, 1862. The same afternoon they went to New York, and sailed for Havana the following Tuesday, accompanied by William's uncle, Mr. David W. Denison. It was a kind Providence that put it into the heart of this Christian gentleman to go with them, for he rendered them such service as none could but a kinsman and loving friend. It was a journey at once of joy and sorrow: of joy to the young hearts that they were united by the closest and holiest of bonds; of sorrow that the sickness of him—the pride and joy of the young wife's heart—might be unto death.

The weather was severely cold, and the ill-furnished and over-crowded steamer promised a voyage full of discomfort. The deck, the only pleasant portion of the ship, was always thronged, many having mattresses upon it. In this state of things, with the rolling of the vessel at times, it was impossible for William to take the exercise he felt to be necessary; nor could he get needful rest in his close state-room in the lower cabin, never reached by fresh air, and almost intolerable when the engine fires had thoroughly heated the iron vessel, and the temperature of the Gulf Stream was reached. Still he was uniformly cheerful and uncomplaining, and occupied himself with reading, talking, and attending to his sea-sick companions. In the afternoon his symptoms were usually unfavourable, and he suffered from chilliness.

On the morning of the 16th December they entered the beautiful harbour of Havana, and in a short time found comfortable apartments at the Hotel Cubano. The rain and dampness, however, confined William to the hotel for days together; and as it was the head-quarters of the Secessionists, he found little pleasure in leaving his own rooms. He was, however, occasionally enlivened by the society of some fellow-passengers, who had proved pleasant companions. When the day was fine he would drive through the city and its suburbs, but sometimes felt unable to leave the carriage to see the various objects of interest, and when occasionally he walked out, he always returned fatigued. After remaining in Havana ten days, and feeling that each one left him weaker, it was determined, by the advice of friends, to go over to Matanzas, there to remain until it should be necessary to embark at Havana for St. Thomas.

On the 27th of December the change was accomplished to the gratification of all, Mr. Denison having, with his usual thoughtfulness, made arrangements in advance for their comfort. The house, though plain, was American, and decidedly Northern in sentiment.

With pleasant drives by the sea-side, the society of the American Consul and a number of agreeable ladies, William passed his time pleasantly; but he did not gain strength, and his cough became very painful, keeping him awake much at night.

The greatest exertion he made while in Cuba was to visit the beautiful valley of the Yumuri, near Matanzas, the execrable road to which fatigued him greatly. The party returned to Havana on the 2nd January, 1863; on the 6th set sail in the steamer "Conway;" and on the morning of the 14th found themselves lying within a stone's throw of the green clad hills and airy palms of Santa Cruz, over which was still shining the beautiful constellation of the Cross, as if to recall to their remembrance that love which extends to the ends of the earth.

Here the travellers hoped to make a pleasant home for a few months, but on landing were dismayed to find that there was no longer a boarding-house in the place. In a short time, however, Mr. Moore, to whom they had letters of introduction, hearing of their embarrassment, offered the hospitality of his house. Mrs. Moore received them in the kindest manner, as did also her husband and sons; and all were unceasing in their efforts to add to their comfort and make them feel at home. Never were travellers more blessed in finding friends. A happy week was spent in their society. Nor did their attentions cease when a person was found willing to open a house for the travellers' accommodation, but daily, indeed almost hourly, did they give some mark of their unwearying kindness.

In their new quarters in Frederickstadt the travellers were again blessed by falling into the hands of an excellent lady, Miss A——, who did everything in her power to promote their comfort. The weather was charming, the mercury never falling much below 70°, and usually standing at about 84° throughout the day. Almost uncomfortably warm as this was for his wife and uncle, coming from the frosty air of the north, William was constantly chilly, and never took off the thick flannels and clothing with which he left home but once or twice, and that for a short time in the middle of the day. The construction of the houses on the island, with windows on four sides, and these without glass, was very unfavourable to one sensitive to the least current of air, and he took cold continually, notwithstanding every effort was made to prevent it.

Before reaching the island, he had purposed riding on horseback every day; but a drive out in a carriage was found to be as much as he could bear, and even this was gradually discontinued, from his increasing weakness. His symptoms became more alarming. His appetite—never remarkably good—began to decrease, and few delicacies could be procured to tempt it. He was obliged to have recourse to anodyne nightly. His sufferings from chills were at times severe, and the consequent fever seemed as though it would consume his wasted body. He no longer felt able to sit at table to take his meals, and he became assured that he would not recover while remaining there.

In those dark hours the thoughts of all turned towards home. The invalid especially longed for it. The physicians at first refused to permit the journey, but after a consultation, said he might depart. Then, like an electric flash, came the thought—*there is no hope.* With apparent calmness his wife prepared for immediate departure, her loving heart strained to the last degree of tension, condemned to bear her sorrow alone, unknown to him who had shared all her griefs and joys from childhood. Well was it for her in those long days of agony that an Almighty Friend was near.

Providentially the packet schooner *D. B. Bayles*, Captain Jayne, with excellent accommodations, was in port, and in a few days to sail for New York; and to make it still more pleasant, the excellent wife of the captain was to accompany him.

With sad hearts they bade farewell to the friends to whom they had become greatly attached, and freighted with comforts and delicacies prepared by Mrs. M—— and Miss A——, they sailed from Santa Cruz on the 17th of February. The invalid seated himself on deck, and as the little vessel moved gracefully off before a fine breeze, he gazed for the last time on the beautiful island, waving his handkerchief in reply to the signals of Mrs. M—— and her sons, feeling that although his health had not been restored, God was merciful in having given him such friends as he was leaving, and such as were conveying him home.

Captain Jayne and his wife were unwearied in their attentions, and no sacrifice was too great for them to make. They gave up their own commodious state-room, and provided many things with the special view of adding to William's comfort.

For a few days after leaving Santa Cruz he was very ill, and it was extremely doubtful whether he would live to reach home. Not knowing what might be the result, preparations had been made before leaving the West Indies to return his body to his home and friends, should God take his spirit to himself while at sea. One evening as the invalid was lying on the upper deck, with his constant companion seated by his side, the thought that he would die far away from home depressed him greatly; and as she wiped the fast flowing tear from his pale cheek, he turned his clear, deep eye upon her and said, with much energy, "Mellie, never let them bury me in the sea." On being assured that they never would, in a moment he was calm; and from that time it was thought he rallied somewhat.

Although exceedingly weak and ill during the voyage, he manifested his usual energy of character. He dressed himself with some assistance, every day, with one exception; and the captain and his uncle Denison supported him to the cabin or deck. He took much interest in things about him, noted the daily run of the vessel, and read several volumes during the voyage. Usually the weather was favourable, but occasionally their progress was retarded by head winds and heavy seas, and when nearly in sight of New York they were becalmed for an entire day; yet not a murmur of disappointment rose from the lips of the sufferer.

Early in the morning of 2nd March the schooner anchored off Jersey City; and the friends of the party in Philadelphia, who supposed them still in Santa Cruz, were startled on receiving the same day a telegram announcing their arrival. Some of the family went on immediately, and the next day accompanied him to his home, from which he had been absent just three months. Great was his joy on reaching it, and being again under the care of his own physician and friend, Dr. Rumsey. New scenes animated his hopes, his appetite improved, and all thought he would soon be better. He was very hopeful of his own condition, and frequently spoke to his wife of his plans for the future, as though he had no doubt of his ultimate recovery. This hopefulness did much to allay her fears; for she felt that, were he drawing near the invisible world, he would have an instinctive sense of his condition; and though he might be beyond medical aid, he was a peculiar object of God's care, and he could and would restore him. He expected in a few days after reaching home to be able to go up to the library and amuse himself with his books and minerals and microscope; but this he never accomplished, and left his room but once or twice when he was wheeled in his chair to the adjoining one. He sat up after he rose in the morning till ten, and often eleven o'clock, conversing with the family or some of his numerous friends—at times recalling amusing incidents, and speaking with as much enthusiasm as his strength would allow. In one of these conversations, he remarked to his friend Mr. James Grant: "If there is one thing more than another which my sickness has taught me, it is this—the *absolute folly* of putting off the soul's salvation to a sick-bed. My mind and body are so weakened that I can scarcely find strength to read my Bible and pray." He noticed the new publications, and several times sent out for new works. He read chiefly scientific books, and amused himself in arranging his collection of stamps in an album. In the news of the day he took a deep interest, and read the morning papers regularly before rising, and even did so on the morning before his death.

After the excitement of his return had passed off, it became apparent that he did not improve. His appetite decreased; he rose later each morning, and never walked across the room, save to reach his arm-chair when he rose in the morning, and to return to bed at night. He manifested a great desire to know what his physician thought of his state; and on being gently told that his lungs were affected, and his symptoms regarded as most serious, he looked earnestly into his wife's face, and with a voice not entirely free from agitation, said, "I might have known it," and mentioned one of the symptoms which he ought to have recognized.

Still he continued hopeful, though it was very evident from his remarks that he felt he might not recover. He longed and prayed to live. Life to him was so full of hope and joy, and he felt he had yet so much to do for Christ, that no amount of suffering could wring from him a wish to depart. Yet there was always a willingness and desire that God's will might be done.

Doctors Caspar, Morris, and Pepper were now called in as consulting physicians. Although they could do nothing more than had been done, even to alleviate his physical sufferings, Dr. Morris, who saw him often, brought the balm provided by the great Physician; and the tones of his voice, and the appearance of his benevolent face, brought strengthening to the hearts of *both* sufferers.

On the night of Friday, April 3, while preparing for bed, William had a dreadful attack, and for ten minutes it was doubtful whether he would live through it. It seemed to be spasmodic, and he felt that he would suffocate. After this he had a pretty comfortable night, but from that time he did not leave his bed.

The next evening he noticed his grandmother talking with Dr. Rumsey, and after the doctor retired she seated herself at his bedside. He asked her what the doctor thought of him, and questioned her closely, saying, "Nanna, I have to screw it out of you." She told him plainly there was no hope of his recovery. He said, "I would like to live to do more for Christ; but it's all right. I am glad you told me all; it is best to be prepared for either event." He then looked up to the head of the bed where his wife was standing, and in a few words expressed the agony he felt at parting from her, adding, after a brief pause, "I hope I am ready."

The next day William expressed a strong desire to see and talk with Dr. Morris. The doctor was soon by his side. After conversing a little about his symptoms, and the probable length of his life, he learned there was no ground to suppose he would pass away during such an attack as he had on the previous night; which seemed to comfort and encourage him. William expressed his desire to live, that he might do something for Jesus, when the doctor replied, "You can trust him." The words seemed to flow like healing balm into the sick man's soul. The kind physician then knelt down and prayed with him, and when he arose stooped and kissed the beautiful face, which even then wore the radiant expression that must belong to the heavenly world.

The day following was the Sabbath. Early in the morning, his wife seeing the tears chasing each other down his cheeks, inquired of what he was thinking. He said, "Oh, I long to go to my mission school!"

During one of his paroxysms of pain he whispered to her, "I keep constantly thinking of these lines:—

'Give me, O Lord, a thankful heart,
From every murmur free;
The blessings of thy grace impart,
And make me live to thee.'"

He was visited this day by Rev. Dr. Wylie and Mr. A. Martin, and gave most satisfactory evidence that he knew in whom he had believed. To his pastor he expressed a desire to live, but said, "If it is God's will, I am ready. I look to Jesus alone for salvation." They prayed and sang with him, and the dying teacher seemed to enter into the spirit of both their prayers, as well as the sweet songs of Zion, of which he was remarkably fond. As Dr. Wylie was leaving, William requested his prayers that afternoon, especially that no presumption might be mingled with the confidence he enjoyed of salvation through the atoning blood of Jesus. Later in the day, while conversing with his father concerning his departure, he said,—

"I would like, papa, that you, Dr. Wylie, and Mr. Grant be a committee to look after the mission school, and see that all goes on right. It must go right, for it was planted with a great many prayers. I do not feel as though God were going to take me away. I have felt since I was a boy that *He* had some special work for me to do. Perhaps the founding of that school was my work."

Monday was a day of great suffering to the dying saint, and had not the hearts of those around been blinded by love, they would have seen God's seal upon his brow. It was terrible to see his patient suffering, and know that everything had been done that could be. He had on this day a sweet interview with his friend Grant (who had been, throughout his sickness, unremitting in his attentions), in which the interests of his school were mentioned, and committed to his care in part. Towards evening his case became very alarming, and Dr. Rumsey was requested to remain all night. At times his mind would wander for a few seconds. He knew perfectly all about him. None of those with him undressed themselves; but towards morning nearly all left the room, as he seemed inclined to sleep. The stillness was soon broken by his pouring forth his soul, stirred to the very depths, in a prayer such as none could utter but one of Christ's chosen ones, to whom the veil was being lifted, and who, standing on the confines of the heavenly world, sees the necessity of committing to the Saviour those who are still subjected to earthly influences. Supported by a bed-chair, with one hand raised toward heaven, he prayed still, "If it be possible, let this cup pass from me; yet not my will, but Thine be done." Oh! how earnestly he prayed for his dear partner—that she might be strengthened to bear all the trials of life, and that they might be reunited in heaven; his family, and the one with which he had become so recently connected; his mission school; the faithful nurse who sat by his bedside;—all were the subjects of earnest appeal to the Mercy Seat. The great difficulty with which this prayer was uttered, the intense effort it cost, added much to its fervour. It had been difficult for him to speak even in whispers throughout the day, and now after every few words his cough obliged him to stop, when in a few seconds he would renew the effort. He concluded this long prayer with that which he had learned in early childhood:—

" Now I lay me down to sleep,
I pray the Lord my soul to keep;
If I should die before I wake,
I pray the Lord my soul to take;
And this I ask for Jesus' sake."

When asked by his wife whether the effort he had just made was not too much for him, he seemed surprised that she had heard him, and said he was much exhausted, but felt better for it. His pillows were then arranged, and he fell into a quiet sleep. Day was beginning to dawn. The dews of death were on his noble brow. Soon after six o'clock his anxious father thought it best to arouse him, lest he should never wake again on earth.

"Willie, my dear son," said he, "I trust Jesus is precious to you."

He recognized the voice, and replied, "Yes."

William then asked, "Do you think me worse? does the doctor think so? tell him to come here." He then asked the doctor himself, and when he heard his affirmative answer, he replied, " I will feel better when I get my breakfast;" and immediately turning to his wife, said, " I wonder if this is death; if it is, I do not know it; I pray for dying grace in a dying hour."

He was so weak, that when his father spoke to him again, he said, "I can't speak now—I'll talk to you all by-and-by;" when, as though the strength were immediately imparted to him, and he felt he must avail himself of the present, he delivered a message, singularly appropriate, to each one that stood around his bed.

To his father he said, "God bless you, my dear papa. I had hoped to have been spared to assist you in your labours."

To his sisters he addressed a sweet word of exhortation, urging them to give their hearts to Christ.

To his brother George* he said, "I hope, my dear brother, you will take my place. Seek the Lord early, and you will find him."

He exhorted his younger brother Francis to give his heart to the Saviour.

When his little sister Patty, not five years old, was brought to his side by her father for a message, he said, "Oh, papa, she could not understand me;" and then added, "God bless my dear little sister."

To his grandmother Denison he said, "Nanna, my devoted Nanna, how can I ever thank you! From your lips I first heard the name of a Saviour."

To his aunt and uncle also he spoke most affectionately. His strength was much reduced by this effort, and after a short silence, he called for his faithful nurse, and after thanking her for all the kindness she had bestowed on him, said, "Eliza,* I want you to read the Bible (one which he had given her,) every day. Give your heart to Christ, and meet me in heaven." She made no answer, when he added, "Eliza, won't you promise me this?" when she replied with sobs and tears, "I will try."

To Dr. Rumsey, his faithful medical attendant and

* George and Eliza have, since Willie's death, united themselves to the Church of Christ.

warmly attached friend, he said, "Doctor, you have been very kind to me since I have been a boy, and you have done all you could to save my life; I have a request to make,—that you will meet me in heaven." The doctor, completely overcome, bent over and kissed the dying youth, and said, "Yes."

To his mother and wife he gave most touching messages, but they are too sacred to be repeated here.

After the delivery of these tender farewells, a solemn stillness reigned. When he had recovered a little from his exhaustion, he asked his father to "pray if it be yet possible that this cup may pass from me." After prayer, in which he joined with much earnestness, there was another pause, when the silence was broken by the dying voice exclaiming, "I know that my Redeemer liveth;" unable though evidently desirous to finish the sentence.

On resting for a few moments, with faltering lips he breathed his last words on earth into the ear of her whom he so tenderly loved—such words as would comfort her heart when he would be no longer with her here.

And now he seemed just ready "to depart and be with Christ." In that chamber of death not a sound, save the deep yet tranquil breathing of the dying believer, could be heard. What peace on that lovely countenance! Watch the last gleam of thought stream from his dying eyes. Do you see anything like apprehension? The world, it is true, begins to shut in. The shadows of evening collect around his senses. A dark mist thickens and rests upon the objects which have hitherto engaged his observation. The countenances of his friends become more and more indistinct. The sweet expressions of love and friendship are no longer intelligible. The soothing accents of tender affection die away unheard upon his decaying senses. The curtain is descending which shuts out this earth, its actors and its scenes. He is no longer interested in all that is done under the sun. Oh, that I could now open to you the recesses of his soul! that I could reveal to you the light which darts into the chambers of his understanding! He approaches that world which he has so long seen in faith. The imagination now collects its diminished strength, and the eye of faith opens wide. Friends! do not stand thus fixed in sorrow around this bed of death. Why are you so still and silent? Fear not to move—you cannot disturb the last visions which enchant this holy spirit. Your lamentations break not in upon the songs of seraphs which inwrap his hearing in ecstasy. Crowd, if you choose, around his couch—he heeds you not—already he sees the spirits of the just advancing together to receive a kindred soul. Press him not with importunities. Urge him not with alleviations. Think you he wants now these tones of mortal voices—these material, these gross consolations? No! He is going to add another to the myriads of the just that are every moment crowding into the portals of heaven! He is entering on a nobler life. He leaves you; he leaves *you*, weeping children of mortality, to grope about a little longer among the miseries and sensualities of a worldly life. Already he calls to you from the regions of bliss. Will you not join him there? Will you not taste the sublime joys of faith?"*

While the clock was striking seven, on the morning of 7th April 1863, without a struggle, he gently fell asleep in Jesus. The soul of WILLIAM DAVID STUART was in heaven.

* Buckminster.

When the emaciated body was prepared for its narrow house, many of his former friends and companions were permitted to see it; and all were struck with the almost heavenly expression and exceeding beauty of the countenance. By invitation, between thirty and forty of the coloured children of the mission school, with their parents, came to look upon the face of the departed for the last time. Their sorrow of heart at the loss of their best earthly friend found vent in sobs and tears. The whole scene was affecting and solemn in the extreme.

The following obituary notice was published at the time in several of our religious newspapers. It was written by Mr. JAMES GRANT, one of William's intimate friends and fellow-labourers, and is given entire, that so just a tribute, from one of his companions, may be preserved in connection with the memory of our friend :—

"I KNOW THAT MY REDEEMER LIVETH."—These precious, soul-comforting words, first uttered in a time of the deepest calamity by the patient dweller in the land of Uz, were the last which passed from the lips of our beloved friend and fellow-labourer, Mr. William David Stuart.

He had suffered intensely in a severe struggle with the last enemy on the night of April 6; but early on the morning of the 7th, when the hand of death had nearly completed its work, a short interval of calm repose was mercifully given him. It seemed as if the work of dissolution had been suspended for a brief space, that he might, as he did, with wonderful serenity and Christian fortitude, give a parting message of affectionate love and solemn counsel to those who were gathered around his bed, and, with his dying breath, leave behind him a peaceful testimony that, amid the swellings of Jordan, he was resting on the Rock of Ages.

But not only when the silver cord was being loosed did this dear young servant of God draw comfort from the consoling thought so beautifully expressed by the afflicted patriarch, but the felt conviction of an ever-living Saviour, and how much he owed him for his personal salvation, was the motive power which impelled him to consecrate all the energies of his short life to the cause of Him who had redeemed him with his priceless blood.

Few young men are blessed with such rare natural gifts as he was. Graceful in form, fair and noble in countenance, courteous in manner, ever cheerful in spirit, amiable and benevolent in disposition, with a mind quick to comprehend and eminently practical in its workings, and a body—till wasting disease prostrated its strength—full of manly vigour and living energy.

Added to these, he had all the advantages of a refined and liberal education; and having travelled extensively and mingled much in society, he possessed wisdom and intelligence far beyond his years.

It is believed that very early in life he became a subject of Divine grace, making a public profession of his faith in Jesus when but sixteen years old. From this time onward his Christian character made its mark, leading him, with singular devotion, to seek the soul's salvation of those with whom he was intimately associated, as well as the perishing around him.

His principal efforts were made in connection with the Coloured Mission Sabbath-School in St. Mary Street, of which he was the founder and superintendent. This locality is one of the very lowest in the city, and to labour in such a district, among such a class, required no little self-denial and zeal. The repulsiveness of the field, however, was entirely overlooked in the desire to elevate the degraded, comfort the distressed, and save the lost. Assuming the management of the school at the age of seventeen, his deep, prayerful interest in it never flagged till, in the bloom of early manhood, he was called to cease from his labours, and enter upon the heavenly rest. When declining health, or absence from home, prevented him from being at his post of duty, he would frequently write letters of kind advice and instruction to the teachers and scholars; and but a few hours before his lamented death, the school and its management, after he was gone, was the subject of conversation and thought.

It was a touching sight, and one which proved how tenderly he was loved, when, on the day of his burial, a band of the coloured children and people assembled around his silent remains—beautiful even in death—and made great lamentation over him. His name, the kind words he spoke, the deeds of sympathetic kindness he performed, will long be remembered in the miserable abodes of the dark neighbourhood in which he laboured.

To us it is mysterious that one so gifted and so useful, with such strong desires to work for the glory of God and the welfare of his race, should be so soon removed; but to use his own words, when convinced of his approaching death, "*It is all right.*" "What I do thou knowest not now, but thou shalt know hereafter." What was said by the biographer of the sainted M'Cheyne, in reference to his brief life, appears peculiarly applicable to him: "Only this much we can clearly see, that nothing was more fitted to leave his character and example impressed on our remembrance for ever than his early death. There might have been envy while he lived; there is none now. There might have been some of the youthful attractiveness of his graces lost had he lived many years; this cannot be impaired now. It seems as if the Lord had struck the flower from its stem ere any of the colours had lost their bright hue, or any leaf its fragrance."

In these unhappy days of war and bloodshed, we hear much of death. When dear William Stuart died an ardent Christian soldier fell, not amid the booming of cannon, the cracking of musketry, the clashing of steel, or the horrible carnage of an earthly battle-field; but peacefully, hopefully, triumphantly, in the home of his childhood, in the twenty-third year of his age, he laid aside the spiritual armour wherewith he was girded, and entered into the joy of his Lord.

May we who remain still in the place of conflict and labour be enabled, by God's grace, to redouble our zeal, and, like him, with unwearied earnestness, "work while it is day," for "the night cometh, when no man can work." G.

The funeral took place on Saturday afternoon, April 11. The hour named was two o'clock, but it was nearly two hours later when the long procession began its mournful movement towards the Woodlands Cemetery. The day was soft and balmy, for the season; and the large concourse in and around the house, and which followed the body to the grave, testified how deeply he was lamented. An aged and devoted minister of Jesus remarked, that he "had seldom, if ever, seen so much respect shown to one so young."

The funeral services at the house were commenced by the Rev. Alexander Reed of Parkesburg, Pennsylvania, who read appropriate selections from the Scriptures. This was followed by an address,* of peculiar beauty and appropriateness by the Rev. Dr. Wylie. Rev. Dr. Boardman then made a short but touching address,† closing with a solemn and appropriate prayer. The coffin was borne by six of his young friends, two of whom, four short months before, had acted as his groomsmen.

In the cemetery, with the large congregation around him, standing by the open grave of him whom he knew and loved in life, the Rev. Albert Barnes made an appropriate address.‡ The Rev. Dr. Suddards offered the concluding prayer; and the solemn funeral rites were brought to a close by his pronouncing the apostolic benediction.

This memorial of our beloved friend and Christian brother would be incomplete without giving the proceedings of several Societies with which he was connected. The proceedings of the Associations connected with the First Reformed Presbyterian Church were published in

* See Appendix. † Ibid. ‡ Ibid.

the *Banner of the Covenant* of May 9, 1863, and were introduced with the following editorial:—

"EARLY RIPE, EARLY GATHERED."

The following are the proceedings of several Societies connected with the First Reformed Presbyterian Church, in relation to the death of Mr. William D. Stuart. Although prepared in the first warm gush of sorrow which his early death has caused, they do not express more than is proper—nor, indeed, do they say enough. The whole-hearted devotion with which our dear young brother served his Saviour has rarely been equalled. With talents and an education which might have gained him the laurels of fame, with worldly resources which would have enabled him to enjoy all that wealth could procure, he engaged in promoting the welfare of a portion of the most degraded and neglected class in the community. Having established a Mission Sabbath-School for Coloured Children, he was always faithful in his duties as its superintendent; and in addition he conducted services twice every week—in the evenings of the Sabbath and a working-day—for the benefit of their adult friends and relatives. He visited the sick and poor among them in their abodes of want, amid circumstances so disgusting, oftentimes, that scarcely any one who had not lived among them would have been able to endure them. By the bedside of those whose occupations almost excluded them from all intercourse with society, he was to be found reading the word of God, and leading in earnest prayer, that souls so precious that Jesus died for them might be saved. His self-sacrificing, unsparing labours, we have no doubt, shortened his life; but though he died young in years, he died old in usefulness. He sought Christ early, and gave evidence that he had found him; and his short but bright career is a most valuable testimony to the reality and loveliness of youthful piety, and presents an example of personal holiness and Christian usefulness which, it is to be hoped, many will endeavour to imitate. Those who have been bereaved may be consoled in their sorrow when they consider what God made him while on earth, and what God has now given to him in heaven.

At a meeting of the Officers and Teachers of the St. Mary Street Coloured Mission Sabbath-School of the First Reformed Presbyterian Church, held on Thursday evening, April 16, 1863, *the following Resolutions were unanimously adopted:—*

WHEREAS it has pleased our heavenly Father to remove from his field of labour our late honoured superintendent, William David Stuart, it is fitting that we, who have been witnesses of his zeal for the cause of Christ, of his kind and loving disposition, manifested at all times, of his self-sacrifice and devotion to whatever good work he undertook, and especially of the lasting interest he took in this Mission Sabbath-School, which he organized, and laboured in long after his health and strength began to fail, should place on record the estimation in which we held our deceased brother. Therefore

Resolved, That in the decease of William David Stuart we have lost a faithful and devoted superintendent, a zealous co-worker, a Christian exemplar, a kind friend.

Resolved, That while we bow in humble resignation to the will of God in this afflictive dispensation, we feel assured that, as for him "to live was Christ," so "to die was gain;" therefore we will cherish the memory of our departed brother, who was endeared to us by his ardent love, manly piety, Christian fortitude, and self-sacrifice in the work of his heavenly Master. "The righteous shall be held in everlasting remembrance."

Resolved, That we recall his devotion to the service of his Saviour, manifested by his abundant labours, "in season and out of season," for the upbuilding of Christ's kingdom in this school, as a bright example for us who remain, while, following in his footsteps so far as he followed Christ, we endeavour to feed the lambs of the flock who were the objects of his prayers and efforts while he yet remained with us.

Resolved, That we deeply sympathize with the bereaved relatives, while we would not intrude on their sacred grief, reminding them that they are not called to mourn as they who have no hope; and trusting that Jesus, who wept at the grave of Lazarus, whose compassions are infinite, will comfort them in this the time of their trouble.

Resolved, That a copy of these resolutions be presented to the relatives of our departed brother, and that they be published in the *Banner of the Covenant.*

JAS. M'LEOD.	ELIZABETH HAZEL.
EPHRAIM YOUNG.	EMILY HAZEL.
JOHN BIGGERSTAFF.	MARY M'CALLA.
EBENEZER YOUNG.	ELIZABETH M'NUTT.
THEO. A. GRAHAM.	MARTHA B. WHITE.
THOS. DONNELL.	HELEN C. BLAIR.

JAS. H. WINDRIM.

Resolutions of the Sabbath-School Association on the death of Mr. W. D. Stuart, Superintendent of the St. Mary Street Coloured Mission Sabbath-School, April 20, 1863:—

WHEREAS it hath pleased Almighty God, in his mysterious providence, to remove by the hand of death into the heavenly rest the beloved superintendent of the St. Mary Street Coloured Mission Sabbath-School, Mr. William David Stuart; therefore it is resolved—

1st, That in his early, but not untimely death, this Association has lost one of its brightest ornaments, and most gifted, faithful, and most active members; one who, by Divine grace, consecrated with singular devotion his great natural talents, his refined and liberal education, his unselfish benevolence, and his remarkable energy of character, to the glory of God and the everlasting welfare of his fellow-men.

2nd, That while we cannot but deeply lament the shortness of his useful life, we render devout gratitude to God for all the Christian labours he was enabled to accomplish; for the peaceful trust in Jesus which sustained him in the dying hour; and for the precious consolation left us, that, freed for ever from sin and suffering, as a good and faithful servant he hath entered into the joy of his Lord.

3rd, That inasmuch as the special object of his love, his prayers, and his unwearied efforts, was the St. Mary Street Coloured Mission Sabbath-School, of which he was the founder and superintendent, we, as an Association, pledge ourselves to sustain it effectively by every means in our power, in the hope that the seed sown by him and his fellow-labourers, and watered with their prayers, may yet spring up and yield abundant fruit to the praise and glory of God.

4th, That we will ever cherish his memory as one endeared to us by many acts of generous kindness and hallowed hours of Christian labour; and that we commend his bright example of youthful, vigorous, manly piety, to the young men of the congregation, urging them to follow him in so far as he followed the footsteps of his Divine Master, who went about continually doing good.

5th, That a copy of the foregoing resolutions be sent to his bereaved relatives, with the assurance of our united prayers, and an expression of our deepest sympathy for them in this season of sad and solemn affliction. And that they be inserted in the *Sunday-School Times* and the *Banner of the Covenant.*

JAS. H. WINDRIM,
JAS. GRANT,
WILLIAM RAY,
JOHN W. FAIRES, } *Committee.*

At a meeting of the Board of Trustees of the First Reformed Presbyterian Church, Philadelphia, held Monday evening, April 13, 1863, *the following Preamble and Resolutions were unanimously adopted:—*

WHEREAS it has pleased God, in his inscrutable providence, to remove from the scene of his earthly labours our late friend and brother, William David Stuart; and whereas it is proper that this Board pay a just tribute of respect to the memory of one who was recently a member and officer of the same; therefore be it

Resolved, 1st, That we bow with humble and willing submission to this dispensation of God's providence, resting assured that "He who doeth all things well" has removed our departed friend from the cares and trials of an earthly pilgrimage to share in the eternal happiness of the redeemed in heaven.

Resolved, 2nd, That in the relation which our departed brother recently sustained to the members of this Board, as well as in that which he bore to them as a fellow-member of the congregation, we had abundant opportunities to estimate his worth, to appreciate those traits of character which endeared him to us by ties of strong, ardent, Christian affection.

Resolved, 3rd, That the Board of Trustees has by this affliction lost one who, by his warm and generous feelings, his amiable and affable disposition, his earnest and devoted Christian activity, gave promise of great usefulness in the Church of Christ ; yet, while we mourn, we can rejoice that our loss has been his eternal gain.

Resolved, 4th, That it is our duty to imitate the example of our departed brother, in so far as he imitated Christ; and, reminded by this sad event of our mortality, to have a greater zeal in the service of our Redeemer, to improve the opportunities for usefulness with which God is blessing us, knowing that "the night cometh, in which no man can work."

Resolved, 5th, That we tender to the family of our deceased brother our warmest Christian sympathy, praying that He who has afflicted them may give them his own grace and strength in this hour of their trial, that they may know "whom the Lord loveth he chasteneth."

Resolved, 6th, That a copy of these resolutions be sent to the family of our departed brother, and published in the *Banner of the Covenant.*

GEORGE GORDEN, *President.*

Attest, WM. J. CHAMBERS, *Secretary.*

At a special meeting of the Christian Association of the First Reformed Presbyterian Church, held Friday evening, April 17, 1863, *the following Preamble and Resolutions were unanimously adopted:—*

WHEREAS, in the mysterious but all-wise providence of God, our late friend and brother, William D. Stuart, has been removed from the scene of his labours and usefulness below, to the mansions of rest prepared for the redeemed in "the house not made with hands, eternal in the heavens;" and whereas the intimate relation which he sustained to this Association, as its presiding officer, renders it peculiarly appropriate that we, the members thereof, should express our sense of his worth, our sorrow at his departure, and our Christian sympathy with his bereaved relatives; therefore be it

Resolved, That this Association bow with humble resignation to the Divine will in this afflictive dispensation, assured that it cometh from the hand of Him "who doeth all things well."

Resolved, That this Association has sustained a loss not easily repaired in the removal of our beloved brother, who, as its presiding officer from the date of its organization, discharged the duties of his office with distinguished fidelity and success, while in his intercourse with his fellow-members he was ever dignified, affable, and courteous, illustrating by his life and manners the character, and displaying the qualities of the Christian gentleman.

Resolved, That this Association will long remember the labours of our departed brother in the cause of Sabbath-school instruction for the neglected and degraded, he having organized, and for five years having had the active superintendence of, the St. Mary Street Coloured Mission Sabbath-School of the First Reformed Presbyterian Church,—a work to which he devoted his living energies and his dying thoughts.

Resolved, That in the life and death of our departed brother we have a convincing proof of the realities of the Christian faith, and a bright example of the power of Divine grace; while in the ardour of his zeal and devotion in the service of the Redeemer, his love for the souls of others, which led him "in season and out of season" to labour for their spiritual good, he furnishes us an example worthy of our constant imitation.

Resolved, That we tender to the relatives of our deceased brother our warmest Christian sympathies, praying that the God of all peace and consolation, who has said, "My grace will be sufficient for thee," will cause them to realize his own declaration, that "all things work together for good to them that love him."

Resolved, That a copy of these resolutions be presented to the family of our departed brother, and published in the *Banner of the Covenant.*

JAMES GRANT,
JOHN W. FAIRES,
SAMUEL YOUNG,
GEORGE S. CHAMBERS, } *Committee.*

The Christian Association of the First Reformed Presbyterian Church of Philadelphia, was organized on the evening of February 12, 1857, mainly through William's instrumentality; the object of the organization, as expressed in the preamble to their Constitution, being "a desire to promote the furtherance of missionary enterprise in the foreign and domestic field, and the inculcation of the spirit of missions upon the young, together with their moral, spiritual, and intellectual improvement." In his assiduous labours for the welfare of this Association, he originated and carried into successful operation a plan of systematic contributions on the part of the members of the Church, for missionary operations at home and abroad. The amount thus collected was nearly $2000 annually; which greatly exceeded their own expectations, and enabled the Church to do her full share in the support of foreign and domestic missions, besides contributing largely towards the support of her own mission schools. On the 9th March, 1857, William was elected the first President of the Association; to which position he was re-elected every year until his death, and in which he was distinguished for his urbane and dignified deportment and his genuine Christian intercourse with his fellow-members. The essays which he read before the society, in furtherance of its literary objects, were characterized by an ease and fluency of composition, and a graceful and effective delivery, that imparted delight as well as instruction. On learning of his death, a special meeting of the Association was held, and the above resolutions were subsequently unanimously adopted.

PROCEEDINGS OF COMMITTEE OF THE YOUNG MEN'S CHRISTIAN ASSOCIATION OF PHILADELPHIA.

PHILADELPHIA, *April* 13, 1863.
ROOMS OF THE YOUNG MEN'S CHRISTIAN ASSOCIATION.

MRS. WM. D. STUART.

DEAR MADAM,—At a meeting of the Hospital Commission, held last Thursday evening, the departure of your dear husband was announced, and expressions of deep feeling fell from the lips of a number of the members, both on account of his loss to them individually, and the cause of the Redeemer; and likewise because of your sore family bereavement.

A request was made by the meeting that I would prepare a letter expressive of their deep sympathy with yourself and the parents, brothers, and sisters, of this beloved friend and associate in Christ.

We regard it as a just cause of human sorrow, when one in the prime of life, possessing so many Christian virtues, with a heart so warm and a hand so ready for every good work, is smitten down under the power of a fatal disease. But we feel it is *then*, perhaps more than at any other time, that the worth of the gospel, which he had received and loved to publish, manifests itself in its sustaining influence upon the soul. It is in the last conflict with the great enemy of our race that the Christian hero is able to say, "I conquer, though I die." Death for a season may separate the soul from the body—the mortal from the immortal part; but at the same time it sends the spirit home to God, to bathe in everlasting light and love. The grave need have no gloom, for Jesus has been there and illuminated it with his presence, and triumphed over it by rising again. It is now to be regarded as the dressing chamber of the soul, where this mortal puts on immortality, where this corruptible puts on incorruption, and where "death is swallowed up in victory."

May the happy life, the peaceful death, and the glorious eternity given by our heavenly Father to this, your beloved, cause your heart to be glad, and enable you submissively to say, "The Lord gave, and the Lord hath taken away; blessed be the name of the Lord."

On behalf of the Hospital Committee,
JOS. PARKER, *Chief of Commission.*

UNIVERSITY OF PENNSYLVANIA.

At a meeting of the Graduating Class of 1859 *of the University of Pennsylvania, convened the* 9*th day of April* 1863, *the following Resolutions were unanimously adopted:—*

Resolved, That we have heard with feelings of unmingled sorrow of the death of our former class-mate, William D. Stuart, whose noble disposition, warm and genial heart, and Christian spirit, endeared him to all in every circle where he moved.

As a college class we had many opportunities of learning and appreciating his virtues, in the intercourse arising in our common pursuit of literature and the classics, and we are unable to let this occasion pass without paying a tribute, however slight, to the ability evinced by him in historical, scientific, and literary studies; and, above all, to the generous impulses of his nature, guided and controlled, as they ever were, by conscientious convictions of duty.

Resolved, That though we recognize in his removal the hand of an all-wise Providence, who walketh in clouds and darkness, and whose ways are past finding out, yet we feel his loss irreparable; and to his parents, his family, and all those most near and dear to him, we tender our sincerest sympathies in this their hour of great affliction

Resolved, That we will attend the funeral of our late friend and brother.

Resolved, That a committee of six be appointed to present these resolutions to the family, and to have them inserted in the daily papers of this city.

HENRY A. CONVERSE, *Chairman.*

CHARLES BUCKWALTER,
THOMAS HOCKLEY,
WILLIAM B. ROBINS, } *Committee.*
G. W. RUSSELL,
ALFRED ZANTZINGER,

From over a hundred letters of condolence received by Mr. Stuart from all parts of the world, on the occasion of the death of his son, a few extracts are made by the editor from some of those whose writers personally knew the deceased, showing the estimation in which he was held by all who enjoyed his acquaintance. It would be gratifying to have given more of these extracts, were it not that our volume already exceeds the limits of its original design. The letters are given in the order of their dates:—

Mrs. Judge JONES, President of the Female Bible Society of Philadelphia, and of the Ladies' Aid Society of Philadelphia, writes to Mrs. Geo. H. Stuart, under date of 7th April, 1863, (the day of William's death):—

I have heard this evening that your dear son has gone to his heavenly home. What inexpressible comfort you have in this sorrow! True, it is a great cloud; but it is a great glory too—a cloud resting upon the earthly home, but a glory in the heavenly. How sweet to recall the days of his beautiful, joyous, useful life,—thanking your gracious Father that you had it in your power to make him so happy; and then to follow his blessed spirit into that land where they shall no more say "I am sick," and exult in the finished redemption that provided such an eternity of blessedness for him! I feel like coming to you and pouring all the tenderness of a heart trained in the school of affliction into yours, but shrink from intruding on a privacy so sacred.

My sympathizing love to all the afflicted circle, especially to the youthful widow. May she be comforted with the comfort wherewith God comforts his chosen ones.

THOMAS NELSON, Esq., of Edinburgh, Scotland, one of William's most valued friends, who showed him, on the occasion of his visit to Scotland, every attention in his power, to make it pleasant and profitable, was on a visit to this country during William's sickness. He saw him frequently during this time, and at the funeral was one of his pall-bearers. He writes:—

NEW YORK, *April* 7, 1863.

What can I say to you, my friend, in this sad hour? God bless you and all your family. May He give you that "strong consolation" which comes to those alone who are His children. Deeply, warmly do I sympathize with you all, and trust that to you and other sorrowing friends this sore affliction may be sanctified.

Poor Willie! loved by every one who knew him in Scotland;—many a kind inquiry was made to me about him, long after he left. I had learned to esteem and love him as one of the most genuine characters I ever knew; and I will cherish the intercourse I had with him in Scotland, as one of the pleasantest of life's remembrances. . . . . .

Rev. ALEXANDER REED of Parkesburg, Pa., writes from his parsonage under date of 9th April, 1863:—

A letter to-day informs me of the release of your dear son Willie. No sadder sorrow has fallen upon my heart since Jesus took our darling daughter home; and yet I can say nothing to comfort you. I know, and you well know, the emptiness of human condolence at such an hour, when God is present in very deed, and His messenger, whom no power can resist, no skill evade, no influence thwart, snaps asunder the fondest ties that earth can know, and leaves our poor hearts *bleeding, broken, desolate.* . . . .

No human ken can comprehend *now* why one so gifted in person, and mind, and heart; so winning, gentle, cultivated, noble, —with a brilliant future opening, full of hope and rich in promise,—with every earthly blessing filling to the brim the cup of joyous life;—no one, I say, can possibly *now* know *why* he *should die!* Yet even in the midst of such a gloom as this the words of Jesus come, full of blessed consolation, "What I do thou knowest not *now*, but thou *shalt know hereafter.*" Oh, how full of hope, how full of meaning to the child of God are such words. "Now it is dark, my suffering children, very dark, but *trust in me*, and by-and-by it shall be light." Surely—

> "God moves in a mysterious way,
> His wonders to perform."

. . . . . More than twenty years ago God gave into your keeping one of *His* immortal children, and said to you, "Take this child and nurse it *for me*, and I will give thee thy wages." He has but taken what He loaned: you were faithful to your trust; you shall yet receive your "wages." Look upward through your tears, and say, "It is the Lord; let him do what seemeth him good." Oh that God may sustain you in this overwhelming sorrow.

My heart bleeds in sympathy with you all—father, mother, sisters, brothers; but for that lonely one, who a few brief months since started out upon life's bright journey, leaning lovingly and trustingly upon an arm now so cold! oh, what can now comfort her? May the "Husband of the widow" be her stay. . . . .

I shall mingle my tears with yours on Saturday around that precious dust. Would God I could do more!

Rev. E. E. Adams, D.D., pastor of the North Broad Street Presbyterian Church, Philadelphia, became attached to Willie in his visits to the family. He writes:—

Philadelphia, *April* 11, 1863.

Great was my surprise when the notice of your son's funeral met my eye. I knew that he was in feeble health, but had not a thought that the hand of death was so strong upon him. He was a noble young man. Short, indeed, his career on earth; but he has left a memory precious to you—to many—of a youth consecrated to great ends, of a manly piety, and of a blessed hope.

There is *a resurrection.* Even the *body* of the saint shall be like that of his glorified Lord; and it will come soon. Strike the balance between this life and death; on which side descends the scale?—

> "*Life* makes the soul dependent on the dust;
> *Death* gives her *wings* to mount above the spheres.
> Through chinks styled *organs* dim Life peeps for light;
> Death *bursts* the involuntary *cloud*, and all is DAY!
> Death but entombs the *body*—Life the *soul!*
> Death gives us to repose in festive bowers,
> Where nectars sparkle—angels minister;
> And more than angels share, and *raise*, and *crown*,
> And ETERNIZE, the birth-bloom—BURSTS of bliss!"

O Death, the palm is thine! The palm is William's. His the gain. Death is *conquered* by *death*. The vine on which life's clusters grow is rooted in the tomb of Jesus. From such clusters only those who die can eat.

Rev. W. J. R. TAYLOR, D.D., Corresponding Secretary of the American Bible Society, was for many years associated with Willie in the Young Men's Christian Association of this city, and became very strongly attached to him. He writes from New York (his present location), under date of April 13, 1863:—

Not until the day of his burial (Saturday) did I learn the sad news of the death of your late dear son William. . . . . You have lost a noble son; one of whom, had his life been spared, you might have expected much good, and an honourable career of Christian usefulness. But, my dear brother, let your heart be comforted with the same comfort wherewith you have often comforted others. He *was* a Christian; he *is* a glorified saint with the dear Saviour, to whom he gave "the dew of his youth." Young as he was, his "works do follow him," and his memory will be fragrant. If it seems strange that he was so soon cut off, it is enough to know that his work was done.

> "A Christian cannot die before his time;
> The Lord's appointment is the servant's hour."

Multitudes of earnest Christian hearts doubtless united their prayers for you and all your bereaved family, when the heavy tidings came that William was dead. Not a few will continually bless God that he ever lived. . . . . .

Rev. M. L. R. P. Thompson, D.D., of Cincinnati, Ohio, has been for nearly twenty years an intimate friend of the family, and became attached to Willie by more than ordinary friendship. He thus writes:—

Cincinnati, *April* 13, 1863.

George and Patty.

My very Dear Friends,—Mr. Denison's letter on yesterday informed me of the death of your noble and much-loved Willie. The intelligence did not take me wholly by surprise. I had learned before, from various sources besides your own letters, of his critical and alarming condition. I was only not prepared for the sad event of his death *so soon*. I supposed you would be able to keep him with you through the summer, and was confidently anticipating the privilege of once more seeing him, and conversing with him. But God has ordered otherwise, and I am sure you will say with me, "*He* doeth all things well."

. . . . . Our hearts bleed with yours; and if by sharing your pain we could in any measure relieve it, we would find a melancholy pleasure in the participation. Yours, however, notwithstanding all human sympathies, is the whole burden, which only the Divine mercy can lighten and make supportable: for that mercy be assured that our prayers ascend with yours. . . . .

Willie had every quality that could endear him to your hearts. Mrs. T. and I have often said, since we saw him last in Buffalo, that he seemed to combine in himself everything best fitted to make him the joy and pride of his parents. And such was the opinion expressed of him by all who then made his acquaintance. But that which chiefly made him dear to you was owing to the grace of God in him, which more fitted him for higher and holier scenes. Let heaven have him, my dear friends, and instead of mourning that he is so early taken from you, be thankful that you had him so many years, and that now you have a son with Christ. . . . . .

CHARLES H. WOLFF, Esq., a merchant of Cincinnati, with whom William kept up a constant correspondence, writes to Mr. D. W. Denison, uncle to the deceased :—

CINCINNATI, *April* 13, 1863.

. . . . . The painful intelligence of the death of our dear young friend Willie reached me several days ago. I loved him as a brother, and mourn him as one of my dearest friends. Aside from his estimable character, there was that peculiar magnetism of love in and around him that drew one imperceptibly to more than value his friendship.

It was one of the happy plans, sprung directly from my heart, to have him visit us here. At first I only included himself, but afterwards her whom he had chosen for a companion through life. This now is all changed, and must be deferred till we meet in that better world. To me, this day there is added a new interest in that heaven above where he has preceded us for a short time only; for these rapid moving moments are short, though they should be lengthened out to three or four score years.

. . . . . Your graphic and delicate description of his last moments is very touching and satisfactory. His pious life was a sure guarantee as to what his end would be. He died in peace, and is now in heaven. "The Lord gave, and the Lord hath taken away; blessed be the name of the Lord." . . . . .

Rev. WILLIAM B. SPRAGUE, D.D., of Albany, N. Y., writes :—

ALBANY, *April* 16, 1863.

. . . . I cannot forbear to write you, partly to congratulate you on your being such a favoured mourner, and partly to express my own personal sense of the loss of one whom I had always thought of as a dear young friend. He made a most agreeable impression upon us all, not merely by his devoted attentions to Dr. Edgar, but by the kindliness, and manliness, and propriety of his whole bearing. His graceful form, and beautiful expression of countenance, and modest demeanour, and fine powers of conversation, are as vividly in my remembrance as if I had seen him but the other day. . . . . You surely have every reason to think of his departure with devout thankfulness, much as your heart may bleed in view of it. That one whose life has been so brief should have accomplished so much for the cause of Christ, and then gone to heaven in a chariot of glory, and been permitted to speak to you of his blessed experience just as he was reaching his glorious home, furnishes an occasion for gratitude which, I venture to say, you reckon among the richest blessings of your life. With all the sadness which his death has brought with it, I cannot doubt that it will make the rest of your pilgrimage the more happy, that you can reflect that you have educated one son for heaven, who has preceded you in the way thither, and will be ready to greet you with his filial benedictions on your arrival. . . . .

EDWARD S. TOBEY, Esq., President of the Board of Trade of Boston, writes :—

BOSTON, *April* 19, 1863.

. . . . What a peculiar and rich blessing you have in the evidence of a triumphal faith in the last moments of your son—in the consoling last words that fell from his lips; and also in the cheering recollection of his holy, early consecrated, and consistent life and character! Truly indeed "the memory of the just *is* blessed." How comforting the thought that he is no longer subject to the sufferings, trials, and many disappointed hopes of a delusive world; but is now rejoicing in the smile of his blessed Saviour, and has securely reached that happy world where there shall be no more sin and no more suffering! . . . .

I do not forget that the loss of companionship and hourly sympathy on earth, of one so pre-eminently qualified to fulfil the fond expectation of a parent's heart, is irreparable; but then, how brief the period before you shall be permitted to be with him! We, dear brother, have arrived at that period of life when we *realize*, as we never could in earlier life, that it is indeed but "a span, a vapour, that appeareth for a little time, and then vanisheth away." . . . .

Rev. Alexander T. M'Gill, D.D., Professor in the Theological Seminary, Princeton, who was one of William's most esteemed friends, thus writes:—

Princeton, *April* 20, 1863.

There are not many houses in which the memory of William is more embalmed than in mine. The visit he made in the summer of 1860 left a memorial with my wife and children, to which they often turned with interest long before we apprehended he would be removed so soon to his home in heaven. I was absent in Europe. A friend of Mary, Miss G—— of Brooklyn, was on a visit; George was at home; Wm. H——, son of Dr. H—— of Philadelphia, was then in the last vacation of his course as a student of the Seminary; and the whole party, Mrs. M'Gill says, were full of life and gaiety.

The family worship was led by Mr. H——, William, and George, in rotation. But the prayers of William were so rich, and pertinent, and full of unction, that he impressed every one with the deepest interest; touched the hearts of the children as well as the mother, and his mirthful companions; leaving on every one the vivid and indelible impression that he was pre-eminently devout in heart. And, though playful as a child, he was even revered by his company for the heavenly fervour with which he would lead them at a throne of grace.

I think it proper to write down this incident, and offer it to you, in the tide of our heartfelt sympathy and condolence. I could say much more—of his kindness to my son at Philadelphia, and the high estimation in which George held both his mind and heart.

We think and talk here every day of your sorrow, and that of your dear family. But oh, what *consolation* you have! Sad as you are, you know how safely that sainted first-born has reached the haven, where no storm or danger of any kind may reach him. . . . . May "the God of all consolation" bless you and yours, beyond what I can ask or think.

Rev. James Moorehead, Presbyterian Minister, Donacloney, County Down, Ireland, who was Mr. Stuart's pastor before his coming to this country, thus writes:—

LAMB'S ISLAND, DONACLONEY,
April 21, 1863.

It is with unusual sadness I sit down to express to you our very deep sympathy under your heavy bereavement. We have just learned that on the 7th instant your gifted, amiable, and sainted son was taken from you by death. Although we had heard his health was not good for some time past, his removal has been a great shock here; and what will and must it be to his parents, and young wife, and tender and attached sisters! He must have greatly endeared himself to all who knew him. His spirit seemed to have drunk in much of the mind of our Lord. His bearing was so gentle and kind, his appearance so prepossessing, and his gifts of thought and utterance so commanding, that we thought him destined for great and lengthened usefulness on earth. Now we see he was only early prepared, and I would suppose well ripened for glory. His eloquent and earnest address to our young people in the Sabbath school, and his captivating deportment for a few hours in our family circle, cannot soon be forgotten by any of us here. We had hoped to see him again in the flesh. The Lord, "who doeth all things well," has ordered otherwise. May he give us grace to be submissive under his hand. I know natural affection is not weakened in the furthest advanced believers here. It will claim, and may have its tears and sighs. The hearts that love Jesus most are most susceptible of tender feelings in their natural attachments. Our Lord wept at the grave of Lazarus, and David lamented sorely the death of Absalom. We may sorrow under such dark and trying providences; but, dearly beloved, I do hope you and yours will not repine. You cannot sorrow as those who have no hope.

Mr. GEORGE MACFARLANE, (formerly of Philadelphia,) a friend and companion of Willie's, and one who frequently accompanied him in his mission school visits and operations, thus writes from Scotland:—

DALKEITH, *May* 4, 1863.

The sad tidings that have recently reached me, that your household has so suddenly been turned into a family of mourners, by the removal of one of its dearest members, came upon me so unexpectedly that I have not yet been able to realize it. I had seen Willie here so lately, and apparently in such good health, and then so soon after heard the news of his happy marriage, that I cannot appreciate the fact that the gushing, joyous stream of his life has so soon fallen into the silence of eternity.

I cannot, I dare not, try to comfort you in this sad bereavement. I know you seek it above, where alone it can be found. Would that I could help to ease you of this weary burden of grief that a mysterious Providence has laid upon you. But I cannot: I can only weep with you. . . . .

My memories of William D. Stuart have been, and shall always be, of the most pleasant character. His kind, affectionate manner,—his warm, impulsive, generous nature,—all added their charms to his character, and made any one happy who could call him *friend.* And when those natural gifts were purified and heightened by the grace of God shed abroad in his heart, no one who knew him could help loving him.

I can never forget the active and intelligent co operation he was ever so willing to lend in every work where the advancement of the Redeemer's kingdom was concerned; and doubt not that his happiness is, and will be enhanced, by the presence of those who through his instrumentality have been led to the Saviour. . . . .

Mrs. NOTT, wife of Rev. Eliphalet Nott, D.D., the distinguished President of Union College, Schenectady, N. Y., writes to Mr. and Mrs. Stuart:—

UNION COLLEGE, *May* 6, 1863.

My first impulse, when I saw the death of your dear son in a Philadelphia paper, kindly sent me, was to write at once to assure you of the heartfelt sympathy of Dr. Nott and myself; but what could I say to comfort those whom God had smitten? I know that the Being to whose service your precious son had early consecrated himself was the only one who could pour the oil of consolation into your wounded hearts; and I believed that he would do so. Has he not?

What joy must have filled your hearts as you heard his dying exclamation,—"I know that my Redeemer liveth!" And *so* the young Christian hero died. The battle was ended, the victory won. "Thanks be to God, who gave him the victory through our Lord Jesus Christ."

Dr. Nott, whose health is very feeble, desires me to say, "that you should be grateful to God for having had such a son." He was deeply affected by the allusion, in the very beautiful memorial in the *Presbyterian*, to the group of coloured children and people who mourned his loss on the day of his burial. Nothing could have been more touching. "Why am I spared, while the young and the gifted are taken? Even so, Father; for so it seemeth good in thy sight," was his language, when I announced to him the death of your son. . . . .

Colonel JAMES GWYN, of 118th Regiment Penn. Volunteers, writes from—

HEAD-QUARTERS, 118TH REGT. P. V.,
CAMP NEAR FALMOUTH, VA., *May* 9, 1863.

I had commenced a letter to you some two weeks since; but the sudden movement of the army, calling me to active exertions in having my command thoroughly equipped, gave me no opportunity of completing it. Amid the din of the late battle-fields I still had time to think of you and your late severe affliction—to feel for and to mourn with you.

Willie was indeed to me as a dearly beloved young brother: perhaps no brother ever loved another more deeply than I loved him. I had known him so long. He had, from a little prattling child, grown up under my eyes to a tall handsome man. As he grew up, he was continually engaged in doing good. Truly the ways of God are inscrutable. The tree here cut down was not cumbering the ground, but bringing forth fruit.

Had I not seen him the last time I was at home, I could not have realized his death; but when I saw his poor emaciated form, I felt that he must soon leave you. I felt sick at heart when I bade him farewell; and never will I forget his warm grasp of the hand and sweet smile, when he said, "God Almighty bless and protect you!—good-bye." With difficulty I restrained my tears, as I left your house with a heavy heart.

But why should you be sad? I am sure he whom you mourn could say with Paul, "I have fought a good fight, I have finished my course, I have kept the faith: henceforth there is laid up for me a crown of righteousness." I need not say to you where you can receive consolation. You have so often pointed out the way to others, that I am sure you have received from God's mercy-seat that rest which he has promised to all the weary and heavy laden.

Please say to Mrs. Stuart and the young widow that from my inmost soul I sympathize with them—I mourn with them. . . . .

CHARLES H. WOLFF, Esq., Cincinnati, in a second letter thus writes:—

CINCINNATI, *May* 11, 1863.

The *Presbyterian* of the 2nd instant is just to hand, containing a notice of the character and demise of my dear friend William. Many young men whom I highly esteemed have gone to the better world, but the death of none of them affected me so poignantly as the death of your son. The brief biography is so touchingly beautiful, and so truthful in all its delineations, that you will much oblige me by giving me the author's name.

Were it not that my heart reposes in the wisdom and goodness of our heavenly Father, it would ask, Wherefore, O Lord, hast thou caused this dire calamity to come upon us? But, with the Psalmist, let me say, "I was dumb, because thou didst it." "The

Lord gave, and the Lord hath taken away; blessed be the name of the Lord."

The loss to your family circle is irreparable, and my deepest sympathies are with you. I cannot write more, my heart is too full. . . . .

Rev. R. MACDONALD, North Leith, an eminent minister of the Free Church of Scotland, and the intimate friend of the late Rev. R. Murray M'Cheyne. He and William visited together the Island of Arran, and became mutually interested in each other.

NORTH LEITH, *June* 17, 1863.

I have read with intense and sorrowful interest all that has been said and written about your sorely missed and beloved son. His unexpected removal, just when he was becoming so eminently useful and so highly appreciated, is a most mysterious providence. Yet I feel sure that, through Christ strengthening you, you will be able sweetly to trust your Lord, even when you cannot trace him, and to say from the heart, "He hath done all things well."

It may be emphatically said of your dear and honoured son, "He lived much in little time." And one striking proof of this is the fact that, young as he was, he has been so universally and tenderly lamented. The accounts given of the feeling manifested forcibly recalled to me the touching words of inspiration,—"Devout men carried him to his burial, and made great lamentation over him."

I will always reckon it one of the privileges of my life that I enjoyed so much pleasant intercourse with him during his sojourn in Arran, about two years ago. He was so sweetly lively in spirit, so enlightened, so large-hearted, so manly, and, above all, so nobly Christian, that it was impossible not to admire and love him. I was greatly struck with what the *Banner* truly calls "his whole-hearted devotion to the cause of his Saviour;" and with his self-sacrificing and unsparing labours as the superintendent of the mission school for coloured children. His labours will not be in vain, and I doubt not that the crown he will receive from the Lord he loved so well will be a very bright one.

I feel very deeply for you, for a sorer bereavement than that you have experienced I cannot easily conceive. Blessed be God, however, you can mingle much joy with your sorrow, for you have the most assured conviction that your loss has been his unspeakable gain; and I have every confidence that you will be able to say with one of your own great American missionaries, when he lost in the prime of life a dearly beloved son—"If my Lord would rather that he should serve him in heaven than serve him here on earth, why should I say nay?"

In the course of my lecture last Sabbath afternoon I especially referred to your dear son by name; and after stating some facts regarding him, earnestly urged the young men of my congregation to follow his bright example. I trust many of them may be moved to do so by the blessed Spirit. . . . .

Rev. JOHN EDGAR, D.D., Belfast, Ireland, Professor in the Theological Seminary of the Presbyterian Church in Ireland, thus writes:—

BELFAST, *June* 22, 1863.

I have often tried to muster courage to write to you. My spirit has been heavily bowed down by the state of your country. A ray of light seems to break in now. God grant that you may soon have once more the blessings of peace. Since I was with you, many of those I saw then I shall see again no more. My dear travelling companion, who was to me as my own son—faithful, attentive, and kind—gone. I shall go to him, but he shall not come to me. It gives me the highest pleasure to hear of his own last scenes and triumphs, and of the very many who rightly prized his worth. The news came on me at first like an electric shock; but it was soothing afterwards to find that you and he had been previously warned that he was a mere tenant at will. The departure at the last was like what Pollok describes his sister's—"calm, self-possessed, cheerful, triumphant." You have a stronger hold than ever both on this world and the next; on this, for usefulness; on the next, for glory. . . . . May God fill you with all joy and peace in believing, and multiply to you and yours continually his great loving-kindnesses. . . . .

EXTRACTS FROM THE DIARY

OF

WILLIAM DAVID STUART.

DIARY.

SABBATH, *June* 8, 1856.—This morning I drove to Rev. Mr. H.'s church in Germantown, and heard him preach a very impressive sermon on the death of Nadab and Abihu for their sin in putting strange fire in their censers to burn before the Lord. The conclusion was especially directed to the unconverted. After dinner retired to my room, where I spend most of my spare time. I have been thinking, especially lately, of my former resolution of turning my attention to the ministry; and after looking at it in every light, have at last concluded, that if it please God to call me, I will offer myself, soul and body, to His service, and thus endeavour to fulfil my engagements, and win souls to Jesus. How much better is the service of God than that of the world!

Sabbath, Aug. 17.—Started for town at 8. At Sabbath school had a class of three. After dinner Messrs. G. and M'F. called for me, and we went first to the carpenter shop, and then to Amita Street. Addressed the latter school for about twenty-five minutes—tried to impress upon them three things: 1st. They are preparing for an eternity either in heaven or hell; 2nd. Love to Christ; 3rd. Each little boy and girl can do something. I felt that I was speaking for their souls, and did my best to produce an impression—hope I was successful. The S. S. teacher has a very important work to do. Sooner or later all must die. Are we prepared? If so, well; if not, *hasten!*

Friday, Aug. 22.—Every day I am more and more impressed with the necessity of studying for the ministry. Oh that God would give me sufficient grace never to look back, but to press forward in His service! and, when the hour shall come that I must be separated from all those who are near and dear to me, may I not shrink back nor falter, but boldly exclaim, "O death, where is thy sting? O grave, where is thy victory?" and ascend to glory, there to wait at the footstool of God, and sing His praises throughout all eternity. I often find great difficulty whilst praying, to keep my heart completely shut from the things of this world, and my thoughts fixed on heaven. I must still persevere, and God will in no wise cast me out. We should be thankful that Almighty God has protected us from pestilence and disease of every kind during the summer, now nearly past. Shall we ever see another? Who can tell?

Tuesday, Aug. 26.—Rose at 3.40. Had worship and breakfast with Nanna. Arrived at Milton at 12. The ride was pleasant, and Nanna enjoyed the scenery very much. I should enjoy walking from Summit to Danville, with my sketch-book and fishing-rod, to contemplate the curious formation of the strata, and to gather for mother the beautiful moss hanging from the trees. It was amusing to watch the various persons in the cars this morning.

Behind us sat a man and wife, of the "would be woulds." Before reaching Reading, we were pretty well posted up in all their family affairs. She made the car her dressing-room. Beside us sat a couple of old maids, who amused themselves with eating all the way;—in front a snobbish young man—his feet on the seats (not a very gentlemanly accomplishment), and answered his sisters in rough yeses and noes. So the time passed.

Saturday, Aug. 30—MILTON.—I have felt more ease of mind for the last day or two. Oh that Christ would shed abroad His glorious light in my heart, and show me the way to heaven.

Sabbath, Aug. 31—MILTON.—Beautiful morning. Very unwell—raging nervous headache. Read to M.;—walked with her and her brother L. to church. Rev. Mr. W. preached a very impressive sermon from the text, "The harvest is past, the summer is ended, and we are not saved." Some of his points seemed to be directed at me. I felt that indeed the harvest was past, and I still out of heaven. Oh, my God, strengthen me. Show, oh show me my Saviour. Teach me to know and feel that I can do nothing of myself, but Christ is all and in all. Make me to feel there is balm in Gilead, a great physician there, who is both able and ready to heal. I hope I have done what becomes a son of an elder, a S. S. teacher, and more than that, one who is looking forward to enlisting under the banner of Jesus.

I wonder how my dear S. S. class is to-day: though not with them in the body, I am in the spirit. Oh that God would make my labour effectual amongst them! Just think! their immortal souls are committed to my care. I must not betray the trust thus reposed in me by my

Saviour. Prayer—constant, earnest, heartfelt prayer—is one of the great means; and God will surely answer. I must set them a consistent, holy example.

The communion is now approaching—the time when, if God spare my life, I intend to make a public profession of my faith in Jesus and dependence on Him. May it not only be a public, but a private profession; may it be a prayerful one; may it be an acceptable one. May I be enabled to say, "Let others do as they will, as for me, I will serve the Lord." Oh may Jesus kindle, with a coal from the divine altar, the heavenly fire in my heart, to feel that to live and die for Him is all my desire—all that I live for. I feel now that I would rather die than deny Christ—that the world can kill my poor mortal body, but, thanks unto God, it cannot touch this soul. Ah, no! it belongs to Jesus: He gave it, and he only can take it away. He will receive a poor sinner like me, if I come in spirit and in truth. "Come unto me," He says, "all ye that labour and are heavy laden, and I will give you rest." I will support you throughout this troubled world; I will be with you in the hour of trial, when the dearest friend has forsaken you; and when the cold hand of death is upon you I will bear you aloft to the mansions prepared for you in glory.

What an honour it is to be a minister—to preach the gospel of Jesus! Would that my life might be spared (if it be His will) to proclaim the glad tidings of great joy to perishing people!

After dinner, retired to my room to read and meditate. Read in "Gleanings among the Mountains, or Traditions of the Covenanters"—a most interesting book. What great persecutions God's people have suffered in defence of his word! Oh, ye who sought to obtain renown by the persecution of the saints, where now is your fame? Your name is a reproach, and only remembered to be despised; while those whom ye considered as worse than dogs—whom ye oppressed and killed by scores as pestilent and worthless beings, are now honoured in heaven. Sleep on, ye bleeding bodies of the saints! sleep in your mossy bed, sleep in the martyr's winding-sheet; and while ye sleep ye shall not be unattended: posterity shall guard your couch, and point out your cot to the passing traveller; and He in whose service you fell, and in whose sight the blood of His saints is dear, will at length raise you from your lowly bed to shine among the sons of light in God's own house, and in His own presence, throughout the ceaseless ages of an ever-blessed eternity. To you indeed to live was Christ, and to die was gain. You shall wear a crown brilliant with innumerable gems, for you counted not your lives dear unto you that you might finish your course with joy.

Monday, Sept. 1—MILTON.—Aunt Mary P. has concluded to go to Niagara, which will make our party still more agreeable. At 12 we went to the Rail Road, and when the cars came, Nellie and uncle D. made their appearance. Reached the Suspension Bridge at 12

Tuesday, Sept. 2—NIAGARA.—Rose at 4. Took a short walk before breakfast to see the sun rise on the Falls. After breakfast we went on board the new steamer, *Maid of the Mist*, and having donned oil-cloth suits, prepared to pass almost under the Falls. How grand! This is Thy work, O mighty God! Went over to Goat Island, and there having rested ourselves a few minutes, we started for the end nearest the American Fall. Here a scene of terrific grandeur burst upon our view : at our feet the centre Fall, the water rushing, tumbling, plunging, as if in wild despair, before making the fatal leap, and then dashing itself, as if in a dying effort, on the rocks below. M. and I went to Prospect Tower, from which the view is equally grand. Goat Island is one of nature's mightiest cathedrals : its majestic pines are its fluted columns ; and its mighty organ pours forth in notes, too grand to be mistaken, the praise of its glorious Creator.

Thursday, Sept. 25.—Went to Y. M. C. A. Debating Society. Declaimed. Elected Corresponding Secretary. Had a spirited debate.

Thursday, Oct. 2.—Went to college as usual. Afterwards painted till 3. In the evening went to Debating Society, and led in the affirmative of a debate on the question, "Has the war with Russia promoted Christianity?" Gained my side.

Sabbath, Oct. 19.—After worship, papa handed me a letter from my dear pastor urging me to join the church. Why should I delay? Life is uncertain; death is sure. I may not live to see another communion season.

Went to the Home* and brought up the children.

Taught my class this afternoon from 1 Cor. xv., and tried to impress upon their tender minds the necessity of receiving Christ. In the evening we had a prayer-meeting for the young men of the church. I enjoyed it exceedingly. Truly this has been a day of refreshing from the presence of the Lord. O God, open mine heart—bring me to Thee. Let me no longer be out of the fold

* The Home for Friendless Children. The children were permitted to come up, under the escort of one of the teachers, to the Sabbath school of the First Reformed Presbyterian Church, on the Sabbath, for instruction.

of Christ, my Saviour and Redeemer. Thou art my Rock and the God of my salvation.

Sabbath, Oct. 26.—Went to prayer-meeting before S. school. Much pleased, and felt fitted for my labours. During the past week J. N. was removed. I hope that through the grace of God I did him good. Afternoon, school. I see W. M. has come back. Oh that he would stay! I think I am beginning to see more of Christ; but still how far from Him am I yet! Prayer is the sinner's only hope. Have mercy upon me, O God. Show me myself. Show me Thyself.

Sabbath, Nov. 16.—After church went to the study [of the pastor] and expressed my desire openly to enlist under the standard of Jesus, for He is our only safety and Rock of defence. Oh that He would give me grace never to dishonour my position, for it is a high one. Just think! a soldier of King Emmanuel! a position which the loftiest of earth's potentates might indeed rejoice in. God has said, "My grace is sufficient for thee." If we only trust in Him, coming with an humble, contrite heart, He will supply us with all needful grace from the fountain opened in the house of David. Went down to Marion Street, and had a very interesting meeting—spoke for about twenty minutes. We know not what good, with God's blessing, may result. We can do nothing of ourselves. I think I am beginning to see some good in my class. W. H. and J. P. both seem to be religiously inclined, especially the former. They are yet young, but not too young to die—not too young to be saved. If there have been impressions for good made upon them, O God strengthen and confirm them. Make them ornaments to Thy Church below and take them at last to

Thyself. I am afraid E. B. is rather wayward; still, I will not cease to pray for him, that God will open his heart to the reception of the truths of the Gospel, to see the awful position in which he is standing, and lead him to the foot of the Cross. God will always answer prayer when He thinks it is best.

Sabbath, Nov. 30.—Preparation Sabbath. Went over to the prayer-meeting, and down to the Home for the boys. Spoke to my class about the salvation of their souls; showed them the difference between the two covenants; and gave them that beautiful verse, "I love them that love me," &c., to remember, and guide them throughout the week. Rev. W. J. R. T. made a very touching address in the church. He showed that the first thing the Christian did when he had found Christ was to go to his nearest and dearest friends and relatives, and bring them also to the Messiah. I thought—It is my duty, and how much would I love to be the humble instrument of bringing my dear M. to the Saviour—to place the crown of her salvation on the head of her Redeemer.

Before tea, went to my room and spent a few minutes in prayer. Went over to the prayer-meeting. It was one of deep interest—the very room seemed fragrant with the air of heaven, a sweet foretaste of the happy, blessed eternity we shall enjoy in the realms of God. Why should we fear to come to God at His holy table, not in our own righteousness, but placing all our faith and dependence on Him?

Thursday, Dec. 4.—Very cold. Went to church. Sabbath will be communion. Oh that God would give me grace to come having on the wedding garment of Christ's righteousness.

Friday, Dec. 5.—Evening, went over to the church and was formally received by the Session as a member of the Church of the living God. I have now taken the step that separates me from the world. It is an important one—one which I shall never, I am sure, regret.

Sabbath, Dec. 7.—Went to prayer-meeting at 9—took part in the exercises. Took the communion for the first time. Oh that God would give me a double portion of His grace to keep my vows—to keep me from sin.

Sabbath, Dec. 14.—Pouring. No class. Evening, went with M'F. and G. to Marion Street—spoke for nearly half an hour on "I love them that love me, and those that seek me early shall find me." I often find great difficulty on the Sabbath in keeping out wandering thoughts. Satan is trying hard to draw me back to himself; but I will pray to God, and He will give me grace to resist him.

Monday, Dec. 15.—Examination with Professor F. on chemistry—written—got through first rate.

Friday, Dec. 19.—Examined by Professor C. at 11. Got through finely. Went to hear Elihu Burritt.

Saturday, Dec. 20.—Professor J.'s examination. Got through.

Monday, Dec. 22.—Rose at 2. Studied my geometry till 7. Examination—did not pass very well. Evening, monthly meeting of the Y. M. C. A.—very interesting.

Sabbath, Dec. 28.—Led in prayer for the first time. S. school—class all present. Tried to impress upon them the necessity of coming now to Christ; and gave them the verse, "Let not your heart be troubled," to remember.

Wednesday, Dec. 31.—Evening, Nellie had a little

company—spent a very delightful evening. The last night of 1856; but time never stops—always runs on, and so our lives.

Sabbath, Jan. 4, 1857.—Spoke earnestly to my boys about love to Christ. Went with M'F. to Marion Street —spoke for twenty-five minutes on the importance of grasping and improving youth ere it be lost in the fathomless depths of eternity. Retired at 11, after earnest prayer to God for my Sabbath class, my night school, ——, as well as all my family.

Tuesday, Jan. 6.—Evening, our soiree came off, and we had a delightful time—the room was crowded. M'F. read a fine report; G. a very good essay; S. P. H. made an excellent speech; and then came mine on "Scottish Martyrs,"—was received with thunders of applause, and interrupted with it throughout my piece.

Wednesday, Jan. 7.—In bed until 12. Severe pains all over my body.

Saturday, Jan. 24.—Rose at 6. Studied my speech —rehearsed "Bernardo del Carpio,"—read "Childe Harold." Went to the Germania—very fine. Walked home with M. and C. Had a long conversation on the necessity of salvation, early—how we should set ourselves against those things which would disgrace the calling of a Christian—against those things that the enemies of Christ might seize upon to sneer at the religion of Jesus. What pleasure can there be in this world if we have nothing to look to beyond—if all eternity lies dark and drear before us? Far better, inestimably better, to have an eternity in view, a heaven as our goal, a Saviour as our eternal companion. Oh how I would rejoice to see

M. a Christian! I will not cease to pray to God on her behalf. He will give answer, and cast off none who come to Him. God is the very embodiment of love. Though we are great sinners, Christ is a great Saviour.

Mrs. F.'s son John is dying from dropsy, arising from scarlet fever. May his soul go to Jesus, free from care, free from trouble, there to rest peacefully for ever.

Sabbath, Jan. 25.—Spoke earnestly to my class about Christ. Told them about John F., how happy he is waiting patiently for Jesus. After church, Mr. H. and I went to see him, and found he was still patiently waiting for his Redeemer. Oh that I were as happy as he! "Watch and pray:" the Son of man cometh in an hour when ye know not, as a thief in the night. Be ready. The tomb has no terrors, for Jesus has made it soft as eider down.

As I stood at the death-bed of that child this evening, how envious was I of him! I said, "John, would you like to get well?" "Oh no," he replied, "not for a thousand worlds; let me go to Jesus!" Here indeed is a case, one of many, in which Christ shows Himself as the support of the dying saint. Oh that M. could have been with me then! I know, I feel assured, it would have done her great good. It would have shown her that death is a blessing to the believer. He has not a cloud to obscure his setting sun: as it darkens to us on earth, it becomes brighter and brighter in that celestial city, until at last it bursts in its glorious, redeemed, and spotless effulgence before God and the Lamb. Soon he will fold his pinions at the gate of the heavenly mansion, and angels will ring the vault of heaven with loud hallelujahs, for the ransomed soul, redeemed from sin tc sparkle in the diadem of Jesus. Happy! happy! happy John! for you "to live was Christ, and to die is gain."

Wednesday, Jan. 28.—College. Wrote out lecture on Sulphur. After dinner went with Mr. H. to see John F. and Mrs. M'B. The former is still living—he has had a severe hemorrhage.....I am troubled with a nervous sick headache, and dull pain all through my limbs. I must do something.....Practised two hours. Read the "Hunter Naturalist." Had a pleasant chat with Mr. H. before retiring. Studied till 1.

God, I think, is beginning to answer my humble and, I hope, heartfelt prayers. I see more of Christ's grace in my heart, less inclination to do evil, and a greater desire to do good during my short stay in this world of care.

Friday, Jan. 30.—Rose at 6. College as usual. Lecture on Phosphorus and Selenium. George not any better. Dr. R. is going to try the galvanic battery. I must begin to study more; indeed I must not be lagging behind. Studied till 2.

Sabbath, Feb. 1.—After dinner went down to see John F. He asked me to kneel down, while he uttered a most fervent prayer. Much weaker—may God sustain him to the end, and as he approaches heaven strengthen his hopes and give him a triumphant entrance to glory. Afternoon, had a new class given me—persuaded all my boys to pray morning and evening. Read in "Heaven, or the Sainted Dead," by Harbaugh.

Monday, Feb. 2.—Very unwell. Did not go to college. Painted all morning at Mr. L.'s—finished my "Brandy Wine." Afternoon, went to see John F. He is much weaker. Studied. Retired at 2.

Tuesday, Feb. 3.—I am out of sorts to-day. I think my health is giving way—I am getting so weak in the chest. It would be a great trial to me to be prevented from becoming a minister; but God knows what is best: He doeth all things well, and we must bow in submission to His will. Very sick this evening. What is the matter with me? Retired at 12.

Wednesday, Feb. 4.—Wrote out chemical lectures. Studied till 1—getting over the blues. George is still the same. I trust God will restore him soon to health and strength.

Thursday, Feb. 5.—Evening, went to Dr. M.'s to a meeting of the young men, members of the church, in college, to establish an organization in the University, called the Christian Brethren.

Friday, Feb. 6.—Went to church meeting to form Constitution for Christian Association.

Saturday, Feb. 7.—Experimented with nitric acid. Wrote the proposed Constitution. Practised. Spoke to M. earnestly about her salvation.

To-morrow will be the Sabbath. May God grant it be to us a Sabbath indeed. May His grace be poured out on our wounded souls like healing ointment.

Sabbath, Feb. 8.—S. school as usual. Damp and rainy. W. J. only present—taught him from John x. May God accompany it with His blessing, without which all teaching is in vain. John F. is better. Oh that God would make me walk closer with Him, and keep my mind more fixed on Jesus. Read in "Hedley Vicars." It is a sweet book—I never tire of it. The more I read of his life, the more I am impressed with the divine love of Jesus. Just see how a young man, depraved, profane, ungodly, when brought under the saving influences of the Holy Spirit, immediately becomes an instrument of good. I firmly believe that God raised him up as a monument, a guide to others to find that blessed Saviour. I have been reading to-day in Pike's "Persuasions to Early Piety." They are indeed beautiful, and should be in the hands of every young person.

Sabbath, Feb. 15.—Before S. school read Pike's "Persuasions to Early Piety." It is indeed a gem, a rare gem. Took a walk with S.—had a long talk about our future lives. I do not think I am called to be a minister. I wonder if M. loves Jesus. Oh that she did!

Tuesday, Feb. 17.—This evening Messrs. H. and S. started for Pittsburgh. I trust S. will do well. May God bless him and go with him, be his counsellor and his guide, his help in this world, and his only hope in the world to come. May he never swerve from duty, and God will prosper him.

Wednesday, Feb. 18.—Went to see John F. He has had a relapse, and the doctor says he can hardly recover. What an instance of grace! Jesus has been with him while his body has been racked with pain. Retired at 2, after study. I wish I could train myself to study—somehow I cannot do it, I get so nervous.

Sabbath, March 1.—Another month begun! Am I nearer heaven? Studied my morning lesson in Daniel. Went to S. school. W. H. has gone to the country. He was a good, obedient boy. May the grace of God be with him. I have prayed more earnestly to-day than usual for my S. S. class. May I see the fruit of my labour, not for myself, but for His glory.

Thursday, March 5.—Worked at my chemicals. Spent

all afternoon in laboratory. Studied. Retired at 3. I do not feel satisfied with myself, somehow. I am entirely bewildered in making a choice for life. I cannot feel at all that I have a call to the ministry. I fear I will not be of any use there. May God give me grace in my choice. May I live entirely for his service: yet all I can do is nothing compared to what He did for me. God give me grace to be humble.

Sabbath, March 8.—To-day my mind has been filled with wandering thoughts, and I have struggled in vain almost to keep them out. I will pray for more grace and strength from God. Would that I were like Hedley Vicars!

Monday, March 9.—Went to the first meeting of our Christian Association; was elected President. Had a very warm debate. Came home, and studied till 3. My eyes are very sore indeed.

Sabbath, March 15.—I feel a voice (or whatever it may be called) within me saying, "Stop and consider what is your duty, to be a minister or not?" O God, give me grace to decide. May I have nothing to influence me but a desire to promote Thy kingdom, and do what I can for Jesus, who has done so much for me.

Thursday, March 19.—College as usual. Came home and made sulphur medals and casts. Went to Debating Society. Chemistry coming along splendidly. Prayed earnestly for a change of heart. Oh, the redeeming love of Jesus! Who, who can form the smallest estimate of it! —boundless, tender, ceaseless, never-changing, good for time and good for eternity. May I have a goodly portion of it, and tell others how it may be obtained. What a precious thing prayer is! It is indeed "the soul's sincere desire, unuttered or expressed." God is very good, and we very ungrateful. Could I but love Him as He loves me, I would be so happy! Make me Thine, O Jesus.

Saturday, March 21.—I do not know what is the matter with me of late: everything I do seems to tire me. I feel unfit for everything. I am unable to fathom it.

Sabbath, March 22.—Went to the young men's prayer-meeting—presided, and led in prayer. Raging headache. To-day I have been unable to keep my thoughts from wandering. O God, assist me; without Thee I can do nothing. Make me one of Thine own anointed ones, loving and serving Thee with all my heart; and may I strive to bring others to Thee likewise—to do what little I can to promote the interests of Zion, and spread the glory of the Cross. How many are there in our very midst who do not care for Jesus, but are going down to death without one ray of hope!

Monday, March 23.—*Swelled neck* and raging headache. Professor F.'s examination—written—got through splendidly—A 1.

Friday, April 3.—There is something the matter with me lately. A voice tells me I am not doing my duty. Am I any nearer Christ than I was yesterday, or even a week or a month ago? I dare not answer the question. True it is that my soul is nearer eternity—my life is every day becoming shorter. Am I nearer God? Oh, may I this night resolve that, in the strength of promised grace, I will not let another day go by without doing something for Jesus. He did very much for me; He has given me many opportunities, and will require much at my hands. It seems strange how so many people go to church, believe in the Bible, heaven and hell, and yet are perfectly indifferent as to the salvation of their souls. What do we live for? To eat, drink, and gratify our lusts? The beasts do that. Why did God give us reasoning powers—make us in the image of Himself—give us an immortal soul? Why, but to prepare us to dwell with Him throughout eternity. Oh, could I be the means of bringing one soul to God—of rescuing one immortal soul—more precious than all the world—from eternal ruin, I would be satisfied.

How happy does the Christian feel when he has been labouring for his Master! He is happy, not only in his Saviour's smiles and approbation, which he feels in his heart's inmost core, but happy in the thought that God will reward him in eternity. There is no real happiness but to the Christian. The monarch on his throne may seem happy; but could we look into his heart, the canker-worm is there. The beautiful maiden, just blooming into womanhood, admired and courted, a lover of pleasure, may indeed seem happy; but go with her to her chamber, and when a thought of eternity comes o'er her, and come it will, no matter how much she may strive to drown it—see her shed tears of remorse. Whence is this? Where are her gay companions? No friend to console and comfort! She has not Christ. Let Him be my friend. When all others forsake, He is near to comfort.

How would I love to see M. come to Jesus!

Tuesday, April 7.—To-day I have been reading Young's "Night Thoughts." They are grand indeed. It makes one's very soul thrill to read them, so full of meaning, such great truths contained in them. Unquestionably they are one of the finest productions in the English language.

Sabbath, April 12.—Low spirited. Raining. Taught with considerable vigour. Read "Hedley Vicars." This book is indeed a treasure. Oh that I were he! but God doeth what is best for both of us. He takes care of His own children.

Sabbath, April 19.—Preparation Sabbath. Spent the time before dinner in private prayer for my class and M., that they may be early brought to Christ. Still low spirited. Because I am so is no reason that Christ is not with me. He hides me in the hollow of His hand, and will not show me His great love. He knows it would be too great for me to bear. He stands knocking at the door of our hearts. He is patient, yet He will not stand for ever. Our death-knell will soon be rung, and then woe if we have not let Him in! John F. is still alive.

Thursday, April 23.—Read my Essay on Electricity before the Debating Society. It was moved that I be requested to repeat it.

Sabbath, April 26.—Rose at 6. Communion Sabbath. Went to prayer-meeting at 9—deeply interesting. Sat down at the first table. Never have I felt the Spirit's presence, and my own weakness, so much as to-day. There I uttered most fervent petitions for one dear unto me, who as yet has not found Jesus. I resolved, in the strength of promised grace, to walk closer with God—to labour more earnestly in the vineyard of the Lord—to do what little I can to promote His glory. Went to prayer-meeting in the evening, and led in prayer.

Saturday, May 2.—Very unwell to-day—cannot tell exactly what is the matter. I feel that I am not living as I ought—am not advancing toward heaven, or doing anything to promote Christ's cause. I must be more active. I have not enough association of the right kind. God help me! I am weak, God is mighty; I am a helpless sinner, He the high and holy God. I wish, I pray that M. may become a Christian—how delightful it would be! I think she is becoming rather more serious. Would to God it were so. All we can do is to pray, and trust the rest to God. How kind, how good He is to us sinners, who deserve nothing but punishment at His hands!

Sabbath, May 3.—Between services to-day I engaged for half an hour in prayer for my class; also for my dearest M., that God would open her heart. Evening, took her to church. After service spent a delightful hour—we had a long chat upon the necessity of early coming to Jesus. I think she is more attentive to the things of her soul. God will say to me at the judgment, "Where is the flock, the beautiful flock I gave unto thee?" May I be able to say, "Here they be, Lord; all redeemed by thy Son." How happy the thought that we who love on earth, shall love still more in heaven! We shall not always be separated.

Sabbath, June 28.—Rose at 6. Church in the morning. After dinner retired to my room and wrote to M. about her eternal salvation; engaged in prayer for her, my S. S. class, and myself. After tea had sacred music. How lovely it is on a Sabbath evening for a family to engage in pouring forth their hearts in praise to their Creator! It makes me think of the eternity we hope to spend around the throne of God. How delightful it is to be a Christian! Oh that I could do more for God!—that I could bring M. to His footstool! I will not cease to pray for her till I get an answer to my prayers. God has promised to hear me if I persevere.

Thursday, July 2.—Rose at 5. Went in to hear the result of the examinations. I am passed to a Junior. Worked all day in the carpenter shop making shelves for my laboratory.

Monday, July 6.—Beautiful moonlight! so calm, so bright, so still. How grand are all thy works, Parent of good, and yet how ungrateful are we, guilty sinners!

Thursday, Aug. 6—ATLANTIC CITY.*—Rose at 5. Rolled ten pins till bathing time. Afternoon took a ride to the dry inlet, round the light-house. Had charades—took several principal characters, with which all were much pleased.

Monday, Aug. 10.—Rose at 6. Worked at chemistry all day. Read Regnault. My seventeenth birth-day! I think there is no better time to make good resolutions than on one's birth-day; and by the grace of God I will endeavour to keep those that I have here set down:—1st, That I will endeavour strictly to adhere to the truth—never make a statement unless I know it to be the truth, never take anything for granted. 2nd. That I will never speak ill of any person—that I will live at peace with all—that I will break off as many as possible of my foolish habits, and remember I have an example to set as a member of Christ's Church. 3rd. That I will love my brothers and sisters more, and make it more my duty to make them happy—will do my share to keep alive the spirit of love and unity in our family circle. Finally, That I will endeavour to lead a more consistent Christian

* One of the watering-places much resorted to by Philadelphians.

life than I have done heretofore, remembering that God's eye is ever upon me, and I must not disgrace His name. All this I will endeavour to do, not in mine own strength, but entirely in the strength of promised grace.

And now, my Heavenly Father, be pleased to look down upon me and bless me. Grant me Thy grace and assistance to carry out what I have resolved. May I from this day live not for myself, but for Thy glory. Bless my dearest M.; guard her and guide her; early bring her into the fold of Jesus. May she be an humble follower of Thee; and when thou hast done with us on earth take us to be with Thee, throughout the ceaseless ages of eternity. Amen.

Saturday, Aug. 16.—Another week has passed—how rapidly! A week more of my life gone—a week nearer heaven or hell. I have a week less to prepare for eternity, a week's more sins to answer for at the judgment-seat of God. Have I improved it? I fear, in a measure, I have not; certainly not as much as I ought to have done. I must try, by the grace of God, to do better. He has done for me very much more than I deserve. I trust M. is beginning to feel that the all-important thing is the salvation of the immortal soul.

Saturday, Aug. 22.—I must pull up and study now for examinations. I am not satisfied with myself. I must and can do better. God is not pleased with me: I am not living as I ought. O God, give me grace to love and serve Thee better; and make my dearest M. a child of Thine. I come, just as I am, and cast all on Thee. O God help me.

Sabbath, Aug. 23.—Lovely morning. Read in the Word until church time. Afternoon, took a nap, and by procrastinating became too late for S. school—a thing that never happened to me before, and by God's assistance it will never happen again. Oh that my heart were more given to Jesus—that I could feel more my need of Him—that I may lose my sinful pride, and come to Jesus, poor and needy, place all my trust in Him, for he has cared for me and has promised to receive sinners, even me, who am as the greatest.

M. gives me much concern. I fear she has as yet not given herself up entirely to the service of God, that she is yet yearning after the world and its sinful pleasures. I will not give up praying for her and speaking to her on the subject: I feel assured that God will ultimately bless my endeavours—that He will reclaim her, His lost sheep, and bring her to His arms. Her companions generally are not such as would bring comfort in a dying hour, and pour words of consolation in to her soul when all is dark around. What would I not give to see her a child of God, an heir of glory! This universe would be a ransom far too small;—but no ransom is required; our Redeemer says, "Ask, and it *shall* be given you; seek, and ye *shall* find." May she find that Jesus who died to redeem her; and may she rejoice in Him. If I see her to-morrow, and an opportunity offer, I will again speak to her on the subject.

Thursday, Aug. 27.—I must really work hard, and do myself some credit at college next year. I have been too lazy and careless. How many resolutions I make and break! I must reform.

Sabbath, Sept. 13.—Read "Night of Toil." Afternoon, went to school—very full and attentive class. I pray that God will bless my labours—of themselves, they are very fruitless. I will make a practice of retiring to my room immediately on my return from the afternoon service, and invoking God's blessing on my S. school labours during the day. I ought and must seek God's blessing and assistance, if I ever expect to succeed in this important work.

Friday, Sept. 25.—Came in at 8. Great excitement in monetary affairs. Pennsylvania and Girard Banks suspended.

Thursday, Oct. 20.—Bought "Attic Philosopher," and Michaud's "History of the Crusades." Went to John F's. funeral—was one of the pall-bearers.

Sabbath, Oct. 23.—Communion Sabbath. Went to prayer-meeting—very solemn. Dr. W. preached on the atonement of Christ. Went to first table. It was indeed a season of refreshing from the presence of the Lord. God's Spirit was in our midst, and the Lord did wonders for us. There did I plead with God for myself, and earnestly for my dear M. I know He will hear me.

Friday, Jan. 1, 1858.—Did not go to early prayer-meeting, on account of a severe neuralgia. Made arrangements for my Anniversary. Got a new room corner 13th and Mariner. Had seventy children present—fed them on mince pies and raisins. Afternoon, went to Parent school. Feel very unwell to-night. Studied until 1—am to be examined to-morrow. I must set out from to-day to serve God better than I have done—must pray that He will give me strength.

Saturday, Jan. 2.—Went to college and was examined, which lasted for two hours. Preceptors said I had done remarkably well. Played chess.

Sabbath, Jan. 3.—Rose at 6. Went to my school—brought them up to the Anniversary—had about seventy-five children. Altogether there were about 850. Mine were the best behaved. They were presented with the "Life of John Fleming."

Sabbath, Jan. 24.—School not as large as I had hoped for in the morning. Took M. to hear Rev. Dudley Tyng—text, "Wherewithal shall a young man cleanse his way?" I feel very sick to-night; at times, low spirited; and again, when I think God does it all—that He is my God and will take care of me—I am happy. Oh that M. were a child of God! then would I rejoice.

Friday, Jan. 29.—Had another discussion with M. to-day about the opera. I think she is beginning to change her views. I hope, I pray it may be so.

Sabbath, May 9.—Attendance at morning school very small—much discouraged—teachers' prayer-meeting after school. We are too self-confident—we must trust more in God. Afternoon, school as usual; attendance seventy.

Monday, May 10.—Commenced study of the Steam Engine. Evening, meeting of Christian Association—appointed to prepare an address to our young friends M'F. and G., who are about to leave us for a season. We intend to present each with a Bible.

Tuesday, May 11.—Went to Guardians of Poor Office to see about getting a poor coloured woman buried. Bought a malachite and agate. Labelled minerals. How weak, and selfish, and proud we are! More and more I feel my own weakness; and more and more I hope I trust in God. What a blessed thing is faith! pure, confiding faith, ever "looking to Jesus." He will help us in weal or woe. He will never leave or forsake us.

Blessed promise! glorious hope! May M. have great faith.

Monday, May 17.—College as usual. Labelled minerals. Lesson in Müller with L.—Spirals with H. Evening, large meeting at the church to bid farewell to Rev. Mr. W. and Messrs. M'F. and G.—read the address to the two latter, and presented each with a copy of the Word of God.

Friday, May 21.—Bought Dana's Mineralogy, and a very fine specimen of sulph. of lead—one of the finest in the country.

Sabbath, May 23.—Evening, took charge of the Boys' Meeting in the carpenter shop—large attendance—very unwell.

Wednesday, May 26.—Rose at 5. Practised. Read. College as usual. Attended noon prayer-meeting—very interesting. God's Spirit was of a truth present with us. Long talk with mother. Lessons L. and H.

Thursday, May 27.—College. Attended prayer-meeting after third hour. Lessons with K. and H. Went to see aunt J., who is very low. Practised. Evening, went to prayer-meeting at E.'s, and what a delightful time we had! God was truly in our midst. Walked home with P. W., who seemed much changed, and was deeply impressed with the meeting. I will continue to pray to God for him, that he may be led openly to profess his faith in Christ.

Friday, May 28.—This afternoon M. was received into the Church. I pray God she may be a bright and shining light—a consistent Christian. Afternoon, went to the Diligent prayer-meeting. The room was crowded. I opened the meeting with prayer. The exercises were deeply impressive, and I came away with my soul refreshed. Evening, went to see M. Now that she has united herself to the Church, I feel a still greater attachment for her. How strong the bond of Christian love!

Saturday, May 29.—Attended noon prayer-meeting. Walked up with F. E.—he is a lovely Christian character. I must from this evening give closer attention to my studies. I will pray God to give me strength and a will to do it.

Sabbath, May 30.—School as usual—had teachers' prayer-meeting. After dinner went to see Annie S. —talked and prayed with her. She is a happy Christian. Went to see Mrs. J. who is sick—she was glad to see me. Called also on Mrs. La M., whose husband is a slave—took her subscription-book to try to raise some money to buy him off. Evening, went down to school—very good attendance—spoke half an hour. Came home very sick. Retired at 10.30.

Monday, May 31.—Went to prayer-meeting at Diligent Engine House—very large attendance—presided—very solemn. Several young men stood up and asked to be prayed for. How wonderful is the working of God's providence! Evening, read Essay on the "True Hero" at Rev. S. H.'s church, before their S. S. Association.

Tuesday, June 1.—Family moved to the country. Nanna and I will keep house alone for a week or two. Went to the "Diligent" at 5—very large meeting, and very impressive. How precious the privilege of spending an hour in communion with God! How we should improve these privileges! God will require much of us. Evening, talked with Nanna.

Wednesday, June 2.—Uncle D. and I went to Mr.

M'A.'s to see his microscope—spent a delightful evening. I could spend hours over the microscope. The more we look into these objects, invisible to the naked eye, the more we admire the wisdom, the goodness, and the power of that God who made them all. He controls the most distant system, and the tiniest insect that floats in the sunbeam.

Thursday, June 3.—College. Attended prayer-meeting. Went out to Springbrook—retired early, very unwell—sorry I could not remain in the city to attend prayer-meeting at E.'s.

Friday, June 4.—Rose at 4.30—slept very little. Visited Annie S.'s. family. She died yesterday, full of hope. "Blessed are the dead that die in the Lord."

Sabbath, June 6.—S. school as usual—very fair attendance. Went with P. W. to Rev. Mr. B.'s. church. It is their communion Sabbath, and my dear M. is to be baptized and admitted into the Church. Mr. B. preached a beautiful sermon on the subject of our Saviour's crucifixion, and then, descending from the pulpit, advanced to her and said, "M. E., I baptize thee in the name of the Father, Son, and Holy Ghost." Oh, how happy I felt; for there I saw what for years I had earnestly prayed and wished for. Truly, God hears prayer. When I saw placed in her hands the emblems of *our* Saviour's dying love, my heart burned within me—I wished to partake with her. Though not with her in the body I was in the spirit.

Saturday, June 12.—Went in to college. Packed minerals, and had lesson with Dr. L. Read Lardner on Steam Engine. Much amused at a young snob wanting another to fight a duel. Read Pickwick, and Humphrey's Glimpses of Ocean Life.

Sabbath, June 13.—Rode into town with papa. Went to see Mrs J., one of my scholars, who is very ill. Very happy to-day.

Wednesday, June 16.—Spent a very delightful evening with M. How beneficial to a man is the society of woman, especially of that one whom he loves! How much that is sinful is he kept from doing by the thought that she would not like it!

Sabbath, Aug. 1.—Read "Pearls of Thought," and Newton's "Cardiphonia." Afternoon, had sacred music. I love it; it seems to lift the soul from earth to heaven, and give it a sweet foretaste of what in a great measure will occupy it in heaven. Evening, went to prayer-meeting—took part.

Monday, Aug. 2.—Read in Lamartine's Girondists. Practised. Read Goethe's Faust; also in Todd's Student's Manual. I consider the latter an invaluable work; every time I read it I get from it some new thought, and some new light is thrown upon my course of study.

Wednesday, Aug. 4.—Packed in a few minutes' notice—came to town at 8, and at 3.30 started for Pottsville. The road from Port Clinton was new to me—the scenery grand and much varied. Now we were in a valley, with the mountains rising three and four hundred feet on either side; again we were upon the summit of the ridge, with the country stretching away for miles at our feet. Arrived at Pottsville at 7.45.

Thursday, Aug. 5.—At 5, took carriages and drove twelve miles over the Broad and Blue Mountains to Ashland. After breakfast, drove to the Locust Run coal mine. For the first time I here entered a mine, and was much interested with the various operations through which the coal passes. We then visited the colliery of Mr. H., where I obtained some fine specimens of coal and slate fossils, which are now rather rare. After dinner, visited the colliery of Mr. R., where I procured some good specimens of variegated coal. Went three quarters of a mile into the breast.

Friday, Aug. 6.—Started for Tuscarora after breakfast—from thence took stage for Tamaqua—there again took stage and ascended the Sharp Mountain, 6 miles to Summit. Here entered the cars, and rushed down the side of the mountain, 9 miles, to Mauch Chunk. We here took the Lehigh Valley Railroad, and reached Easton at 2, where we took Central Railroad for New York.

Saturday, Aug. 7.—At 5 P.M. we left the Harlem Depôt for Lake Mahopec—arrived at 8.30, very dirty and tired. Dressed. Saw aunt A. and cousins.

Sabbath, Aug. 8.—Took a walk before breakfast. Went to church at 10. Walked home along the lake. This is a poor place to spend the Sabbath. No one seems to know or care that it is God's holy day—laughing, reading novels, and flirting, seem to be their occupations.

Monday, Aug. 9.—Uncle D., the boys, and myself rowed six miles and took a bath before breakfast. Started at 8 for Peekskill, 16 miles distant—took the Hudson River R. R. for Garrison's, and thence the ferry to West Point. The view from the Parade ground is remarkably fine. Visited Kosciusko's monument. As I looked at it, Campbell's lines came home to me,—

> "Hope, for a season, bade the world farewell,
> And Freedom shrieked as Kosciusko fell."

Truly the great and good will never be forgotten. Left at 2.30 for New York.

8

Tuesday, Aug. 10.—Left New York at 4.20 P.M. for Boston. Read "Knickerbocker" in the cars. My eighteenth birth-day! God grant me grace to dedicate myself anew to Thee, and live a more consistent life.

Wednesday, Aug. 11.—Went on board the *Europa*—was disappointed in her accommodations—bade my friends good-bye at 12, and then the vessel headed for "Old England." At 4.20, left Boston, viâ Fall River, for New York.

Thursday, Aug. 12.—Arrived in New York at 8, and at 4 left for home, sweet home. Read the Life of John Stevenson in the cars. Reached home at 7.40—found all well, and of course glad to see me.

Tuesday, Aug. 17.—Did not go to town. Spent two hours in cleaning my minerals. The Queen's message was received to-day, thus proving the complete success of the Atlantic Telegraph. Planned an Essay to be entitled "Young Men—their Influence."

Friday, Aug. 20.—Rose at 6. Did business for father. Read "Tom Brown's School Days." Came out at 4—found all the family had gone to J.'s. Read. Took tea all alone, after which sat on the porch and thought of M. I pray that God will give her grace to resist all the temptations with which she may be surrounded during her absence.*

August 24.—Rose at 6. Went to the house to see mother and grandmother: the former very well; the latter—oh, it pains me to say it—not as well as I would wish to see her. It makes my heart bleed at the very idea of

* M. was to sail for Europe in a few days, and expected to remain abroad for two years.

parting with her; and that, I was going to say, for ever; but, no! blessed be God,—

"The good shall meet above."

Went to the store, and to Jayne's Hall prayer-meeting —very interesting. Dined at home. Had a long talk with grandmother. Went up to Lansdowne at 4. Retired at 11—very unwell indeed.

Friday, Aug. 27.—Rose at 6. Came in with P. at 8. Heard the news that I have a little sister. God grant that her life may long be spared, and that she may be a bright and happy Christian.

Sabbath, Aug. 29.—Lovely morning. Mr. Scott preached on the observance of the Sabbath. Sat in the lawn until dinner time. After dinner, retired to my own room to read and meditate. Read in "Kennedy's Divine Life." Deeply interested. Am I a Christian? True, I am a member of the visible Church; but that will not save me. Have I experienced that change of heart which marks the true believer, and which alone can secure salvation? I trust I have. I love Jesus, and look to Him only for salvation. "Lord, I believe; help thou mine unbelief." Open mine eyes, and show me Thy law. I find Jesus more precious to me now than ever before. Daily I feel my own insufficiency, and endeavour to rest with more assurance upon the Rock of Ages.

If God spare my life, in one short year I will have entered the school of the world, whose lessons, (alas, how hard to many!) are taught by the stern rule of experience. Soon I must be exposed to all the taunts and temptations of a jeering, godless world, under whose bitter scoff too many have fallen. How consoling is the thought,—

> "From every stormy wind that blows,
> From every swelling tide of woes,
> There is a calm, a sure retreat;—
> 'Tis found beneath the mercy-seat."

To-day is M.'s last Sabbath at home. May it be to her a precious day of grace. How joyful to think that our prayers, though uttered at points far distant from each other, will come nearer and nearer as they approach the mercy-seat, until blending together they reach the ear of the Lord of sabaoth, who will grant us our petitions as it seemeth best unto Himself. Spent some time in the woods in prayer, previous to going to church.

Thursday, Sept. 2.—Made tow wig and whiskers. Evening, went to B.'s—had tableaux and charades. I impersonated eight characters, much to the pleasure of my audience, but not to my own. My heart and thoughts were not in it. Retired at 12, very unwell.

Friday, Sept. 3.—Went to town at 8 o'clock. Very unwell. Came out at 4. I have yet much of my procrastination to break off. God grant me grace and strength to resist it and other sins to which I am subject.

Saturday, Sept. 4.—Saw Mrs. W. T. W. on the boat. Had a long talk with her. She is a lovely Christian.

Sabbath, Sept. 5.—Rose at 6. Went down to my school. All were very glad to see me. How happy am I in that God has spared me to return with new zeal to my labours. Mr. M'E. preached for us a very able and instructive sermon from the text, "Ought not Christ to have suffered these things?" He was what I would term a clear preacher, leaving no doubt in my mind in regard to the subject on which he preached. After dinner, went to my school as usual. I taught the boys' Bible class. All seemed very attentive and desirous to learn. Mr. M'E.

preached in the afternoon from the text, "Ye must be born again," if possible a more able sermon than in the morning. He has got hold of the matter, and speaks like one who has experienced in his own soul all that he says. At 7, W. M. called for me, and we went to see Mrs. J., one of my scholars, who is dying of a very rapid consumption. She was not only in great bodily pain, but in great mental agony. She said, "Oh, I cannot, I cannot find Jesus." I told her how and where she could find him. She exclaimed, "Oh, I have not been worse than anybody else—why cannot I find Jesus?" I then told her she must come resting alone on Jesus for salvation. I prayed with her for a long time, and was frequently interrupted by her cries for mercy. After prayer, we sang the hymn, "Just as I am." Never before did I feel the necessity of seeking Jesus ere laid upon a dying bed. Lord grant that I may have laid up *now* my treasure in heaven, and that I may rest my all on Jesus. How sweet the name of Jesus! May I be His child. Oh, that I were like Him! Went to my school at 8 o'clock, and had a very good prayer-meeting. I spoke to them from the subject of Paul's interview with Felix. They listened with marked attention, and seemed much impressed.

Wednesday, Sept. 8.—Went to town at 8. Learned the sad news that Mr. A. R. is no more. He died suddenly of apoplexy at their country seat near Auburn. He was preparing for a trip to the south, when suddenly he was cut down. Truly, "in the midst of life we are in death." What a warning to us all to be ready, with our lamps trimmed and burning, waiting for the coming of the Master! He was a truly Christian man. None knew him but to love him. College began. Got books. Made arrangements with Mr. G. to enter his laboratory.

Sabbath, Sept. 12.—Went to my school. Attendance small in the morning. Afternoon, much larger. After tea, went for G. M'F. to go with me to see Mrs. J. We found her very happy. When I entered the room her eye kindled, and she said, "Oh, Mr. Stuart, I have found Jesus—yes, I have found Him; He is my only Saviour!" We both prayed, and sang several hymns with her. How we should thank God for what He has done for her; and what an encouragement should this be to us in our work and labour of love! Truly, God is the hearer and answerer of prayer. We have but to ask, and it shall be given. God's delays are not denials. In His own good time we shall have what we have asked, or what we ought to have asked.

Monday, Sept. 13.—Sat with mother and nursed Pattie until 8.30. Went to college—from there to the laboratory.

Wednesday, Sept. 15.—Heard that Mrs. J., my S. S. scholar, died in peace.

Sabbath, Sept. 19.—Lovely morning. Walked in the woods. Went to church. After dinner, retired to my room—read and prayed. Went to Mr. S.'s Sabbath school—taught a class of coloured children. They seemed much interested in what I said. Came home very tired.

Tuesday, Sept. 21.—Went to laboratory. Analyzed Lythia Mica—very difficult. Got flower of the aloe preserved in spirits. Came out at 4. Worked at chemistry and blow-pipe until 9.30. Studied. Saw the comet very distinctlv this evening with telescope. Moonlight.

Sabbath, Oct. 3.—Rose at 6.30. Drove to town with father. Attendance at school small. Dr. L. preached from Joshua xx. 1–5, a most impressive and heart-searching sermon. May it be of service to many souls. God bless it to my own. Afternoon school attendance very good. Taught my Bible class. To-day my friend P. joined the Church. I pray that he did it with a sincere and honest heart, trusting only to the merits of Jesus for salvation. Drove out at 6. How many darling sins have I yet to mourn over. I would do right, but "evil is present with me." My old habits cling to me—hard, hard is it to shake them off. O God, grant me Thy Spirit's assistance, that I may have this hard and stony heart of mine cleansed from every sin; and may I take delight only in the ordinances of Thy grace. Of myself I can do nothing; but do Thou make me clean. May I daily grow in grace and in the knowledge of Thy holy word. May I have strength to resist all the temptations with which my path is beset—to restrain my evil passions and temper—to speak evil of no one, but rather love my enemies; and may I never in any way disgrace the name of Jesus, but ever walk an humble, devoted, earnest Christian, having my heart and hand in my Master's work. Hear and answer me for Jesus' sake.

Saturday, Oct. 9.—Bought mineral cases and arranged minerals. Evening, saw the comet. It reaches its perihelion to-night. One of the grandest sights I ever beheld. God's works proclaim Him divine. Studied. Retired at 11.30.

Wednesday, Oct. 13.—Rose at 6. Raining very hard. College as usual. Wrote out Greek. Came out at 2.30 P.M. Father had a dinner party, at which were present

Dr. M'C., Prof. G., Mr. J. C. and son from Edinburgh, Dr. W., and several other clergymen. I showed my minerals to Mr. C., who is much interested in such things. Retired at 12.30.

Thursday, Oct. 14.—Came to town at 8. Did not go to college. Went with Mr. C. to the Academy of Natural Sciences, with which he was much pleased. From there we took a cab and drove over to the Insane Asylum. Dr. S. showed us all through the buildings, and paid us great attention. We then went to see Rev. A. B., who gave us a very warm reception, and we spent a very agreeable half hour in his company. I was very much pleased indeed with Mr. C. He is a perfect gentleman—a man of great learning, and withal one of most unaffected manners—all rendering him one of the most agreeable and attractive men I have ever met. On returning from our ride bade him farewell, as he leaves this evening for New York. Gave him some minerals.

Friday, Oct. 15.—College. Bought minerals. Worked at laboratory. Came out at 4. Rolled ten pins with E. B. Nursed sister Pattie. She is a sweet darling baby. Evening, labelled minerals and wrote letters.

Monday, Oct. 18.—College. Wrote out chemical notes. Read in Plattner on Blow-Pipe. Feel very unwell this evening. I must control myself more in my words and actions.

Tuesday, Oct. 19.—Rose at 7. Very heavy fog. College as usual. Went with W. to the reception service in honour of Prof. G. and Rev. Mr. M'C. The room was very elegantly decorated; entertainment good, and addresses most capital, especially that of Dr. L. I enjoyed myself very much.

Friday Oct. 22.—Did not go to town. Very unwell. Worked all day in my laboratory, which was not beneficial.

Saturday, Oct. 23.—Rose at 6. Went to town and college. Very sick. Cold very bad indeed, which with weak eyes, renders me quite miserable. Came out at 2.30. Worked all afternoon in laboratory. Studied until 11.

Sabbath, Oct. 31.—Drove to town. Weather cool and clear. Attendance at school small, both morning and afternoon, but very attentive. We must not be discouraged, but rather go on with more zeal and with more prayer. We do not pray enough. We are not earnest as we should be in this work.

Friday, Nov. 5.—To-day is mother's 38th birth-day. God grant that she may live to see many more, and long be preserved to us, for what is home without a mother? Evening, went to hear B. T.'s lecture on Moscow. Not much pleased. Retired at 12.

Sabbath, Nov 7.—Weather clear and cool. Went down to my school. Had teachers' prayer-meeting—very solemn and interesting. Evening, went to my school—addressed them from parable of Dives and Lazarus. Meeting one of very deep interest. I pray that much good may result. How solemn the thought! —immortal souls committed to our care!

Thursday, Nov. 18.—Wrote at my Essay, "The Dignity of Labour," until church time. Thanksgiving day. How much have we to thank God for! How very much have we received of which we were not in the least worthy! Mr. Faires preached a very fine sermon, indeed the best I ever heard from him. Text, Ps. lx. 4. Evening, had prayer-meeting at church—deeply interesting—addresses by many young men. I spoke from text, "Jesus of Nazareth passeth by." Felt much in the spirit.

Friday, Nov. 19.—Rose at 6. Did not go to college. All day in the laboratory. After tea went over to prayer-meeting at the church. Very interesting address by Mr. Mingins, the converted infidel. I do not feel that I am living up to the requirements of God's law. I am not as much of a Christian as I ought to be—do not feel earnest enough when I pray; or if I am earnest in private it does not go with me into public life. I have prayed faithfully, I trust, to God, but from this night resolve that in the strength of promised grace I will do more than I ever have done to know and spread the name of Jesus—I will live a closer walk with God.—Pour out upon me, heavenly Father, thy Holy Spirit: come and dwell in my heart: cleanse me from all sin, and may I be in truth a follower of the meek and lowly Jesus. Have mercy upon me, O God: rescue me as a brand from the burning: assist me in following after Thee, for I can do nothing of myself; and may I from this moment be born again. "The Lord bless me, and keep me, make His face to shine upon me, and so I shall be safe." Bless my dear M.: preserve her in all her wanderings: may she daily grow in grace and in heavenly wisdom. Lord, hear me, and grant an answer in peace.—How careful should we be, lest while teaching others we ourselves should be cast away! Let us make sure our own salvation, and see that we are not indulging a false hope, but may Jesus ever be our friend. We may be members of the Church, and associate with God's people; but this will not save us.

Saturday, Nov. 20.—Rose at 7. Just after worship was seized with severe dizziness, which rendered me very sick. Wrote up lectures on mathematics. Read Pope's "Essay on Criticism"—much pleased with it. Read in chemistry. Labelled salts. Practised. Wrote at my Essay. Dined at 4. Made blow-pipe analysis of Phos. of Pl. Dr. M'G. is to preach for us to-morrow, which will be our preparation Sabbath. If one listens to the voice of procrastination, how little he accomplishes! How much more might I have done to-day than I did, just from this very thing! We should guard against this; it is dangerous—not only the thief of time, but also of eternity. God can and will deliver, us if we ask Him.

Sabbath, Nov. 21.—Weather cold. Raining. Dr. M'G. preached a most impressive sermon, well calculated to prepare the mind for holy sacramental communion. Afternoon, taught female Bible class. Went to visit L. S., one of my scholars, who is quite sick. Dr. M'G. preached from Isa. xxviii. 17, if possible a still more impressive sermon than the morning one, urging us to self-examination, and to build for ourselves no hiding-place but Jesus Christ. God is blessing us in a remarkable manner. We are indeed a favoured people; but we must remember to improve all these precious privileges, for "to whom much is given, of them much will be required." Went home and prepared my address for the evening. Took for my subject Christ healing the ten lepers, as mentioned in Luke xvii., especially that verse, "Were there not ten cleansed? but where are the nine?" Had a small but deeply interesting meeting. God was with us. Came up to prayer-meeting at church. I must try, by the grace of God, to have many seasons of sweet communion during the present week, so that on the coming Sabbath I may fully enjoy the Saviour's presence.

Saturday, Nov. 27.—Rose at 7. Very sick. Went down to store for letters. Wrote until dinner time. Read in Benvenuto Cellini—a most interesting book. Afternoon, went to church. To-morrow will be our communion Sabbath. God grant that it may be a day of joy—that I may feel more than ever my own weakness—place more faith in Jesus, and resolve to live a closer walk with God.

Sabbath, Nov. 28.—Rose at 7. Cold and snowing. Went down to S. school. Dismissed school early—came up to prayer-meeting at church—heard letter from Dr. W. read. Dr. M'L. preached from Solomon's Song i. 12, a sermon well calculated for a communion Sabbath. Went to first table. Have enjoyed to-day great peace of mind. I feel very happy, trusting only in God for grace and strength. Came home immediately after the service, and retiring to my room spent some time in prayer, that God would bless to me this solemn ordinance—hear the prayers I had offered at his table, and give me grace to carry out the resolutions there formed. Taught school in afternoon. Evening Dr. M'L. preached the funeral sermon of Rev. A. B. Retired very unwell.

Monday, Nov. 29.—Rose at 11, feeling very unwell. Had lesson with Dr. L. at 5. Evening, went to church. On account of my recent ill health, after careful consideration, I have determined to give up my chemistry for the present. It is a hard thing for me to do, for I take great delight in it; but duty calls me to make the sacrifice, and I will do it.

Sabbath, Dec. 5.—Rose at 6. Raining. To-day is the Anniversary of my Sabbath school. God has indeed blessed us, and if any good has been done, to His name be all the glory. I trust that we are all resolved, if spared to see next year, to do more than we have ever done in time past. May we ever abound in the work of the Lord. Attendance in the morning quite large. Dr. M'G. preached from Ps. lvi. He is such a simple, earnest, solid, yet withal charming preacher—laying down his Master's law so plainly as not to be mistaken by the most ignorant. Went down to my school at 1.30, to prepare for the Anniversary. Though the weather was very disagreeable (just such a day as when we commenced), the attendance was very large. We were addressed by Messrs. H., F., G., B., and father. I added a few closing remarks. The scholars manifested the most marked attention, and their conduct was most gratifying to me and to my teachers. The singing also was very good.

Monday, Dec. 6.—Rose at 4.30. Wrote at my Essay until 7. College as usual. Recitation with Dr. L. at 5. Evening, monthly meeting of Christian Association. Read my Essay on "The Dignity of Labour." Being very unwell, I hardly did myself justice. Retired at 12.

Wednesday, Dec. 8.—Rose at 6.30. Raining. College. Wrote out astronomy. After dinner studied Greek, and recitation with Dr. L. Took a short walk. A. S. came to tea—was very glad to see him. He has become much changed. I have good reason to believe that he is a true child of God. He is one of my earliest friends, and I have great regard for him. Evening, studied, wrote. Retired at 12.

Thursday, Dec. 9.—Rose at 6. Weather clear and very cold. College. Studied all afternoon. Evening, went to prayer-meeting held at J. W.'s, Clinton Street. J. D. presided. I addressed them briefly from the words, "Is it well with thee?" Spent the rest of the evening very pleasantly at Dr. B.'s Retired at 12.45 very much worn out.

Friday, Dec. 10.—Received letter from L. A. of Louisville, Ky., pressing me to visit them at Christmas; which I answered in the affirmative.

Sabbath, Dec. 19.—Rev. Mr. W., our dear pastor, whom God has graciously restored to us, preached a most impressive and appropriate sermon. Evening, went down to mission school. Spoke from John iii. 16. Felt much of the Spirit's power with me. I hope and pray I am daily growing in grace. I feel concerned about my S. S. teacher, ——; he is so careless and indifferent to spiritual things. He is a good-hearted, clever fellow; but that will not save him. I will continue earnestly to pray for him, and I feel assured that God will hear my petitions. He has heard them before, and I trust will again. "Hide not thy face from me, O God, neither take thy Holy Spirit from me."

Tuesday, Dec. 21.—Bought books. At 3.30 bade all good-bye, and started for the west. At the depôt fell in with Messrs. S. and T., who were going to Cincinnati. I joined their party, and we found in each other very sociable companions. Left in a pouring rain. Reached Harrisburg at 9, Altoona at 1 A.M. T. and myself got on the back platform of the cars, and rode over the mountains. The scenery was grand beyond description —to me more beautiful than by daylight, as the full moon shone brilliantly through the leafless branches. We had a very fine view of Conemaugh and the Pack

Saddle, and I felt repaid for standing in the cold for two hours. Retired to my chair for a nap.

Wednesday, Dec. 22.—Awoke at 3. Arrived at Pittsburgh at 6. Paid fifty cents for not eating a miserable breakfast. Left at 6.45, viâ Fort Wayne and Chicago R. Road for Crestline. Arrived at 2.45. Took Cleveland and Columbus Road for Columbus. Arrived at 5. Sat down to a miserable excuse for a tea. Left at 5.30, viâ Little Miami Road, for Cincinnati. Arrived at 10.30. Took passage in Ohio and Mississippi Road for Seymour. Arrived at 2 A.M., and instead of starting immediately for Louisville, we had to wait until 7 o'clock for the St. Louis train. Got nothing to eat. Slept in the cars.

Thursday, Dec. 23.—Awoke at 4, after two hours' miserable sleep. Left for Louisville at 7.45. After various delays arrived at 11.30. Went to Louisville hotel. Dressed, and called on my friends, who seemed very glad to see me. Brought my trunk to Mr. A.'s. Mr. and Mrs. G. called to see me.

Saturday, Dec. 25.—Rose at 7. At 11 went to church. Home at 12. Sat in parlour with company until 2. Went in to Mr. G.'s. All the family received me very cordially. Met Miss L. and Miss ——. With the former I was much pleased, she is such a courtly, refined, intellectual lady, possessing none of those affected graces which make so many young ladies disagreeable. Dined at Mr. G.'s. Came home at 7. Very severe neuralgia. L. and I had a long discussion as to the propriety of church members going to the opera when away from home.

Monday, Dec. 27.—Drove with the young ladies to the Cave Hill Cemetery. The location is very beautiful, and the grounds are laid out tastefully. Very severe neuralgia to-day. Wrote letters home. Went to tea at Mr. P.'s. Spent a very pleasant evening indeed. Home at 12.

Thursday, Dec. 30.—Walked with L. and G. A. to the Artesian well, 208 feet deep, situated on 10th Street, near Main. The old coloured fellow who takes care of it is a comical genius, always talking about "de melodeus and harmonius water." It tastes as though strongly impregnated with sulphurated hydrogen. I could not drink it. Bought ticket for Philadelphia. Called on some friends. With Mrs. R., Mrs. A.'s sister, I was much pleased. After tea went into Mr. G.'s, and bade them good-bye. Spent my last evening most delightfully. At 10.30 the coach came for me, and I bade a long farewell to all my dear friends, who had been so kind to me during my stay. My trip is ended. I would fain stay longer, but Duty calls me, and her stern voice must ever be obeyed. Louisville and its people stand high in my regard. After being in the ferry-boat for half an hour, reached Jeffersonville, and started, with not the most pleasant party, for Seymour.

Friday, Dec. 31.—Reached Seymour at 2.30. At 4 took train for Cincinnati—reached there at 8. Took train on Little Miami Road at 9 for Crestline. Reached Xenia at 2, for dinner; Columbus at 3, and Crestline at 5. Changed cars for Pittsburgh. Reached Alliance at 9, where we took tea. Again we started, and I fell sound asleep.

Saturday, Jan. 1, 1859.—Awoke at 6.30, and found that we were nearing Pittsburgh. Reached there at 1.45, and started at 2 for Philadelphia. Again I slept; and when I awoke we had reached Altoona, where we breakfasted. The ride was long and tedious. Reached Philadelphia at 4. I was very cold and tired. Found N. and G. sick with measles. All very glad to see me, even dear little Pattie, whom I found to have grown very much in my absence, and to have got a tooth. Another new year begun! God grant me grace to walk a closer walk with him, "redeeming the time." May I be spurred up to more zeal in my Master's service. May this year be one of special outpouring of God's Holy Spirit upon all lands and people! Being worn out, took a warm bath, and retired at 12.

Sabbath, Jan. 2.—Went to my school as usual. Attendance very good. No teacher absent. I intend during the present and all future time to insist more on the punctuality of my teachers. Afternoon, brought all the children up to the Anniversary in the church. Their good behaviour was remarked upon by all.

Friday, Jan. 7.—Evening, went to prayer-meeting at "Warren Hose." Led the meeting—very large and solemn—addressed them.

Saturday, Jan. 8.—College. Bought Life of Zwingle, and coal for mission school. Went to Germania concert —very fine.

Sabbath, Jan. 9.—School as usual. My dear friend P. W. united with us as a teacher. Afternoon, went with him to church. Rev. Mr. B. preached, from Eph. v. 11, 12, a very solemn sermon, warning us all of the snares and wiles of Satan. I was struck with the fact that he did not nail his sermon home with this, namely, that we only can be freed from these assaults by the assistance of Christ Jesus, our only Saviour. He seemed to leave the subject as though we could free ourselves in

9

our own strength. In short, he did not hold up in his sermon, as I thought he might, that which is the great end of the Christian ministry, "Christ Jesus, and Him crucified." I know Mr. B. is a man of such piety that he would by no means omit this intentionally. I may be mistaken, but thought had he done so his sermon would have been complete. At 6.30 J. M'A. called for me, and we went to visit L. S., one of his class, who is dying of consumption. He was so weak, and in such pain, as to be unable to speak to me. He was an attentive, regular child at Sabbath school, and I trust loves Jesus, and desires to go to be with Him, which is far better.

Monday, Jan. 10.—Cold and clear. Thermometer 4° below zero. After dinner went with M'A. to see L. S. Found him very low. He did not know us. Left his mother some money and jelly. Lesson with Dr. L. at 5. Studied character of Calvin. Evening, went to prayer-meeting at D. B.'s—very solemn and interesting. Had a long discussion with J. D. and F. E. in regard to "predestination."

Friday, Jan. 14.—Felt very sick. Did not go to college. Made out S. S. roll-book. Read in D'Aubigné's "History of Reformation." Planned and commenced a lecture on Luther.

Friday, Jan. 21.—College. Wrote Christian Association business. Read Gibbon's "Rome" in regard to the taking of Constantinople by Mahomet II. His description is very simple, yet grand and impressive, carrying you back to the scene of action, and making you as one of the spectators.

Saturday, Jan. 22.—College. Went to noon prayer-meeting—deeply interesting. Came away feeling that it was indeed the house of God, and that it was good to be there. Evening, went to Zelosophic Society meeting. Read an essay, and took part in debate. Very spirited meeting.

Sabbath, Jan. 23.—Slight flurry of snow during the night. L. S., my sick scholar, is rather better. Sermon by pastor, Heb. i.; an able and eloquent discourse, full of sound reasoning, deep thought—yes, full of Christ Jesus, the aim and end of all preaching. Afternoon, school; attendance very good. Distributed eight prizes for regular attendance. Went with P. W. to hear Rev. Mr. B. He preached from Eph. vi. 18, 19, 20. Subject, prayer. 1st. How we should pray. 2nd. What we should pray for. After showing us clearly our duty as to prayer, and impressing upon us its importance, he closed with a most earnest appeal to the unconverted ones present to hasten to call upon God ere it be too late; to bend now the knee in prayer, if they had never done so before; to flee imploringly to that God who holds their eternal destiny in His hands. Walked home with C., and stayed there to tea. Took her to hear Rev. Henry Martyn Scudder. His text was Ps. cx. 1. His sermon consisted of a complete analysis of the whole system of Hindu theology, together with their caste, and the hardships of the missionary. I was chained by his discourse. Although I have heard scores of missionaries speak about India, never before did I hear the dogmas of their religion so clearly set forth; never did I hear such grappling with error, such a demonstration of the subtlety of their arguments and sophisms; and never did I realize the hardships, opposition, and labour to which the faithful missionary is subject.

Tuesday, Jan. 25.—College. Went to prayer-meeting at the Diligent—very solemn and impressive. It was indeed "the house of God, and the very gate of heaven." Very much impressed with the question put by our Saviour to Peter, "Lovest thou me?" It is ringing in my ears—"Lovest thou me?" Would that I could with Peter triumphantly answer, "Yea, Lord, thou knowest that I love thee." Why is it that I cannot answer this satisfactorily to my own soul? "Lord, save me, I perish!" "I believe; help thou mine unbelief."

Thursday, Jan. 27.—College, &c. Afternoon, read. At 4.30 went to Diligent prayer-meeting—led the meeting. The hour was one of deep solemnity, and the Spirit of God seemed to be indeed moving amongst us. I trust I came thence a better man, feeling more than ever my dependence on Jesus. Evening, took C. J. to hear Everett's lecture on Franklin—not so fine as his discourse on Washington. Retired at 12.

Friday, Jan. 28.—Damp and raining. College. Bought "What will he do with it?" and "N. Am. Review." Very unwell. Read until 5. Lesson with Dr. L. How much I learn from him! He is a capital teacher, and the cleverest kind of a fellow. Evening, called on Mrs. G. A.—a charming lady, and one of the few whom I take great pleasure in visiting.

Saturday, Jan. 29.—Went to noon prayer-meeting—took charge of it—very deeply interesting. Went to Diligent prayer-meeting.

Sabbath, Jan. 30.—S. school as usual. Rev. Mr. B. preached a very good sermon in the morning, but spoiled it by mannerism. Afternoon, wrote out a few thoughts from which to speak at Diligent to-night. P. W. went with me to prayer-meeting. I presided, and addressed them from the words, "God is love." I had intended to speak but a few moments, but the subject widened so before me, that ere I knew it a half hour had slipped away. What a precious meeting we had, and what good news it will be to tell M. to-morrow when I write! If we could only dwell more on the love of God, the very essence of the Divine Being!—Love, pure, holy, matchless, infinite love! We know not God's love, because we have never made use and trial of it as we should. *Our* love may fade and die, but His cannot. Once in God's love, we are ever in it. Give me grace and strength to know and experience Thine everlasting love.

Tuesday, Feb. 8.—College. Made electrotype casts. Studied. Evening, went to hear Prof. Mitchell's lecture. Was delighted. He has a very fine voice, commands the choicest language, and makes the most difficult things plain. He gave us a general view of the universe.

Thursday, Feb. 10.—Went to Diligent prayer-meeting. It was of deep interest. Three men stood up and desired the prayers of the meeting on their behalf. How I felt the power of God's Spirit in that meeting! It was indeed good to be there. Evening, took Miss A. to hear Prof. Mitchell. His subject was, "Is the Great Architect of the heavens the God of the Hebrew Scriptures?" The lecture was one of great depth and power.

Saturday, Feb. 12.—College as usual. Went to noon prayer-meeting—crowded, and deeply interesting. How refreshing to step in an hour from the noisy, bustling highway of life, and drink of the fountains which God has opened for his people! Afternoon, took C. J. to the Germania. Evening, took her to hear Prof. Mitchell. His lecture was grand beyond conception. Who can look up into the heavens and deny that there is a God! Well can we say, with Young:

"An undevout astronomer is mad."

Sabbath, Feb. 13.—School as usual. P. W. absent by reason of a severe cold. After afternoon church went to see him—sat with him an hour. After tea went with M'F. to his school. Found a very large and attentive audience—addressed them. Visited the step-father of G. S., one of my pupils; found him very low with pleurisy, and apparently near death. His mind was nearly gone, so that we were hardly able to talk with him. After prayer we left him, promising to return.

Monday, Feb. 14.—College. Came home at 12. Worked at electrotyping until 5. Lesson with Dr. L. Went to see P. W.—found him much better. Evening, first Anniversary of our Christian Association. We met in the church. I took the chair precisely at 8 o'clock, and commenced by reading Rom. xii. The Annual Address was then read by the secretary. Addresses delivered by Rev. Drs. W., L., and F.—all stirring and eloquent. Studied. Retired at 1.30.

Wednesday, Feb. 16.—College. Electrotyped. After dinner worked with batteries, and read until 5. Lesson with Dr. L. on Reformation in France. Practised until 8. Wrote speech for college on "Labour" until 11.30.

Friday, Feb. 18.—Rose at 6.30. Weather raw and rainy. College. Not being able to get to the public prayer-meeting, I spent half an hour in singing, reading, and prayer, and found that sweet communion with God in private is a most delightful exercise. It stimulates and sanctifies the soul, lifting it above earthly to heavenly things. Lesson with Dr. L. Read Autobiography of Arago—very much interested in it. Messrs. B. and G. came to tea. The former leaves for Europe to-night. I am sorry he is going so soon. We have all enjoyed his society very much. May God protect him while he journeys, and bring him home in safety. Wrote out mathematical problems. Retired at 12.

Sabbath, Feb. 20.—Rose at 7. School as usual. P. W. absent. Went to see him. Found him very sick, in bed, and threatened with inflammation of the lungs. God grant that his life may be spared, and that he may become a bright and shining light in the Church. Suffered much all day from indigestion. Evening, prayer-meeting at 7 o'clock.

Monday, Feb. 21.—College. Went to see new Sabbath-school room. Lesson with L. Evening, college prayer-meeting at our house. C. M. presided.

Tuesday, Feb. 22.—Went to college, and heard an oration on Washington, by Hodge. To see P. W. Found him a little better, but far from well. Went to noon prayer-meeting. The room was crowded, and oh, such a meeting! the day of Pentecost could hardly have surpassed it, it made me feel so very happy. Afternoon, went to opening of National Sabbath-School Convention, and entered as delegate from my mission school. Gor. Pollock was appointed President. Messrs. Chidlaw and Trumbell of Hartford came to tea. Evening, went to Convention. We were addressed in the most soul-stirring manner by Mr. Pardee, Alfred Cookman, Dr. Tyng, and Bro. Chidlaw.

Thursday, Feb. 24.—Went to prayer-meeting at the Y. M. C. A. Rooms, and to Convention. Meeting very interesting. Noon prayer-meeting crowded. A brother, who once had been the president of an infidel club, addressed us most feelingly. Mr. Lambert, acting Vice-President of the Association, Mrs. L., and several gentlemen, came to dinner. Afternoon, Convention met at 4. About twenty-five new resolutions were presented and laid on the table. The discussions were very spicy. Went with Bro. M'C. to the Y. M. C. A. Rooms, and to the Diligent prayer-meeting. Evening, Convention at 7.30. Many addresses were delivered. A most touching one from Gor. Pollock, in reply to a vote of thanks tendered him. Ralph Wells of New York made a short but stirring address. Studied English Literature. Retired at 11.30.

Sabbath, March 6.—Rose at 6.45. Weather clear and warm. Opened my new Sabbath-school room at 1324 Carpenter Street—a much better place than where I was before. Went to see L. S.—found him almost well. Evening, went to prayer-meeting at mission school—attendance large—addressed them from Titus ii. 13—spoke about forty-five minutes. Had very sore throat when I stopped. Came home at 8.30, and feeling very tired went to bed almost immediately.

Tuesday, March 22.—College. Noon prayer-meeting, and came thence much refreshed. Went to J.'s—spent a very pleasant evening talking with and reading to C.

Sabbath, March 27.—School as usual. P. W. still absent from sickness. Evening, usual prayer-meeting at mission school—very large and deeply solemn meeting. I addressed them from the words, "Search the Scriptures," &c. Many were moved, even to tears. I felt that it was not I who spoke, but God speaking in me. Made —— the subject of very special prayer.

Saturday, April 9.—Another week has rolled round, and here I am alone in my study, thinking whether it has been to me mis-spent time. How many good and laudable plans do we form, to be carried out during a week, but Procrastination, that most insidious servant of the Devil, subtle as the arch-fiend himself, comes in, robs us of time and willingness to work, and would fain wrest from us eternal happiness and salvation. For two weeks past I have been resolving to visit my S. S. scholars—procrastination has tempted me to put it off from day to day, and here I am—another Sabbath has almost come, and the work not done. Fain would I say, "Get thee behind me, Satan." God give me grace, if spared to see another week, to labour with my might. "Whatsoever thy hand findeth to do, do it *quickly*." I have been privileged to attend very regularly the noon prayer-meetings, and find them a source of much joy. They are a sort of spiritual fountain, to which the soul, weary in struggling with sin and the world, can go, and drinking deeply of its reviving and enriching waters, go forth refreshed. Oh, that I had more of the spirit of prayer and of Christ—a deeper feeling of sin, and a firmer dependence on Jesus as my Saviour! "Lord, I believe; help thou mine unbelief." Took tea this evening at J.'s. After tea had a long conversation with C. She seems to have a proper view of the subject. I pray that she may be a bright and consistent Christian. I wish my own sisters had more serious thoughts.

To-night, I suppose M. is near Mount Sinai. As she

treads the earthly footsteps of her Saviour may she also be treading the path to heaven. As she stands on Mount Calvary, and in the Garden of Gethsemane, may her heart overflow with love to that blessed Saviour who bled and died there that she might live. The Lord be with her and bless her; cause her daily to grow in grace and in the knowledge and love of God; preserve her in all her wanderings, and restore her at last to her home and friends.

Sabbath, April 10.—Weather cloudy and very raw. Capital to catch cold. P. W. resumed his S. S. duties to-day, after an absence of more than two months. How thankful we should be to God that He has spared his life and brought him safely through a disease which has proved fatal to so many! Afternoon, went with P. to hear Rev. Mr. B. He lectured on the 6th Psalm, and a most beautiful lecture it was. One thought struck me very forcibly. It was, that although the Christian will be engaged in higher and more exalted duties in heaven, yet there is one duty which he cannot perform there, and which, if not attended to while on earth, will be to him a source of constant regret, namely, the privilege that he has enjoyed of leading a brother, a sister, or some near and dear friend to the Saviour. It must be done in *time*, for in eternity it will be impossible. Oh, if Christians would speak more of Jesus with each other, and with those who are strangers to His pardoning grace and love! Evening, prayer-meeting at mission school. Messrs. G. and H. addressed them.

Monday, April 11.—Rose at 7. Pouring rain. Read "Waverley." College at 11. Home. Studied mineralogy. Bought a magnificent specimen of "Brucite"—the finest in the country. Lesson with L. Evening, college prayer-meeting at D. B.'s—sixteen present—among them A. Z. and E. B. I led the meeting. It was one of very deep and solemn interest. What delightful hours these prayer-meetings are! How they lift one's soul above the world, right up to his God! Happy! happy! happy hours! Oh that M. were home now to enjoy with me this out-pouring of God's Spirit, and to unite with me in praising God for his goodness. Came home and found E. Club prayer-meeting at our house. About 180 present—among them I noticed Messrs. J. and M'M.

Thursday, April 14.—Rain, rain, rain—a disagreeable April day. Arranged, labelled, and tested minerals. Read. Did a great many things, and yet might have done much more but for procrastination. What a curse it is! God preserve me from its baleful influence. Evening, Mr. B. came to tea—very much pleased with him, he is so artless and unsophisticated. We had a long talk about minerals. Read Plattner on Blow-Pipe. Very painful neuralgia. Retired at 11.

Friday, May 6.—Having finished my appointed Greek lesson this morning, I wandered about the house for something to do—too unwell to go out—too nervous to read. What shall I do? The thought struck me, Where is my Diary? I have not written in it for a long time. Away I posted up stairs, three or four steps at a time, unlocked the drawer—the "sanctum sanctorum," where I keep my private letters and other et-ceteras, and there lay the Diary, just as I had left it nearly a month ago, the cover brown with dust. As I took it from its hiding-place, it seemed to reproach me for my long neglect. Well, old friend, I am glad to see you once again—you, to whom I have committed in safe keeping my varied thoughts, and who have kept them so well. I cannot tell you all that has passed through my mind, or all that has happened to me since I last had a chat with you; but I will begin now and try to be more confiding, and more punctual in waiting upon you. Since I wrote last I have been very sick, first with neuralgia, then with abscess in the roof of my mouth, and lastly with severe diarrhœa; so you see I have run a pretty fair rig. All the time of my sickness I was very busy doing nothing, except occasionally reading a little of a novel, which is next door to idleness. If you ask me how I got sick, I will tell you that last Monday week I went out boating, to search for minerals along the Schuylkill. I found nothing curious except a dead horse, against which I ran my boat, mistaking him for an island! For that little pastime I have paid with nearly two weeks of suffering—an exemplification, I suppose, of the old saying, "They that dance must pay the fiddler." My fiddler was so expensive that I do not think I will employ him again. Day before yesterday I read "Guy Mannering"—need I say, as hundreds have said before me, how charmed I was with it? What between book-wormish, simple old Dominie, never or rarely getting beyond "Pro-dig-ious!" and wild Meg as she mutters her curse upon the Laird of Ellangowan (he having turned her and hers from their squattings at Dencleugh), I think the tale inimitable. What sad pictures of crime Glossen and Dirk Hatteraick!

Since I last wrote in you, I have not purchased, or got in any way, a new mineral. What do you think of that? The reason may be that funds are low, and I owe enough already for minerals bought.

Rose this morning at 7.30. Slept well all night—a new thing for me. Not well enough to go to college. Studied Greek. Read Nichol's "Architecture of the Heavens."

Saturday, May 7.—College. Seemed quite natural to get back again after a long absence. Had lecture by Prof. F. Met Dr. S., who took me to his study and showed me his exquisite chromo-lithographs of sea ferns, medusæ, polypi, &c. The grouping and other work reflect great credit upon the Doctor. Went to Germania with Miss M. and sisters—very fine concert, especially the Symphony in C— by Beethoven. Went to Mrs. J.'s, took tea with them, and spent a most delightful evening. Talked with C. on the subject broached by some of her friends, as to whether Christ, when on earth, did not lay aside his divine nature—a most dangerous and soul-destroying doctrine to be held by any one. Had He died for us only in His human nature, where was there that which was remarkable? Will not husband die for wife, and son for mother? We have numberless cases on record. Where was then the efficacy and the wonder of the atonement? It was that the Son of God, as God, —still in possession of His divine nature—still co-equal with God the Father—still God, eternal, omnipotent, and omnipresent, came into the world, died, triumphed over death, and ascended gloriously to heaven, carrying captivity captive. Thought much of M. I fear that the war now bursting out all over Europe will seriously impede their progress, especially in the south of Europe. But I have no fear. I have committed her and her companions to the keeping of the "Shepherd of Israel, who slumbers not nor sleeps."

Wednesday, May 11.—Rose at 7. College. Stayed to prayer-meeting. Came home—practised—taken with severe attack of vertigo, which rendered me very unfit for study. Lesson with L. To-day is the twenty-second anniversary of mother's wedding. May God spare her to see many, many more; and may her children be such as will cheer and comfort their parents in their declining years.

Saturday, May 14.—College as usual. Went to noon prayer-meeting. Read. Spent evening at aunt F.'s, to meet Miss D. A. and her sisters—a very pleasant evening. This night two weeks I will have finished college, and that for ever. Joyous, yet sad thought! The first great era in my life has closed—the preparation is done—the strife must now begin. Thus far, in a measure, others have thought for me, now I must think and act for myself. The world lies before me, with its two great paths; the one, broad and smooth, crowded with seekers after pleasure; the other, a narrow road, with here and there a traveller. Which! the right or the left? Let me say, with Joshua, "Let others do as they may, as for me I will serve the Lord." May God give me grace to carry out this noble resolution, for without His strengthening Spirit I can do nothing.

Sabbath, May 15.—Rose at 7. One of the most beautiful Sabbaths I ever saw. School as usual. Afternoon, taught male Bible class—spoke to them very earnestly on the subject of prayer. Evening, prayer-meeting at mission school—addressed them from Luke xix. 10—spoke for almost half an hour. Read Col. i. Retired at 11.15. Verse to think about during the week, "Let your conversation be such as becometh the gospel of Christ."

Monday, May 16.—Rose at 6.30. Weather cool and beautiful. College. Prof. F. showed us experiments on polarized light. Went to see about having class photograph taken. Evening, attended Anniversary of Sab. School Association. The exercises consisted of voluntary addresses from S. S. teachers, interspersed with singing. The statements were deeply interesting and thrilling, and two hours very quickly passed away. We do not realize as we should the importance of this work,—that the great King has committed to our care these gems, precious gems of immortality. When we leave our classes on Sabbath we know not but that ere another comes round, Death may steal in and snatch away the lamb. We should ask ourselves each Sabbath, Have I done this day all that I could to bring my class to Jesus? Have I prayed for them as I should? If you can with a clear conscience say, "I have," then happy, thrice happy, thrice blessed Sabbath school teacher: yours will be indeed a rich reward.

Tuesday, May 17.—College as usual. Went to the Academy of Natural Sciences with uncle John—spent much time in wandering about there.

Wednesday, May 18.—College. Went to see about class photographs. Called to see A. S., who had a hemorrhage of the lungs last Saturday, and has been very low—found him better. Took tea with uncle John. News just arrived of the death of Humboldt. The greatest man of the nineteenth century is no more! His knowledge is gone, and he sleeps quietly and unconsciously as the humblest peasant. Death is truly the great leveller of all men. J. T. of Buffalo spent the evening with us.

Thursday, May 19.—College as usual. Last day I will ever be there to recite. Feel sad at leaving, although I would be very unwilling to stay another year.

Sabbath, May 22.—School as usual in the morning—attendance small. Afternoon, much better. Heard Rev. M. B. lecture on Ps. ix.—was delighted with him, as indeed I always am. Evening, addressed S. school from the words, "Watch, for the night cometh." Attendance small, but very attentive.

Saturday, May 28.—Rose at 7. Went to town at 8. College. Passed—all right—an A.B. Hurrah! During the past week I have been unable to write in my Diary as I desired, owing to my examinations. They were as follow:—

Friday..........Prof. V.—Our Government.
Monday........Prof. F.—Physical Geography.
Tuesday........Prof. C.—English Literature.
Wednesday....Prof. J.—Horace, Ars Poetica, and 8th Satire of Juvenal.
Thursday......Prof. K.—Calculus.
Friday..........Prof. A.—Plutarch's Vita Caesaria.

I got through very well, and am now A.B. Since I last wrote we have moved to "Springbrook." Rev. Dr. T., wife, and J., from Buffalo, are staying with us for a few days. To-night, as venerable V. would say, "I step up a step and am one of the alumni."

Sabbath, May 29.—Church in morning. Read in "Footsteps of St. Paul." Walked in the woods. Spent some time in prayer.

Tuesday, May 31.—Went to Synod. Heard Report of Committee on Union, and addresses from Drs. M'L. and H. M'M. Father invited all the Synod to spend the afternoon at Springbrook. They arrived at 4 and went in at 10. Spent a very delightful afternoon.

Thursday, June 2.—Went to Synod. Worked in laboratory. Arranged finally to start on my western trip next Wednesday. Read in Collins' and Gray's Poems.

Sabbath, June 5.—Drove to town with father. Went to S. school—found everything going on as usual. Bade Phil. good-bye. Drove out with father. After tea had sacred music. A thought struck me to-day, and is worth remembering. When our Saviour was walking with the disciples on the way to Emmaus, on reaching that place He would fain go on, but they constrained Him to come in and sup with them, for the day was far spent. They constrained Him to come in and dwell with them, and what was the consequence? He blessed them. Jesus is walking with us now—have we asked Him—are we asking Him to come in and dwell with us? If we do not, He may pass on and never return. The day, to us, may be far spent. Oh, let us look carefully to it that we constrain Jesus to come in and dwell with us! He has given us the blessed assurance that He will come and make His abode with us. I am much discouraged with myself that I make so little advance in Christian grace. I fear I trust too much to myself—too little to God.

Sabbath, June 12.—How weak I feel in my Christian faith! What a mere child I am! Every step I take I falter. When I pray, my thoughts wander over the hills of vanity. Truly, "when I would do good, evil is present with me." I pray God that all the support I am tempted to place on my weak self may be removed, and that I may rest solely upon the Rock of Ages—that

Rock which is higher than I. Oh, that I might live more above the world, and not in the world. What is there that requires sucn careful watching as the human heart? Man cannot control it but by the grace of God. Conducted family worship.

Sabbath, June 19—MILWAUKIE.—In the morning went to hear Rev. J. C. R., of the Episcopal Church, who was the most eminent man in that Church in the North-west; but, alas, his mind is failing. Severe study has bent the bow of reason beyond what it could endure. The discourse was from Gen. i. 1—very rambling—perfect blasphemy in the pulpit. The man is more to be pitied than condemned. What a difficult place a hotel is to keep the Sabbath in! One needs to keep his Christian graces in very lively exercise. Read Rev. xi., and retired at 10. Text for this week, "Watch and pray."

Monday, June 20.—Wandered about the hotel until dinner time. Took the 3.15 train for Racine. There took the train on the Racine and Mississippi Road for Beloit. The ride was through a country singularly beautiful, and I enjoyed it greatly. Arrived at Beloit about 8—took tea, and at 10.30 started for Belvidere. Again took the cars on the Galena and Chicago Road for Freeport. At the last place took the Illinois Central for Warren. About 1, I began to sleep.

Tuesday, June 21.—Awoke about 3, and found we were approaching Warren. Going from the cars we found the morning very cold, and were glad to gather around the fire at the Burnett House—a rather mean little shanty in the middle of the prairie, where we got a very mean breakfast. At 7.45 started for Mineral Point. After a beautiful ride through a hilly country, diversified with prairies, we arrived at noon. Our friend Mr. B. met us at the depôt, and escorted us to the hotel. Here we have as comfortable a room as a man can wish for. After partaking of a very good, substantial, country dinner, we started on horseback for the copper mines. Hardly had we left the hotel when my horse fell, and I barely saved myself from being seriously injured by leaping over his head. Safely ensconced on his back, we pursued our way to the mines, which lie about a mile and a half N.E. from Mineral Point. The largest shaft is about seventy feet in depth—the copper is in the form of pyrites, very rich, interspersed with iron pyrites, known to the miners as "mundic." After a tour of inspection through the grounds, with which we were highly pleased, we returned to the hotel.

Sabbath, July 10.—MILWAUKIE.—Went to hear Rev. Mr. B. preach—text 2 Chron. xxxiii. 12, 13—subject the conversion of Manasseh, showing how true his repentance was, in contrast with that of Ahab, and how God revealed himself to him in his affliction. Heard Mr. B. again in the afternoon, being so much pleased with his morning discourse. After tea, we walked to the bluff overhanging the lake, and sat there for several hours, enjoying the scenery and watching the moonlight as it rose over the waters. Involuntarily my thoughts sped to the loved ones at home, and lingering there a while, flew onward with unerring aim to that land rendered sacred by the footsteps of the blessed Jesus; and there they rested fondly and happily on her who to me is above all else earthly. How far we are separated! A thousand miles from home, five thousand from her I love; yet the same God watches over us—the same omnipotent hand is ever stretched out to save us, and will ever guard us from danger, and in due time unite us again. Thrice have I been at the very gates of death, I might say, yet God has kept me. What can I render to Him for all His goodness? All He asks is my heart.

Monday, Sept. 19.—More than two months have passed since I opened my Diary: so much for neglecting it a single day. From this time forth I trust it shall be kept more punctually. Began Essay on the "North-West," to be read before the Christian Association.

Friday, Nov. 4.—Again I open my Diary after a long silence; but now that I am settled in town I trust it will be faithfully kept. Went to the store as usual. Came home with a lame foot, and labelled minerals, arranged books, and wrote. Have a prospect of going west next week as far as Louisville and Chicago, but nothing definite is decided yet. We have still with us the Irish delegation, consisting of Dr. Edgar and Rev. Messrs. Wilson and Dill. It is with Mr. Wilson that I propose to go west: he will be good company.

Saturday, Nov. 5.—Went to Germania for the first time this season. Took tea and spent the evening with C. J. Another week has passed, and I am yet spared in life. When I look back over it, I feel that indeed I have left undone much that I ought to have done, and done much that I ought not to have done; and this night my prayer is, "Lord, increase my faith"—perfect my trust in Thee—wean my thoughts and affections more from the world, and centre them on Thyself—make me a new creature in Christ Jesus, and may it be my meat and drink to do my Master's will. May I live unto the Lord, and not unto myself, ever striving to get nearer and nearer to my God, and let no opportunity of serving Him pass by unimproved.

Sabbath, Nov. 6.—Sabbath school as usual. Attendance large. After school had a prayer-meeting—addressed by Messrs. H. and G. I find it very hard to deal with the boys: they are wicked beyond description, and need much patience and prayer; both of which if persevered in will do much to solemnize their minds and bring them to Jesus. Took C. J. to hear Rev. Mr. Dill—found church so much crowded as not to be able to get in.

Saturday, Nov. 12—NEW YORK.—Rose at 7. Started at 11 for Albany. Cloudy and rainy, so that we had no pleasure in viewing the scenery. Arrived at 5.30, very tired. Dr. Sprague met us at the depôt, and took us to his house—very much pleased with him.

Wednesday, Dec. 21.—Rose at 6.45. Read Job, 9th chap. Went to store. Read in Humboldt's Views of Nature. Went to noon prayer-meeting and to see if C. J. would go with me to hear Rev. Mr. Guiness. Heard from S. W.—she is sinking slowly. What is our loss is her inestimable gain. She is a bright, consistent Christian. Would that I were like her! Evening, went to hear Mr. Guiness—text, "If I regard iniquity in my heart, the Lord wlll not hear me,"—a solemn, searching sermon. I trust I am beginning to see more of Jesus. God has been hiding His face from me, but if I persist in earnest supplication he will make me to rejoice. I fear that I regard iniquity in my heart—that there is something that I love better than Jesus. If there be such in me, O God,

> "Help me to tear it from Thy throne,
> And worship only Thee."

I feel that in times past I have become cold and indifferent, and God has punished me for it; and now my heart's cry unto God is, "Lord, what wilt thou have me to do?" Am I now in the line of duty? If not, direct me, O God—lead me in the way in which Thou wilt have me go, even the way everlasting.

Thursday, Dec. 22.—Weather clear and cold. Went to noon prayer-meeting—very interesting. From every place the cry of the revival comes, and the anxiety of awakened souls. Afternoon spent with N. R.—a lovely girl, for whom I have a high regard. Went with sisters to Miss M.'s annual party—pleasant evening, but do not like parties. Home at 11, tired and sleepy. Retired at 12.

Saturday, Dec. 24.—Rose at 7. Store as usual. Went to noon prayer-meeting—did not enjoy the exercises as I usually do—fear I was not in a proper frame of mind. God grant me more grace. Afternoon, went Christmasing with N. After tea spent Christmas Eve, as we always do, in looking over and talking about our presents. How grateful should we be to God that He has preserved us to see another Christmas in health and prosperity! and should we not make Him the only present that He asks from us—our undivided hearts? It is the least that we can do. He has done much for us—should we not do thus much for Him? Retired at 11.30.

Sabbath, Dec. 25.—Weather clear and cold. School as usual. Attendance good. Afternoon, second Anniversary of our Mission—attendance large—addresses by Rev. Dr. W., Rev. S. P. H., and J. G. Evening, presided at Diligent prayer-meeting.

Monday, Dec. 26.—Went down town with G. W., and

to noon prayer-meeting—attendance very large, and deeply interesting. Afternoon, spent playing with the children and talking with Rev. S. P. H. Retired at 12, and thus ended Christmas 1859. Another year has gone—another Christmas passed! Who shall see the next? Not one of us can tell. It becomes us then to be up and doing, now while we have life, and health, and hope—to give ourselves away to the Lord Jesus in a covenant never to be forgotten.

Sabbath, Jan. 1, 1860.—Weather clear and very cold. "A Happy New Year," I hear from every side. The happiest they can wish me is that I might live nearer to God—that I might have more faith and earnestness. That would indeed be a happy new year. S. school as usual. Afternoon, annual sermon by Mr. Guiness—attendance very large. Our school mustered eighty—behaved very well.

Wednesday, Jan. 11.—Weather damp and raw. Suffering much from sore throat. Store as usual. Attended class meeting of my fellow-students—a very pleasant reunion. Afternoon, store—very busy. Evening, went to mission school—spoke from Job xxviii. 18–28. Met C. J. on my way home—went in and sat an hour. Mrs. W. is sinking rapidly; but the change will be a glorious, happy one. Would that I were like her! but I must take no pattern save Jesus. Would that I had more grace—more of His Spirit! In a week M. will be with me, and I shall see her face to face. I wonder if she will be much changed. A brighter, better Christian, I hope.

Tuesday, Jan. 24.—Weather clear and mild. Went to

see A. and M. who returned from Europe last night. M. goes to Milton to-morrow to see her sister S. It is sad indeed that they have come home only, as it were, to see her die. God grant that as she nears the tomb her faith may become brighter and firmer—that daily Jesus may be more and more precious unto her soul; and that at last, in full assurance of hope, she may enter her Father's house, there to dwell with Him who loved her and gave Himself for her, throughout eternity.

Sabbath, Jan. 29.—S. school as usual. Addressed News Boys at their Home, 237 South Third Street. Took for my subject the character of Samuel, as one eminently worthy of their imitation—spoke for nearly half an hour—felt very deeply what I said. They listened with serious attention. Evening, went to J.'s to hear how Mrs. W. is. They heard yesterday, when she was free from pain, but very weak. Sat with Mrs. J. and C. all evening—had prayers with them. Spent, I trust, a profitable evening.

Saturday, Feb. 4.—Very cold. Felt very happy this morning. I believe God is answering my prayers, and that indeed I am beginning to enjoy more of His Spirit's presence. As I read my morning psalm, in regular course, I felt tears of happiness and peace starting in my eyes. Oh, may I daily have a closer walk with God! What happiness I would then have! and why should I not have it? I am daily nearing eternity, should I not be also daily nearing heaven, and getting closer to God? Store as usual. Went to noon prayer-meeting—enjoyed it much. God's Spirit was there, and where that is, God's people will be happy. Afternoon, suffered much from dyspepsia. Evening, read M'Clintock's Narrative of a

Search for Sir John Franklin—a deeply, sadly interesting book. What a blessed thing it is to have that peace of mind and joy which passeth all understanding! I feel of late more waked up to duty than ever before. A great work is to be done—there are but few to do it. I hear a voice from heaven crying, "Work! work! work, while it is day." God grant me grace and strength and energy to engage more deeply in His service.

Monday, April 30.—This day two months ago I attended Mrs. S. W.'s funeral; and to-day we have been called to follow the remains of our dear friend Mr. J., [her father,] to their final resting-place. How mysterious is the providence of God! How are His ways past finding out! This night a week ago I took tea with him—he was in perfect health; now the grave has for ever closed over his remains! How crushing to that family, so dearly loved, and whose heart-strings were and are so tenderly wound about him. Yet why should they mourn? Rather should they rejoice that he has passed from the land of the dying to the land of the living. I doubt not but that he was an humble child of God. May God bless this sad affliction to every one of them.

Saturday, June 16.—Rose at 6. Damp and foggy. I fear I do not grow in grace as I should. I am not as earnest in prayer as I ought to be. God grant that I may ever be looking more and more unto Jesus. As long as we keep our eyes and our trust fixed upon Him, so long will we continue to grow; remove them, and our steps are backward.

Monday, July 9.—Went to J. T.'s funeral. We laid him in his grave at Woodlands, there to rest until the last trump shall sound and the dead be raised incorruptible. After the funeral had dispersed I walked over to Mrs. J.'s lot, and for some time gazed upon the little mounds beneath whose grassy tops rest the beloved forms of M.'s father and sister. They were dear to me as well as to her. Often have I felt my heart rise and swell within me as I talked with that sister (Mrs. W.) about heaven and Jesus—so precious to our souls. Oh, that I may follow her as she followed Jesus! Her race is run, her conflict o'er; would that her mantle might descend upon me, that I might have that peace and happiness which she so fully enjoyed. Picked for M. a sprig of fern from their graves. Back to the store. Home at 4. Worked with microscope until 6.

Monday, July 16.—Rose at 4, intending to write. Bathed. Found it so hot when I dressed that writing was out of the question. Sat under the trees and read "Quits." Went to town as usual—took music lesson. At 4 went to Lansdowne. Conducted family worship. What a consolation the doctrine of the recognition of saints is! It binds us closer to the dear ones here, to think that when re-united after the short separation of death, it will be never to be torn asunder.

Sabbath, July 22—LANSDOWNE.—Rose at 6. Weather clear and cool, after the showers of last night. Breakfasted at 7.30, after which retired to my room and spent a delightful half hour in prayer to God. Rose from it much refreshed in spirit—felt as though I had been heard, and that this Sabbath is indeed going to be to me one of precious nearness of God's Holy Spirit. I know God is always with me, yet I do not always feel His presence as I would desire. Sometimes I call, but He answers not—I seek His face, but in vain; yet I know He is with me, for he has promised "I will never leave thee nor forsake thee."

At the usual hour went to church. Mr. H. preached. Sermon good; and though hardly as clear and concise as I would have desired, all was amply compensated for in the fact that his words were those of one who felt what he said, and who earnestly desired the salvation of his hearers. And this, after all, is what the Church needs—an *earnest* ministry. When men are less in their studies and more among their people; when they labour more and strive harder to save souls than to polish their sermons, then will the Church of Christ go forward and take her stand first, and over all the so-called religions of the earth.

Read a very beautiful book entitled "Life's Morning." The chapter which particularly interested me was headed, "What have I done for Jesus?" The question struck me forcibly, and came home to my soul with solemn and momentous import, affording me food for an hour's deep, and, I trust, profitable meditation. After the children's usual singing, had family worship, which I conducted, reading Eccles. xii. Retired thinking on this verse, "The love of Christ constraineth us."

Friday, Aug. 10.—My twentieth birth-day! Rose at 6. Spent a precious day with M., and left at 4 P.M. for New York, to meet father, who is expected to-morrow in the *Adriatic.* Well! twenty to-day! What a change even a year makes! Here I am, almost of age, engaged to be married, and in business. Has the same happy change come over my spiritual life? I am nearer eternity! am I nearer to God? Are my views of eternity and hopes for heaven brighter and clearer than they were a year ago? What have I done for God during the past year? Have I done what I ought, and what I easily might have done? Ah, no! I feel that I have come far short of my duty to God and to those around me. I have wasted many precious hours, and frittered away many heaven-sent opportunities. What is to be done? I cannot mend the past! No; but this I can do—resolve, in the strength of promised grace, to do more during the present year than I have ever done before. Almighty God, pardon my shortcomings, and give me grace to live nearer to Thyself, and to work more earnestly in Thy glorious cause.

Sabbath, Aug. 19.—Very warm. Church, as usual. After dinner, I took up and read a new book which father brought home, entitled "London by Moonlight Mission," by Lieut. Blackmore—an account of his labours for thirteen years among the unfortunate females of London. As I read its thrilling pages, and saw the earnest avidity with which they seized upon his offer to save them, together with the dangers which beset them, and the few who care for their souls, the old desire rekindled in my bosom to do something for them in our own city. Poor unfortunates! literally, no one cares for *their* souls. Our mothers, wives, and sisters will have nothing to do with them. If their salvation is ever effected, and they are ever snatched from a life of wretchedness and an eternity of woe, it must be done by the sterner sex. A year or so ago this idea forced itself strongly upon my mind; but I felt that I was too young, and did not at all see my way clear. Now that it has come again, shall I resist the call? O God, show me the right way, and then give me grace to press forward in it. I will write to Lieut. Blackmore soon, and inquire of him fully as to his plans; and then, if I can enlist G. or some other of my *working* friends, God and eternity only will know the result. I do not intend that this shall at all interfere with my mission school work—by no means; but I am sure I can devote one night a week to it. I will make this the subject of special fervent prayer to God. Having taken the necessary steps, I will leave all in His care, knowing that He will direct me to do that which will be best for myself, and best for the promotion of His kingdom. "Work while it is day: the night cometh."

Wednesday, Aug. 22.—Rose at 7. Went to town at 8. Weather very oppressive. Business dull. Went to Mercantile Library, where I spent an hour profitably. Left town at 4—reached Lansdowne at 5.30. After retiring to my room, planned my Essay on "The Microscope and its Revelations." Did not get to bed until after 1.

Thursday, Aug. 23.—Rose at 7. Overslept myself. Had a severe storm in the night, which I, as usual, unconsciously slept through. Business dull. Came out at 4. Very hot. Worked till tea time with microscopic objects. After tea, lit my lamp to continue my work, but hardly had I begun when the perspiration began to stream down my forehead. In disgust I blew out the lamp, and, book in hand, went to find some cooler spot where I might study; but between bugs, heat, and the talking of those around me (I fancy they would not like to see this latter) I was obliged to give up microscoping as a "bad go," for one night at least.

Sabbath, Aug. 26.—Rose at 6.30. Not remarkably well. Weather delightfully cool and pleasant. Church in the morning as usual—a good practical sermon. After dinner retired to my room and wrote two little snatches, one on "God's Threatenings," the other on "God's Chastisements." Had a severe attack of diarrhœa, from which I suffered much all afternoon. M. is much in my thoughts to-day. It is one of sadness to her. This day six months ago her dear sister died; and this day four months, her father. Thus in half a year God has seen fit to take from that household two of its much-loved members. Yet how consoling the thought of which M. and I were speaking the other evening—that none of the sorrows from heaven but have their more than redeeming joy! Blessed provision of a loving Father!—when He smites, He at the same time pours in the healing oil.

Sabbath, Sept. 2.—Rose at 8. Felt much refreshed and ready for a good day's work. Went to school at 9, and was most heartily welcomed back by both teachers and scholars. Dined with G. Afternoon, school—attendance very good. After school, in company with Wh., M., and W., started for one of the courts near the school, to hold an open-air prayer-meeting. Having found a place, and obtained permission to use steps as a pulpit, we began to sing the hymn "Just as I am," &c. Immediately the crowd began to gather, and before we were done singing we had an audience of one hundred. I then led in prayer, and never with more pleasure and comfort. After singing and reading, Wh. addressed them, then M. and myself. We continued the exercises three-quarters of an hour, and then distributed tracts. From thence we went to 12th and Brinton Streets, where we held a much larger meeting, there being about three hundred and fifty present. I addressed them from the words, "He will by no means clear the guilty." Many were in tears. In the evening held our regular prayer-meeting, when my text was, "Consider your ways." Came home at 9.30, rejoicing in my heart for what I had been permitted to see to-day. It is a day long to be remembered. I feel my soul refreshed and strengthened.

Sabbath, Sept. 16.—Went to church at Holmesburg, and heard a most excellent sermon from Rev. Mr. B. He dined with us. Went to Nanna's room, and sang with her and the children for an hour. Have thought and prayed much for M. to-day. Would that I had more grace. I do not find Jesus as precious as I would like Him to be; nor have I that pleasure in prayer which I would desire. O Lord, why hidest Thou Thyself? Why dost thou any longer tarry? Come, come quickly! Warm and invigorate my cold and deadened soul. Even this night lead me nearer to Thyself than I have ever been before. Thou, O Christ, art all I want. Thou alone canst satisfy the cravings of my soul. Come and dwell supremely in my heart, driving sin and sense for ever from it, and making it Thine own dwelling-place. I feel my own weakness. Often have I resolved to do good in my own strength, and as often have utterly failed. Now I cast myself upon Thee, and upon *Thy promises.* Save me, for I trust in Thee. Elevate and sanctify all my thoughts and affections. Cause my heart to go out in love to Thee and my fellow-men. Quicken all my energies, and make me to labour, so that when I come to die my regret shall not be that I had not done as much as I could.

"I travel through a desert, drear and wild;
Yet is my heart with such sweet thoughts beguiled,
Of Him on whom I lean, my strength, my stay,
I can forget the sorrows of the way."

Tuesday, Oct. 16.—Last evening heard Gough. He has lost none of his magic power, but thrilled us all, as of yore. Received this morning my consignment of Bennet and Adams' linens. Now is my chance to start, and make myself a name. I pray God that I may never, either by word, equivocation, or mental reservation, in order to make a sale, swerve in the slightest from the truth; never sacrifice integrity to the "almighty dollar;" but so act as that I shall have the perfect confidence of all with whom I have to do; never be so wrapped up in business as to forget the interests of those who have higher claims upon me.

Sabbath, Oct. 28.—Our communion. Rose at 6.30, feeling very well. Mission school as usual. I had feared that being so much worried about our lectures,* I would not enjoy the day; but as I conducted the opening services I felt my spirit rising. I felt the love of Jesus thrilling my heart anew. It continued; and when I took my seat in my pew, how happy I felt! Surely this was an answer to the prayer of some one. Need I go far to find the loving heart that I know was pleading for me at a throne of heavenly grace? Had a beautifully appropriate sermon by the Rev. A. M. S., from 2 Sam. xix. 10. Just what we needed for the solemn occasion. Went to the first table, and enjoyed it more than words can tell. I felt a greater leaning on Jesus than ever before. More humble in my own sight.

Thursday, Nov. 1.—Rose at 6. Not much trade stirring. Dined at aunt F.'s. Read in Quatrefage's "Rambles of a Naturalist"—charmed with the book—

* A series of lectures to be delivered by John B. Gough, under his direction, for the support of his mission school.

talked a long time with Nanna in the library. Evening, father returned from New York. Had a long discussion on the merits and demerits of High Church Episcopacy. Wish my eyes would become stronger—as they are I can do nothing of any account. But what I wish for more than any earthly or bodily blessing is, that I might have more of Jesus, my blessed Saviour. If I could only love Him as he deserves, and as I desire, how much happier and more joyful I would be! Almighty God, help me to lean more entirely upon Thee. Be Thou in my waking thoughts—continue ever uppermost with me throughout the day, so that every action may be done as in Thy sight—not to please men, but Thee; and when I lie down to rest, be Thou with me then—help me to review the actions of the closing day with truthful candour, to repent of sin, and resolve to do so no more. Be Thou ever with me, and then what need I fear! "Make me to understand the way of Thy precepts."

Sabbath, Nov. 11.—Rose at 7. Cloudy and raw. School as usual. All my teachers present. Afternoon, there being no preacher in the coloured church, I officiated, taking for my text "Abide in Me." My earnest prayer before commencing was that I might have utterance given me boldly to declare the whole counsel of God; and I believe my prayer was answered. The attendance was very good, and they listened eagerly. I felt that it was not I who spoke, but God speaking in me, with an earnestness which I rarely have. Many came to me at the close and thanked me for what I had said. If any good has been done, to Thy name, O God, be all the glory; for if I have power to speak, Thou hast given it to me.

Monday, Nov. 12.—Rose at 6. Went to Academy of Music to arrange about tickets. Very busy all day about this lecture business. I heartily wish it were over. Had a long talk with Mr. M'A. as to the practicability of applying the microscope attachment to the magic lantern. After a full discussion of the subject and a consultation of the best authorities, we jointly concluded that it would be an useless and expensive experiment, in which, judging from the experience of others, we would signally fail.

Tuesday, Nov. 13.—Gough lectured for my mission school in the Academy—full house.

Sabbath, Nov. 18.—Raining. S. school as usual. Went visiting with S. W. Had a long conversation with the mother of one of our scholars, and with the greatest difficulty persuaded her to come to our meetings. How hard the soil is in which we have to work!—greater the glory to God if good is done. Lord, help us to work and persevere even unto the end. Make me Thine—entirely Thine; control every thought; guide every action. Perhaps if the struggle is hard I will but love my Saviour more. Do with me as seemeth best in Thy sight. Evening, went to mission school prayer-meeting—very interesting.

Thursday, Nov. 22.—Weather cold. Called with N. on Mr. and Mrs. J. A. from Louisville. Store as usual. Bought a Smee's Battery, which I might have done without. Set to work electrotyping. Left store at 5.30. Went to M.'s—read to her and A. for an hour from Motley's "Dutch Republic"—deeply interested. Eyes still inflame every evening, and are a source of great trouble.

Friday, Nov. 23.—Store as usual. Home at 3. Not feeling very well did not go back. Wrote at my Essay on the Microscope. Went to M.'s—continued our reading in Motley—am becoming more and more fascinated. Our subject this evening was the meeting between Don John of Austria, lately appointed Governor of the Netherlands, and the Commission of Nobles for the ratification of the Treaty of Ghent; and also the efforts of the crafty Don John to win over the high-minded, noble, patriotic William. Came home at 11, and found that George had been taken sick about tea time with a sore throat and vomiting. The doctor is treating him for diphtheria. How sad it makes us all feel. We earnestly pray that God's will is, that he may be spared. Made him a subject of special prayer.

Saturday, Dec. 15.—Bitter cold. Trade dull. Money market easier. Southern prospects not much better. Came home at 1. Talked with grandmother. Read in "Rambles of a Naturalist" both before and after dinner. Suffered much from dyspepsia. Bought stereoscopic views. Went to M.'s. Played games until 9. Read in "Dutch Republic," commencing with the rule of Alexander Farnese in the Netherlands. Saw very brilliant Aurora Borealis. Very unwell.

Oh for more of Christ!—Christ in every word—Christ in every thought—Christ in every action—Christ all and in all! I do not feel that I want Him, as I should—I do not feel his need! Grant me, O God, to feel how needy and helpless I am. Give me a burning, increasing desire to have Jesus as my friend. Cleanse this wicked heart from every sin. Prepare me for death, judgment, and eternity! Make me ready! Reign entirely in my heart, and make me, O God, for ever and for ever Thine!

Monday, Dec. 31.—11.45 P.M. 1860 is just passing away—passing into eternity, with all its blessings and privileges, never more to return, carrying with it many unpardoned sins—all gone to God's judgment-seat. We cannot call it back—never! never! But we can improve the future. Such should be our earnest desire—such is my prayer this night. I ask for pardon of every sin and every shortcoming. I ask for a rich blessing on ——, on all I love, and on myself. May all our sins be pardoned, for they are many! I ask a blessing on ——; he needs it. O God, touch his heart with the influence of thy Holy Spirit! Watch over him, and for *Jesus'* sake —*Thine own Son's sake*—save his soul from going down to death. Have mercy upon him, and lead him to Thyself. (I now spend the remaining moments of this year in prayer.)

Saturday, Feb. 2, 1861.—At it again! What changeable beings we are! One day a desire comes and burns in our bosoms that it may be fulfilled; another, and it is gone, or has become of little or no interest. So have I been on the Diary question, and so will (I fear) ever be. The fever has now come,—let me make the best of it. Rose this morning at 7.30, feeling much better than I have for a week past, owing to a severe cold and bilious attack. Went with Rev. Mr. Fisch to call on Drs. Brainerd, Boardman, and Jones—found all at home, and spent a few moments very pleasantly with each. Dr. Brainerd showed us the Diary of the celebrated David Brainerd, missionary to the Indians. It contained his religious experience, and it was delightful to look at the records of God's dealings with so great and good a man.

Sabbath, Feb. 3.—Weather mild and cloudy. Rose at 7. Afternoon school rather noisy: expelled a very bad boy. Not feeling very strong, did not visit.

Sabbath, Feb. 10.—Suffering much from my cold. Morning school as usual: received four new scholars, all girls. Went to church as usual, but feeling quite sick, was obliged to come home. Took medicine, and dozed until dinner time. Have thought much of M. to-day. My earnest prayer for both of us is that we may grow more in Christ. We are growing in years, and must be advancing in either sin or godliness. I am often led to despair of myself; I am such a wanderer—such a sinner. Often when I kneel down to pray, I cannot fix my thoughts upon God—I cannot pour out my soul to Him as I would desire. So it goes on! Oh that I knew more of Christ—that I felt more my heavenly Father's love! I am such a *weakling* in grace. I know so little of Jesus and His precious love to poor dying sinners like me. Yet withal I cannot but believe that I am one of His children. From what I have tasted of God and of His precious grace—from the joy that I have felt when engaged in the ordinances of His house, and from the sweet hours of communion in prayer which I have enjoyed, I cannot but believe that I am one of God's own children; and though He may hide His face from me for a while, yet He will not cast me off for ever.

Sabbath, April 21.—Rose at 6.30. Weather cloudy, but afterwards a lovely, clear day. To-day is preparation Sabbath, but the doctor has positively forbidden my going to church. How hard it is to be deprived of the ordinances of God's house! I long to return to my Sabbath school, and resume my labours. This is a severe lesson, and I most earnestly pray that to the fullest extent it may be blessed and sanctified to me. Dressed and walked to M.'s, arriving just before they returned from church: had a delightful chat with her before dinner. Talked with Miss L. until church time, and then read in a most interesting and instructive book, entitled "Success in Life," by Dr. Tweedie. My book was so interesting, that before I knew it the hours had slipped by, and the family had returned from church. After a few moments' conversation, started for home with M., and had a delightful walk together.

In reading that book this afternoon, how much I felt the power of prayer! If I could only pray as I want to; but I cannot. My thoughts fly from me when they should stay: I cannot fix my mind, and I even forget what I am saying. How long shall these things be? "Oh, that I knew where I might find Him, that I might come even unto His seat! then would I order my cause before Him: I would fill my mouth with arguments." So do I cry, as did Job. He found Him. Why shall not I?

Monday, April 22.—Rose at 6.30. Read with interest and faithfully the morning papers, though they contain but little news. Had a long talk with the doctor on our government. We both fully agreed in the centralization of power, and reduction of the right of suffrage—introducing property qualification.

Wednesday, April 24.—This afternoon read in the Life of Captain Hodson, of Hodson's Horse—a charming biography of a Christian, and a gallant, noble-hearted soldier. Had a talk with the doctor.

Poor me! If I were only better than I am. If I could only accomplish half what I desire. I sometimes feel that I will never do much good in the world; yet I ever hear a voice within me saying, "Persevere! press on! the end is not yet." If I could only be the Christian I want to be, and love to pray as I desire, what a burden would be taken from my soul! Oh how I desire something better, nobler than I am myself! May I be guided to that course by pursuing which I may accomplish the greatest amount of good. That such guidance may be given me is my most earnest prayer.

Thursday, April 25.—Fast day. Rose at 6.30. Finished the Life of Captain Hodson, and turned from it feeling I had learned something. How these

> "Lives of great men all remind us
> We can make our lives sublime."

They show of what human nature is capable, and what may be done when the energies are properly governed and controlled.

Sabbath, April 28.—To-day is our communion Sabbath. Read in the "Well in the Valley," by Dr. Smyth—a very interesting and instructive work, well calculated to awaken us to the solemn responsibility resting upon us as immortal and intelligent beings. At dinner time it began to rain, and I was deprived of the privilege of the communion. After dinner, slept: suffered much from pains in my side and breast, and from oppressive breathing. Dr. Wylie and Mr. Herron came to tea—had a long talk with them.

Sabbath, May 5.—Rose at 7. Read John xviii. Read Dr. Scoresby's letter to his sister on the subject of religion. It is one of the most concise, comprehensive, and beautifully expressed letters I ever read. Every word comes from the writer's heart, and much, if not all, is the result of his own personal experience. Written as it is with all the tenderness and love of a brother and a Christian, it cannot fail to impress every one who reads it with a right motive.

In looking over the past week, I find that, as ever, I have much to be thankful for. My health has been greatly improved, and I have been blessed with precious seasons of prayer. If I only had more faith: could I but trust Christ more and myself less: ah! this faith is what I need; here is my stumbling-block—want of proper confidence in God. I do not keep Christ prominently before my mind: I forget that it is only through Him I can approach the Father; only by trusting entirely in Him that I can attain unto eternal life. I can say with the Psalmist, "My soul cleaveth unto the dust." How much I need the reviving, quickening influence of God's Holy Spirit, that I may be led in the way everlasting!

I trust that M. finds great delight in calling upon God. It is to me such a source of inexpressible happiness to think that she has a hope beyond this world. I never can believe that they who live only for the present life, and who have no abiding hope for the world to come, can be as happy as they whose confidence is fixed on God. True, they may love as well as sinful hearts can love, but there is a source of happiness which they know not of—a fountain of living, purest love, from whence they cannot draw. The love of Christian hearts increases with their love to Christ: as grows and increases their love to their Saviour, so does their affection for one another deepen and strengthen. This is the inexhaustible source of the Christian's love, from whence it ever draws, and nourished by which it increases and goes on from strength to strength, until at last it arrives at its perfect fulness in the presence of Him who is the author of this greatest of earthly blessings.

At 11.30 went to M.'s. Soon after, they returned from church. Went to my mission school, from which I have now been absent three months. All, both teachers and scholars, welcomed me back most heartily. Heard an excellent sermon from Mr. Barnes, containing much food for thought.

[There is no entry in William's Diary until the 17th November, and instead of writing up his Diary, he kept, during his six months' absence, a full journal for the use of his family, from which the following are extracts:—]

Aug. 10, 1861.—My twenty-first birth-day. In company with Mr. T. N. I left Edinburgh at 10 o'clock *en route* for Arran. The morning was clear and beautiful. We arrived in Glasgow at 11.30, and at 2 went on board the steamer *Juno*, bound for Lamlash Bay, Arran. As we passed down the narrow Clyde we met many large vessels inward-bound, and at the moorings the *Scotia*, preparing for sea. Soon the high crag of Dumbarton, upon which Dumbarton Castle is built, came in sight; and then having passed Greenock, the birth-place of James Watt, we were fairly out on the Firth of Clyde. And now what a change came over the scene!—the sky became obscured; the waters which an hour or so before were calm and smooth, were crested with foam; and the rain and sleet came down in torrents: the consequence of which was, considerable uneasiness was felt by many of our passengers, and sundry stone China basins were in constant demand. After passing the Cumbraes we headed across the Firth for Arran. Soon a thick mist gathered round us—the storm redoubled its fury; but we were not to be put back. Like "a thing of life," our little steamer cut through the waves, and soon we were under the lee of the mountain Goatfell. Passing Brodick Castle, we were soon at our anchorage in Lamlash Bay. The wind was blowing such a gale that our steamer could not land, and we were compelled to go ashore in small boats. Of course we were drenched. We found Mrs. N. expecting us, with a nice warm tea prepared.

Aug. 11, *Sabbath.*—When I arose it was raining in torrents. About church time it moderated, and I started off with Mr. N. to the Free Church of Invercloy, 3 miles distant. The preacher was the Rev. Mr. Macdonald of Leith. His text was 2nd Peter i. 10. A more earnest, simple, faithful discourse I have rarely ever heard. After church we walked back to Lamlash, over a hill covered with most beautiful ferns.

Aug. 12.—When I arose this morning it was raining so heavily that even the fences were quite invisible. Suddenly, however, the rain ceased, the clouds rolled away, and a more beautiful day was never seen. After breakfast we took a boat and sailed to Whiting Bay, a distance of about 4 miles. Here we left our boat and walked about 2 miles up a beautiful glen called Glen Ashdale, to see a fine waterfall. We had a delightful walk: the hills were covered with the rich purple heather, now in full bloom, while on the banks of the little streams ferns were growing luxuriantly. After dinner we all sailed about 4 miles to the fishing ground. Here we caught many fine large cod, and in an hour had as many fish as we could conveniently carry home. The sun was just setting as we left our boat, the long mountain shadows were stealing across the bay, while far beyond the hills the pale beams of the new moon were playing upon the water. Thus ended our first day in Arran.

Tuesday, Aug. 13.—Another beautiful day. Went out to sail with Mr. N. in his new yacht, which arrived during the night from the Forth. She is a fine large boat, very graceful, and of great speed. The wind was blowing very fresh, so that we sped along in gallant style. After sailing round the bay all morning, we returned to Lamlash to dinner; after which we again took the boat, having with us Mrs. and Miss N. It was a lovely afternoon—not a cloud to be seen as we sailed out of the harbour; so clear was it that we could distinctly see the Ayrshire coast, where a faint line of smoke marked the town of Burns. Before us lay Bute, while in the background were the hills of Argyleshire, among which towered Ben Lomond. As we cleared the harbour the wind freshened, and often we were covered with spray. We now entered Brodick Bay, and after a little tacking succeeded in landing on a ledge of rocks. Here we each one betook ourselves to our favourite studies, the ladies to the ferns and mosses, while I wandered amongst the rocks in search of sea-weed and marine animals. Here, in little pools clear as crystal, covered in by dark damp weed, I found many beautiful plumose anemones, their delicate thread-like tentacles waving to and fro with the slightest ripple. Here, on a barren rock, where man seldom comes unless to study nature, nourished by each flowing tide, these exquisitely beautiful and delicate creatures exist and perish. As I looked at them I thought of the words of the poet,—

> "Full many a gem of purest ray serene
> The dark unfathomed caves of ocean bear."

The rapidly setting sun put an end to our soliloquy, and warned us to hurry back to our boat. The wind had now quite died away, so that we were nearly two hours in reaching the entrance to Lamlash Bay. We were now compelled to take to our oars, and after a long tedious pull got back to the moorings about midnight. As we entered the bay we noticed how beautiful the phosphorescence of the water was. At each dip of the oar the water fell from it like silver rain, while the bow flashed and sparkled as though studded with diamonds.

Let me now say a word or two in regard to Arran. It lies in the Firth of Clyde, having on one side the Mull of Galloway and on the other the Ayrshire coast. It is about 80 miles from Glasgow. Its extreme length is 20½ miles, its breadth 6½. The north end of the island is a huge mass of rugged, lofty mountains, the highest of which is Goatfell (height 2,875 feet.) The southern end is a gently rolling country. Thus the island affords every grade and description of scenery, from the gentle to the sublime. The rocks are a complete epitome of the geology of Britain. There is no such collection of ferns in the three kingdoms. Insects are abundant, while the shells, sea-weed, and marine animals are of the rarest and most beautiful kinds. All these combine to render Arran by far the most interesting spot in the British Isles to all lovers of nature, no matter what be the form. It belongs to the Duke of Hamilton, who has erected a fine castle on the eastern shore.

Thursday, Aug. 15.—A clear, beautiful morning. About 11, Miss N., her brother, and myself set sail for King's Cross Point, to gather ferns and sea-weed. The wind was very gusty, so that often our boat heeled over to the water's edge. In about twenty minutes we reached the rocky ledge which served us as a wharf, and soon were on our knees peering into the little pools in search of sea-weed and anemones. Besides the ordinary red anemone, which is to be found here in great perfection, we found also a very beautiful delicate brown variety, which is rather rare in this locality. Having dislodged it without any material injury, it was transferred to our vasculum, together with a very lively little prawn, who by his own activity had made himself our prisoner. Slowly we walked along the beach, peering into every little pool, and carefully turning over every mass of weed in search of something new and rare. At last we reached King's Cross Point, a cluster of rocks jutting out into the sea, famous as the place from which Bruce set forth in his memorable expedition to Scotland. On these rocks we found very beautiful yellow lichens, specimens of which we cut from the rocks "In Memoriam." After damaging our understandings slightly on the slippery rocks, we returned to our boat, and the wind having moderated, concluded to try dredging. So sailing over to Holy Island, the sole occupant of which is Dr. Carpenter, the great physiologist, we borrowed from his son his dredge, and fastening it with our anchor rope, heaved it overboard. After letting it drag for a few moments, we began to haul. It was one thing to let it down, but quite another to pull it up ;—so *we* found.

Our first haul was a very rich one, including several varieties of star fishes, a fine sea urchin, hermit crabs, and lovely anemones. Down goes the dredge again, and away we sail. This haul brought us a beautiful goniaster, as well as a very fine trochus and many beautiful shells. After three or four hauls we sailed home to dinner.

After dinner we started for a drive to Brodick, thence to walk up Glen Rosa. Hardly had we got a mile from home when the rain came down in torrents, and as we were in an open car we were drenched. Nothing daunted, however, we pushed on, and in an hour were at the mouth of the glen. Here we left our car, and consoling ourselves with the fact that we were about as wet as we could be, started. When we had gone about a mile another storm broke upon us, and indeed it was a ludicrous sight to see our party crouched here and there under the rocks seeking shelter. After being prisoners for about half an hour, the storm cleared away, and we pressed on to a beautiful waterfall called the Rocky Burn. Here we remained for a while to see if we could be favoured with a view of the summit of Goatfell, now hidden amongst the clouds. Strange to say, the patience of our ladies gave out first, and they left us. In a few moments the misty curtain lifted, but for a little, and the lofty summit of the mountain stood out in bold relief against the sky. After another drenching we reached Lamlash about 9 P.M., and putting on dry clothes, we were soon busy around a cheerful fire arranging our ferns.

Saturday, Aug. 17.—And still another cloudy, cheerless day. I am told that August is the most delightful month in the year here—is it? I wonder what the worst is like, if the best is far behind our worst. After various delays and sundry detentions, we took a small row-boat and pulled over to Holy Island. Here we landed to visit St. Molio's cave. St. Molio was the friend and companion of the pious Columba, and at the instigation of the latter selected this island as the scene of his labours. He was one of the Culdees (corruption of Cultores Dei = worshippers of God), and lived to the advanced age of 120 years. He is buried at Strickam, and his tomb is still to be seen. The cave is about 25 feet above the water level, and has evidently been worn out by the action of the water. On the walls are several Runic inscriptions, which have a very antique appearance. At the mouth of the cave is a spring of most delicious water, where no doubt often the old man refreshed himself during his labours. Above the cave are some very fine basaltic columns, in the clefts of which are many fine ferns. On our way back to the boat, we came across a good sized adder. They are very common in this island, and are often found three feet long.

After dinner, in company with the Rev. Mr. Macdonald we rowed to the fishing ground, about 2 miles distant from Lamlash. Here we anchored for about two hours. Our success was poor;—owing to the weakness of our lines the finest fish got away. After pulling home again, we found ourselves very much fatigued, having rowed a heavy boat, well filled, about 5 miles against a very heavy sea.

Sabbath, Aug. 18.—On looking out this morning I found a fearful storm had been raging all night, and as yet had not abated. The bay was filled with ships which had sought shelter during the night; and so great was the fury of the storm, that the bay, usually so calm and peaceful, was so lashed into spray as to render the vessels at times quite invisible. Of course we could not go to church, but drew on Mr. N.'s large library for a good store of reading.

Monday, Aug. 19.—To use a very classical expression, day broke very pluvial. The most of the morning was spent in writing, and reading the news from America just come to hand per *Arabia.* After an early dinner, and in the midst of a pouring rain, we took the steamer for Corrie, distant about 9 miles, to ascend Glen Sannox, famous as one of the wildest glens in all Scotland. Our party consisted of about twenty, and despite the storm, was a very merry one. When we reached Corrie it was still pouring, and we were obliged to land in a small boat. One of our party fainted, so much did the little skiff toss up and down upon the waves. Our boatmen were very skilful, and though it appeared at one time as though we would surely be dashed upon the rocks, the next moment we shot into a little cove, just wide enough to admit our boat, and were washed high and dry upon the beach. After getting a conveyance for the ladies, we gentlemen started to walk to the mouth of the glen. Along the road were many exposures of the rock, peculiarly interesting to the geologist: on one side the ferns were growing in rich profusion, while on the other, rocks were strewn with beautiful sea-weed. A walk of 2 miles, most of it through a driving rain, when umbrellas were quite useless, brought us to the little footpath leading up the glen. Our attention was first called to the little burial-ground: it is of great antiquity, and is said to contain the remains of St. Molio, of whom I have before spoken. On a hook set in a slab of stone beside the gate hung the key, and above it carved the request, "Please lock the gate;"—certainly showing that the people have great confidence in one another. And, in fact, I have noticed the people here, how kind they are to one another. Crime is almost unknown, and no one seems to think it any trouble to assist his neighbour, no matter to how much trouble he may have to put himself in order to do it. Many of them, especially in the interior, live in a very primitive condition, and are quite ignorant of what we would call the ordinary comforts of life. But while I am peering over this old wall, the rest of the party, not having very antiquarian tastes, are almost out of sight; so I must hurry on. We soon stumble upon the remains of an old mill used for grinding the sulphate of barytes, found in the valley. It is used as a cheap substitute for white lead in paint. About a quarter of a mile further on, we came to the mine from which the barytes is taken—and here we were obliged to stop, as the rest of the way was knee deep in water, owing to the recent unceasing rains. What a picture of wild solitude! what sublime simplicity! as though daring man's ruthless hand to mar its primeval grandeur. On our right rose the rugged, inaccessible sides of Caim-na-Cailleach; while like a giant keeper Kir Vohr sat enthroned in awful silence at the head of the glen, and overtopped all the lichen-covered summit of Goatfell. After gazing for a long time on this imposing scene, and being favoured with the sight of the gathering and bursting of a heavy storm on the mountain-top, we hastened back to Corrie, where we arrived just in time to be re-drenched on our way out to the steamer. We reached Lamlash in time for tea, and after changing our clothing we all adjourned to Mr. Stevenson's, where we spent the evening.

Tuesday, Aug. 20.—Pluvial again. Toward 11 the sky began to break, and tempted us away to sail in the boat. Our party consisted of four, besides ourselves there being the Rev. Mr. G. (U.P.), from Liverpool. The breeze was stiff, and before many minutes we were at King's Cross Point, where we landed; and while some of the party indulged in a dip I wandered over the rocks in search of sea-weed. Nor was I unsuccessful, for in less than half an hour several beautiful specimens of sea-weed and zoophytes found their way into my impromptu vasculum. When in the middle of the bay, on our return home, a fearful storm of rain and wind caught us. Our little skiff rushed through the water at a fearful rate, her bulwarks at times under water; and had I not had great confidence in Mr. N. and his boatman, I would have been very much alarmed. The storm soon passed away, and when we reached our moorings every vestige of it had disappeared—the sky was clear and the water scarcely disturbed by a ripple.

In the afternoon we sailed to the fishing ground, and were very fortunate, catching in about an hour a large silver haddock, several sole and fine flounders, and sundry cod. Hardly had the sun set, when, like a shield of burnished silver, the moon rose over the top of Holy Island, and now as I write its pale beams are dancing merrily on the water, and the gentle breeze is sighing among the trees, and the stars are one by one beginning to peep out over the Ayrshire hills.

Friday, Aug. 23.—The same old entry, a wet day. As

there were some signs of clearing, we took the steamer after dinner, and sailed to Brodick; from which place we walked home over the hills. The hills of Arran are all covered with a most luxuriant growth of heather, now in its prime; and I know of no more beautiful sight to gaze upon than a hill-side clad with this rich purple, in striking contrast to the deep green underneath. After tea went out in the bay to try fly-fishing, and would have had good sport had not the storm driven us home.

Tuesday, Aug. 27.—Since my last entry nothing has occurred worthy of mention. The weather has as usual been wet, only more so, and we have been confined to the house, except when, unmindful of rain, we have gone along the shore in search of sea-weed, or out in the boat fishing; in both of which pursuits our success has been various. This morning there were some signs of clearing up, so we went out sailing, and in the afternoon took to fishing again. Although our success was poor, we caught one fish for which I would willingly have given all the rest—not on the score of its edibility, but in order to see that of which I had read so much and such varied accounts. After we had been on the fishing ground about an hour, Mr. N. felt something tugging very hard at his line. As it neared the surface, water was squirted into his face with such violence as to compel him to let go his line;—fortunately it was secured to one of the belaying pins, and one of us again drew the fish to the surface. As it came near we could see its eyes flashing like rubies, and we had hardly time to draw back when it again squirted an inky substance (which is poisonous) all over the surrounding water and into the boat. A few blows of the boat-hook rendered it senseless, and we drew it up on the gunwale. It proved to be a large cuttle-fish. Though the body was scarcely longer than one's fist, the arms or feelers were at least two feet long; and from the manner in which it flashed its wicked eye, and endeavoured with its long slimy arms to lay hold upon us, I could well believe all that travellers have told us of such creatures in the tropical seas. It was, without exception, the most hideous-looking creature I ever saw, and after watching it for a few moments to see some of its peculiarities, I was glad to throw it back into its native element. It is very voracious, and gets its subsistence by pouncing upon the unwary fish, biting a piece out of its back, and then ejecting this inky fluid, surrounded by which it swims away from present danger, and then returning finds its victim poisoned.

Aug. 20.—At 2.30 bade farewell to Arran, and started in the steamer *Spunkie.* We coasted along the shore for about 10 miles to Corrie, lying at the base of Goatfell, from which point we headed across the Firth to Bute. As we receded from Arran the view was very fine, the rugged hills, pierced at intervals by the deep, wild glens, presenting a scene not to be witnessed everywhere. It was what an eminent professor of theology in Edinburgh would call "a pleasing object." This learned gentleman, Prof. C., has no feeling for nature, and whether you call his attention to a roaring cascade or a little mountain rill, a green hill-side or a rugged crag, a perfect calm or a raging storm, his exclamation invariably is, "A pleasing object." About 6 o'clock we entered Rothesay Bay, and having sent our luggage to the hotel, went to dine with a most excellent, good man, the Rev. Mr. N., pastor of the Cameronian church in Rothesay.

Rothesay is situated on the island of Bute, about 50 miles from Glasgow. The climate is very salubrious, and it is much resorted to by invalids. On the outskirts of the town are the ruins of an old castle once occupied by the Kings of Scotland. It figures in history first about the year 1225, passed by conquest into the hands of Robert Bruce in 1311, and was bestowed upon his grandson, Prince David, who was styled the Duke of Rothesay, —the first dukedom bestowed in Scotland.

Aug. 29.—Left Rothesay at 10 A.M., in the swift steamer *Iona.* We soon entered the narrow strait lying between Bute and the mainland, called the Kyles of Bute. It is a narrow, tortuous passage, hemmed in by steep crags, whose bleak tops are covered by the many-coloured lichens. As we entered the Kyles, on our left was Loch Striven, and a little further on, Loch Riddan, famed for their beautiful scenery. On a little island at the mouth of Loch Riddan may be seen the ruins of an old fortress, built in 1685 by the Duke of Argyle, when he attempted the invasion of the kingdom. And now, as we swing round a narrow point, Arran with its lofty peaks comes in full view; while further still we see the coast of Kintyre, and the ruins of Skipness Castle, supposed to have been built by the Danes. We are now exposed to the full swell of the Atlantic, and as the day is by no means the calmest, many poor unfortunates are called upon to settle their accounts with Neptune, Esq. Up to this time the day has been beautifully clear, but now, just as we are entering the Highlands, a famous Scotch mist sets in upon us, and the scenery is totally obscured.

About 1 o'clock we reached Ardrishaig, where we left

our steamer and took a canal boat for Crinan. . . . . . Shortly after leaving Crinan the island of Iona comes in full view, then the island of Scarba; between which island and Iona is the much-dreaded whirlpool of Corrievreckan. Passing through the Sound of Luing, we come in sight of Ben More (3,170 feet)—the highest mountain in Mull. We now come to Easdale, where 400 men are employed in working the slate quarries. Leaving Easdale we skirt along the precipitous shores of Seil, against which the waves are dashing most furiously. This lasts but a little, for we are soon under the lee of the island of Kerrera. . . . . . We reached Oban at 7 o'clock, and found most excellent quarters at the Caledonian Hotel. Here the proprietor (of course his name is Campbell, for all are Campbells here), learning that I was a Stuart, took me to his room and showed me the identical coat which Prince Charlie threw off when he donned the dress of Flora M'Donald, and was hid by her in the cave on the coast of Skye. There is no doubt of the genuineness of this relic, as it has been in the M'Donald family ever since, to which clan Mr. Campbell's wife belongs. Oban is a beautiful town, and a great central place for Highland tourists. Nothing could be more beautiful than its situation. Climbing the hill back of the town, a fine view is obtained of the surrounding country. In front are the lofty hills of Mull, with the green island of Lismore and the ruins of Dunstaffnage and Dunolly Castles at your feet. The situation of the latter is wildly beautiful. Its massive ivy-clad walls tell of days when they gave back the echo from the footsteps of mighty chieftains—the home of a clan mighty and brave enough to confront and defeat Robert the Bruce. Dunstaffnage, a few miles further on, is famed as being once the repository of the Destiny Stone. . . . . .

Friday, Aug. 30.—Rose at 4.30, and at 5.30 took the steamer for Ballachulish on Loch Leven, where we would take stage for Glencoe. The morning was cloudy—almost as bad as usual. . . . . As we advance, the scenery becomes wilder and more picturesque, until we reach Ballachulish, famed for its slate quarries. Here we leave the steamer, which awaits our return, and take a coach to Glencoe, distant about 9 miles. Soon after leaving the town the rain came down in torrents, and as our coach was all outside there was no shelter. However, we were in for it. For about 5 miles we skirt along the edge of the loch, then turning inland around the base of the hill of Glencoe, we are soon hidden amongst the hills. The cluster of mountains which here rear their rugged summits to the sky have not been inaptly termed the Alps of Glencoe, for here they have been heaped together in wild confusion, and down their barren sides a thousand mountain streams are rushing, mingling their roar with the piercing cry of the eagle as he soars away to his eyrie in the Black Rock, in the steep face of which, near to the summit, is shown a cave said to have been the hiding-place of Ossian. Leaving the coach half way up the pass, we walk to the dividing ridge. This spot is called the Meeting of the Waters, where three streams, one from the top of the glen and the others from the opposite mountains, unite amid the black rocks, and form the Cora or Coe, which at the foot of the glen expands into a lake called Loch Treachtan. A little above this are to be seen the ruins of the houses of those who fell in the fearful Massacre of Glencoe in 1692. This sad historic incident, coupled with the wild grandeur of the glen, renders it a place of peculiar interest.

Having spent about an hour in the glen, we returned to our coach, and drove back to the steamer. Continuing our way up Loch Leven, we come to Fort William, lying at the foot of Ben Nevis. Here we leave the boat, and prepare to make the ascent of the mountain. Having secured a good guide—who is, by-the-by, a namesake of my own, and declares he never had as much pleasure in the thought of going up the mountain as now that he is going to take a "Stuart"—we set off on ponies up Glen Nevis, from the head of which we begin to ascend the mountain. Glen Nevis, through which runs the river of the same name, is one of the finest glens in all Scotland. It is entirely unlike Glencoe. The latter is wild, bleak, and barren, while in the former the hill-sides are covered with rich purple heather and luxuriant ferns. Ben Nevis rises 4,404 feet above the level of the sea, and it's a long long, weary climb. . . . . For about 1,700 feet our course lay over heather and long grass. At this height we come to a wild tarn called Loch Nevis. Here all vegetation ceases, and a strange scene of desolation presents itself;—we meet, as it were, with a new mountain, with its huge porphyritic rocks covered with lichens and white reindeer moss, looking as though the refuse of creation had been heaped and piled up in wild confusion. We look in vain for some signs of vegetable life, for all is barren, save where here and there the little Alpine plant puts forth its modest blossom between the rocks. At last we reach the top, after a weary pull of four hours, and sit down upon the cairn. To our left is a sheer precipice of 1,700 feet—all round us desolation reigns—the rocks are covered with snow, and there is not a sign of life. Approaching darkness warns us to leave, and we begin the descent, which, though accomplished in much less time, is as fatiguing as the ascent, if not more so. Weary and worn, in the midst of dense mist and heavy rain we reach the base, and after sundry stumbles over rocks and into creeks, find our ponies and reach the hotel at 11 P.M., having been out since 2. The toil is soon forgotten over a comfortable fire and good supper, after which we retired to rest.

Saturday, Aug. 31.—Rose at 4.30. Very stiff and sore from last night's exertions. Went on board the steamer *Mountaineer* for Oban. Arrived there at 8 o'clock, and at once went on board the *Pioneer*, bound for Staffa and Iona. Our party was a very large one, consisting principally of a company of South Englishers, who had come in delaines and dress coats to "do" the Highlands. They were what might be called a queer lot, and we who had been together for some days past had plenty of sport. After passing out of the Sound of Kerrera, we coasted along the southern shore of Mull. Here we met the unbroken swell of the Atlantic as it comes rolling in from the far off coasts of America. Our vessel of course began to roll, and many of the fair damsels were becoming quite uncomfortable. Descending to the cabin, the scene was to a well person ludicrous in the extreme. The poor unfortunates were strewn about the floor in every imaginable position, each one holding on firmly to his basin, lest some one should snatch it away. As I was returning towards the stairs, I heard a faint voice calling me from behind the door. Looking round, I saw a poor unprotected creature, evidently very sick. "Pray, sir, will you call the steward?" she said, in a very pleading voice. —"Steward, you are wanted," says I.—"Can't come, can't attend to everybody," he gruffly replied.—"Oh, sir," she said, in more pleading terms, "won't you get me a dish, or plate, or even a coffee cup would do." I procured her a soup plate; after using which she said, "Won't you please to hand it to that gentleman over there, may be he'd like to use it for a little."

About 11 o'clock we came in sight of Iona, whose ruined cathedral we could see standing alone upon the rocky shore. We landed in the ship's boat and hastened to improve our hour among the ruins. I need hardly say that upon this island the pious Columba landed in the year 565 and founded the college from which he sent forth preachers and teachers throughout Britain. As we trod the sacred soil we could not but feel as Dr. Johnson did when he said, "That man is little to be envied whose patriotism would not gain force upon the plains of Marathon, or whose piety would not grow warmer amid the ruins of Iona." In the grave-yard we saw the tombs of the first Scottish, Irish, and Scandinavian Kings, and also that of the Lord of the Isles. But the spot where we lingered longest was at the tomb of Columba. There is no doubt of the exact spot, as a few years ago the Duke of Argyle, the lord of the manor, gave permission to the Scottish Archæological Society to search for the tomb of the saint. Here they found a stone coffin, having his name and the date of his death engraved upon it. They opened it carefully, and in it found his dust. Having satisfied themselves as to the accuracy of the inscription, they carefully reclosed the coffin and placed it in its original position. Here, then, lived a man who, under God, became the means of converting to Christianity the greater portion of the Pictish race; who, though his life was threatened, though the gates of the king's palace were closed against him, and he was denounced by every priest, persevered in his arduous labours, until, having overcome every opposition, he saw paganism and idolatry fading away, and in their stead the gospel of Jesus Christ reigning over the hearts of the people

A sail of about two hours from Iona brought us in full view of Staffa. The first object we could see distinctly was Fingal's Cave, and we felt that indeed the half had not been told us of this wonderful formation. Staffa, lying about 8 miles west of the coast of Mull, is about a mile and a half in circumference, and is uninhabited save by a herd of cattle. It is rock-bound, and there is no cove where a ship can safely run in. Our vessel lay about a mile from shore, and we went in life-boats. The sea was running very high, and had we not been in very experienced hands we would have had good cause to be afraid. As we neared the shore, we discerned a little hollow between two ledges of rock, barely wide enough to admit a boat: into this our boat shot upon the crest of the advancing wave, which left us high and dry among the rocks. We walked from here across the island, until we came near Fingal's Cave, when we descended a steep staircase, and clambered along the tops of the basaltic columns until we arrived at the mouth of the cave—a mighty archway 70 feet high and receding inwards about 250 feet. Along the side there is a narrow path, the side of which is washed by the black, angry waves. The entire front and sides are composed of ranges of countless basaltic columns, beautifully joined and of most symmetrical though varied forms. The roof exhibits a rich profusion of overhanging pillars incrusted with lime; the whole forming a picture of unrivalled grandeur, and when once seen cannot soon be forgotten. It was such a sight as I never expect to see again unless I go back to Staffa, this wondrous arch, through which the wild waters ever urge their way, its dark depths ever and anon rendered visible by the flashing light reflected from the surge of the advancing waves, whose wild yet mellow and sonorous moan rises and falls in measured cadence on the ear. With feelings of wonder, and having our minds deeply impressed with the grandeur of the works of God, we slowly retraced our steps from the Cave Cathedral of Staffa. Continuing our course we soon enter the Sound of Mull, and are in full view of Duart Castle, the strength of the M'Leans of Duart, famous for their prowess in battle. Soon we pass the "Lady's Rock," where one of the M'Leans exposed his wife to be drowned by the rising tide. His wicked design, however, was frustrated by some fishermen, who, hearing her cries, rescued and carried her to a place of safety.

Monday, Sept. 2.—Raining as usual. Left Oban at 9. A.M. in the coach for Inverary, distant about 40 miles. About 20 miles from Oban we entered the Pass of Awe, through which runs the river of the same name, famed for its salmon fishing. On our left was Ben Cruachan, its summit capped with clouds. The mountains round the head of the loch were once in possession of the Campbells, whose slogan was, "It's a far cry to Loch Awe;" indicating the impossibility of reaching them in the mountain fastness. Skirting along the shores of this beautiful loch, we come to the inn of Dalmally, at the mouth of the Vale of Glenorchy, where we dined. Resuming our seats, we pass along the opposite side of the loch, in full view of the ruins of Kilchurn Castle, a wild yet stately ruin, built in 1443 by the lady of Sir Colin Campbell, the Black Knight of Rhodes. Ascending a steep hill we stop to view the charming scene. Well has this vale been called the Hesperides of the Highlands, for never was a fairer scene than this. Descending into Glen Aray we are soon at Inverary, where is Inverary Castle, the magnificent summer residence of the Duke of Argyle.

[*Sept.* 3.—He reached Glasgow, where he parted from Mr. N., and took the train at 8 P.M. for Manchester; which place he reached next morning, just in time for the British Association, of which he was a member.]

Manchester, Sept. 6.—Since I came I have been attending the different meetings of the Association, which are very interesting. Last night we had a Microscopic Soirée, which was a most interesting affair. I have heard papers from Du Chaillu of gorilla fame, Sir Roderick Murchison, Armstrong of gun notoriety, Sir Chas. Napier, Owen the great naturalist, Lord Stanley, Brewster, and many other lesser lights. To-morrow I leave for London, spend Sabbath there, and start for Paris early on Monday morning.

Sabbath, Sept. 8.—Arrived in London late last evening. This morning we went to Westminster Abbey, where we heard a very excellent sermon from "the Very Rev. the Dean of Westminster;" immediately after which we were hustled out of church like a flock of sheep by the beadles, of whom there were not a few. At 5, started across the river to hear Spurgeon. A ride of half an hour over Black-friars' Bridge brought us to the door of his Metropolitan Tabernacle, where we were obliged to stand for about an hour, while the congregation was admitted by tickets at the back. At 25 minutes past 6, just five minutes before the commencement of service, the doors were opened, and we all rushed, as fast as respect to the place would allow us, for the few remaining seats. We were fortunate in being just at the door when it was opened, and consequently got good seats in the centre of the house. Whilst waiting for the appearance of Mr. Spurgeon, I had an opportunity of looking at the building. It is of an oval shape, and has two galleries running all round. Jutting out from the first is a semicircular platform, having a sofa and a small walnut table, on which rests the Bible: this Mr. Spurgeon uses for a pulpit, and as there is no desk between him and his audience, his movements are much freer than they otherwise would be. Punctually at 6.30 Mr. Spurgeon rose, and in a rich, clear voice, read the first hymn. His manner was calm and very impressive; his style of reading much superior to that of the ordinary run of preachers. The congregation rose, and he read each stanza before it was sung. After this he read the 32nd Psalm, accompanying each verse with a few explanatory remarks. Many of them were very striking, and although I cannot remember the best, the following is one which will show somewhat of their character. In speaking on the second verse, as to the necessity of being convinced of sin, he said: "Brethren, we must go into the stripping-room before we enter the robing-room; we must be sick before we can be healed." After reading he announced the hymn beginning, "Children of the

Heavenly King;" and then made a brief but most earnest prayer. His manner of prayer partakes largely of the colloquial, and was such that even the most careless could not but have been impressed. After singing another hymn he announced his text, Job viii. 13, 14, "*The hypocrite's hope shall perish: whose hope shall be cut off, and whose trust shall be a spider's web.*"

The sermon was not what could be called a grand one, but a most earnest, faithful, affectionate appeal. His arguments were very closely followed, and yet so simple that a child could understand them. His illustrations, both in the way of similes and anecdotes, were appropriate, and were put with great power. All this coupled with a magnificent voice, and a great natural earnestness of delivery, gave him a perfect mastery over his audience, so that when he sat down, after speaking for more than an hour, we wondered at his brevity, and were astonished to find he had been speaking so long.

One most pleasing feature of Mr. Spurgeon is, that at least to all appearance he has not been spoiled by his popularity. Everything about him seemed so natural, and he had none of that self-sanctified manner so disagreeable in the preaching of some. He is a wonderful man. Every sentence bears the impress of a giant mind; and yet, judging from what we heard this evening, he does not make this a reason for meeting his people unprepared and trusting to the impulse of the hour, but rather presents them with a carefully studied, well digested discourse.

Sept. 9, 1861.—Left London at 9.50 for Paris viâ Folkestone and Boulogne. A ride of two hours through a very well cultivated country brought us to Folkestone

Harbour, where we embarked in one of the little cockle-shell Channel steamers for Boulogne. . . . . We reached Boulogne in about two and a half hours after leaving Folkestone. . . . . At about 3 o'clock started for Paris, distant about 160 miles. . . . . At 8.30 entered that city, and after sundry delays reached the Hotel du Louvre. Having secured our rooms we started out to see the city. Although it was almost midnight, the streets were crowded: long rows of lamps extend as far as the eye can reach, while the Boulevards in many places are lighted with the electric light. Started through the Palais Royal and along the Champs Elysée, and back to the hotel, where we got to bed as the clock was on the stroke of one.

My first impressions of Paris are very pleasing. It is a very magnificent city—by far the grandest that I have ever seen; and yet I am far more content to live in my own beloved land, and would deeply regret the necessity that would cause me to live, or even spend any length of time, in this too gay city. All that I have seen only makes me love and appreciate my own land the more.

Left Paris at 7.30; travelled all night.

[*Sept.* 11.—He arrived in Geneva and presented his letter to the Evangelical Alliance assembled there. Visited the Meeting of the Waters, tombs of Sir Humphry Davy and John Calvin; also the houses of Voltaire and Lord Byron.]

Sept. 12.— . . . . . We left Geneva in a two-horse volante for Chamounix at 7 A.M. The morning was all that could be desired, not a cloud was to be seen, and it was warm without being uncomfortable.

The first village we approached was that of Chesne on the Seine: this stream is the dividing line between Savoy and Switzerland. Our course now lies along the banks of the Arve, a muddy, swift stream, which has its source in the glacier Mer de Glace. At 11 o'clock we reach the village of Bonneville, where we rest for an hour.

Though the beauty of Swiss scenery is unrivalled, much of the charm is taken away by the poverty of the inhabitants, which presents itself at every step. One cannot travel through a village, however small, without seeing dozens of women disfigured by goitre. In many cases this is most disgusting; and as they make no attempt to conceal it, one cannot avoid seeing it as it hangs down from their cheek or chin, sometimes being as much as a foot in length. There are also many of the Cretins, those poor, miserable, half-idiotic creatures, whose life seems to be to them a very burden, and to whom death would be a blessing. To see one of these beings lying on the roadside asking for alms, is one of the saddest sights I ever witnessed; and it is indeed a blessing that such a fearful scourge is confined to a very small section of country.

After leaving Bonneville, our road lay up a most beautiful vine-clad valley, having on the one side the Mont Brezon, whose fir-clad peaks tower to the height of 2,000 feet above the valley. Crossing the Arve, and passing through the village of Cluses, we enter a deep defile through which the Arve rushes—the pass is barely wide enough for the narrow river bed and the road, and is overhung by steep Alpine precipices. A few miles from Cluses the pass opens out; and in the face of the cliff, 800 feet above the valley, is the Grotto of Balme. It extends about 2,000 feet into the mountains, and from the mouth a magnificent view may be had of the Jura Alps. About a mile from this cave there is a beautiful waterfall, the

Nant d'Asperzas: the stream is quite small, and is lost in spray long before reaching the bottom.

One most interesting feature in this pass is the wonderful contortions in the strata as exposed in the face of the cliffs, showing what a power must have been exercised during the volcanic era when these huge masses were heaved up.

A sudden turn in the road brings us in full view of the range of Mont Blanc, crowned by the majestic peak of the mountain of mountains itself. The sky was a rich deep blue, the sun shining as it only does in Italy and America;—that mountain of purest snow, with its glaciers flashing like diamond points, its majestic form, its deep, dark ravines, penetrating into the very bowels of the earth, was the grandest sight I ever beheld. Involuntarily we lifted our hats, and stood for more than twenty minutes transfixed by the grandeur of the scene. We could not but exclaim with the poet,—

> "Mont Blanc is the monarch of mountains
> They crowned him long ago,
> On a throne of rocks, in a robe of clouds,
> With a diadem of snow."

It would be the height of presumption for me to attempt to describe this scene. Man has not words for it, —the imagination of the poet cannot grasp it. To feel what it is, you must yourself stand as we stood, upon the little stone bridge of St. Martin, and gaze upon the majestic panorama. About an hour after leaving St. Martin we ascended a steep hill, from the summit of which we had another splendid view of the mountain, no longer white, but reflecting the roseate hues of the setting sun.

Descending into the valley, a drive of half an hour brought us to Chamounix, where, after supper, we soon retired; and as we lay in bed we could see the full moon shining upon the summit of the mountain.

Sept. 14.—Another splendid day. At the breakfast table we formed a party of seven to ascend the Montanvert and view the Mer de Glace. At 10 we started, our ladies mounted upon mules. There is a very good mule path to the summit of Montanvert, made lately by Napoleon at great labour and expense, in many cases being blasted out of the solid rock. As we approached the summit, the ascent became very steep, the road being a succession of steps in the rocks, many of them three feet in height. . . . A climb of two hours placed us on the summit of Montanvert, with the Mer de Glace at our feet—before us, stretching up the hollow, was this Sea of Ice; here it divided, one branch running past the Col du Géant up almost to the summit of Mont Blanc, the other extending round the Aiguille du Dome to the Jardin. All round us rose the unclimbed rocks known as the Aiguilles. They shoot up almost perpendicularly from the mountain-side, and are, as I have said, inaccessible. Having engaged a guide, we prepared to cross the Mer de Glace, leaving the ladies on the heights to await our return. Looking well to our shoes and the spikes of our Alpine stocks, we descended upon the ice. Advancing about 20 feet, we came to a crevice about 2 feet wide; lying down upon the ice, we looked in to see the deep blue colour which is so remarkable in this glacier. We then took a stone, and dropping it in, listened for some seconds until we heard it plunge into the water below; and we thought what a dreadful death to fall into such a place, and may be linger for days and hours in agony, being gradually crushed by the closing ice, and no one able to render relief. Arriving at the middle of the glacier, the real work began. Here we were obliged to cut steps in the ice and walk along in single file, sometimes ascending and sometimes descending, until we reached the edge of a large crevice, which had opened but a few days before. Lying down upon the ice, we looked into this, and it made us shudder to think of the fearful depth, which we found by measurement to be over 700 feet.

These glaciers form a subject of most interesting study, and have attracted the attention of the most eminent scientific men. It has now been determined that they move, and that their motion is from 12 to 20 inches a-day. This was practically proved a few days since, by the discovery of the remains of some persons who had been lost forty years before at the head of the Glacier de Boissons. Prof. Forbes told the guides repeatedly that in about forty years from the time the party were lost their remains might be looked for at the foot of the glacier; calculating that it would take the ice in which they were imbedded just that time to work itself from the head of the glacier. This discovery has proved the correctness of his theory.

Returning to the Montanvert, we descended the mountain and reached the hotel at 5, just in time for the table d'hôte, which our sharpened appetites enabled us to do full justice to. After dinner we walked round amongst the shops, and went to see the clothing of Balmat, which, as I have mentioned, was found a few days ago. This Balmat made the first ascent of the mountain in 1798, and was for many years the only one who could be found willing to undertake so hazardous an adventure.

Sabbath evening, Nov. 17, 1861.—Six months, and not a word in confidence to you, my old valued friend! I have wandered through England, Scotland, France, Germany, and Switzerland, and have not told you a word of it. Well, here I am again, home, *in health.* How much has transpired since I talked with you last! Loved ones have passed away, strange sights have been seen, and I am *older, nearer eternity*—I hope better than before. Still, I feel my soul clogged by sin; sinful thoughts, and from them sinful pleasures, trammel my soul, and cut short its flight. Too much of the world—too little of Jesus. How hard it is for one to exercise faith as it should be exercised! We all talk about it a great deal, but when it comes to a real, severe test, how it falters and doubts! as if such an anomaly can exist—a *doubting faith.* Such as this will not save us. To be efficient unto salvation, it must be such as will carry us through the very gates of death, shouting loud hallelujahs to a Saviour King.

To-day was to me a pleasant one. The school was good both morning and afternoon. I felt my soul much benefited by the remarks of Mr. Van Meter, of the Wanderer's Home, New York. In the afternoon, Rev. J. Morrison, of the Lodiana Mission, N. India, gave us a most interesting address. Did not go out in the evening, but after worship sang hymns with the children—

> "Oh, the sweet joy this sentence gives,
> *I know that my Redeemer lives.*"

Retired early.

Sabbath, Dec. 1.—A bright clear day. Held the fourth Anniversary of our Mission School in the afternoon. There were present 180 children and 40 visitors. Addresses were delivered by Dr. Wylie, Dr. Faires, Father Martin, and Heber Newton—all most excellent, and were very attentively listened to by the children, whose good order was remarked by every one. We feel greatly encouraged in our labours, and go forward with greater zeal in our Master's work.

Tuesday, Dec. 9, 1862.—More than a year has passed since last I opened a thought on these pages. What events have been crowded in that year! A merciful God has protected me in my journeyings on the mighty deep and in a distant land; friends, familiar faces, have passed from earth to heaven; means of grace have been embraced or neglected; my life has been spared, and even though my health has not been in full measure continued to me, God has given me, to be my partner in life, her on whom my boyish hopes were fixed, and who was the choice of my riper years. Yes, she is mine, and I am hers. "What can I render unto God for all his benefits to me?"

Now we are leaving New York in the steamer *British Queen*, for Santa Cruz viâ Havana. The day is clear and very cold. Good-byes are said, the steamer moves slowly down the Bay, and soon Sandy Hook is lost in the distance. It is a most beautiful afternoon, and the sunset is most brilliant. Our quarters are none of the best, either for eating or sleeping; still we will try and put up with them for the short voyage.

Tuesday, Dec. 16.—Entered the harbour of Havana

about 8 o'clock in the morning, and anchored at 9. The forts at the entrance look more picturesque than formidable. Getting our baggage in one boat and ourselves in another, after a row of a mile and a half, we reached the Custom House Wharf. Here we pay $2 each for permission to stay in the city, and after the usual examination of baggage, take a volante and drive to the Hotel Cubano. We find commodious rooms, and soon make ourselves at home. Oh, the luxury of getting off a ship, to get a good wash, be able to turn round and stretch your legs, and get on some clean clothes! After a lunch, we left M. for a while to her meditations, and went to present some letters of introduction. . . . .

In the afternoon we drove beyond the walls, along the Paseo de Jacon, past the Archbishop's Palace, to the residence of Madame Herrera, a widow, having neither kith nor kin, and the possessor of one of the largest estates around Havana. Uncle D. and M. walked around; I being too weak stayed in the carriage. Very extravagant, but with an utter want of taste—a thing which seems to be quite unknown in Cuba. As we drove in, we saw the señoritas sitting in their parlours protected by iron bars, and shopping in their volantes.

Sabbath, Dec. 21.—A beautiful clear day. After breakfast retired to my room—read and prayed. Tried to feel the solemnity of the day, but could not fix my thoughts, as at home. No Sabbath sun shines on this beautiful island; over it hangs, in heavy folds, the black, loathsome mantle of Popery. Thought of Heber's missionary hymn, especially the verse beginning, "Salvation, O salvation." Read in "Memories of Gennesaret,"—a delightful book by Macduff. Had a sweet talk with M. before dinner. Enjoyed that meal more than any time since I landed;—feel a little better to-day, as it is bright. How strange that the weather should thus affect the health of an invalid! Thought much of home—the family altar—the gathering in church and meeting familiar faces; especially thought of and prayed for my mission school: I cannot think that that little band will be left without a leader: God will raise up some one who will better fill my place, and the work *will* go on.

About 5 o'clock walked to the Promenade by the sea with uncle D. and the Messrs. R.—my first walk for three days. Came home in about an hour, pretty well fagged out. Throat a little sore.

Wednesday, Dec. 24.—. . . . . I can scarcely believe that this is Christmas Eve—so different from the scenes of home; yet I know, as those circles are gathered together this evening, we, the absent ones, are often and lovingly spoken of, and the places we filled are not forgotten.

Thursday, Dec. 25.—Christmas Day! Damp and dull as usual. M. and uncle D. went out to see some churches whilst I wrote letters. Dinner very late, and supposed to be very grand.

Friday, Dec. 26.—A beautiful clear day. At 11 ordered a carriage, and taking Don John as valet, started out for a drive. From Christmas to Sabbath are feast days, and no one does any work. Drove to the Captain-General's gardens, on the Paseo de Isabel—were charmed with what we saw—long avenues of stately palms, a beautiful aviary, cotton and coffee in full bloom, pine apples in every stage of growth; and in the midst of all a summer residence, which, however, is not open to visitors.

From the gardens we drove over a most break-neck road to the Cemetery. This is indeed a strange place. Imagine a large grassy quadrangle surrounded by a white stone wall about 25 feet high and 12 feet thick. In this wall the bodies are deposited, feet outwards: the openings look like windows rounded at the top, and are filled up with a slab of marble, or slate, bearing the name of the deceased. For the use of one of these repositories the friends of the deceased pay $200 for ten years: if at the expiration of that time the payment is not renewed, the body is taken out and thrown into one of the large pits in the centre of the quadrangle, where paupers are buried. At the end of a certain time these pits are re-opened and the contents sold to vegetable growers to fertilize their gardens. Returned to the hotel at 1.30—very tired. Uncle D. returned with a good account of Matanzas, so we will all go down to-morrow.

Saturday, Dec. 27.—A very warm day. Felt very poorly. Left Havana for Matanzas at 3.25—country very monotonous—arrived at 6.40—beautiful moonlight night—went at once to the Hewitt House, where we found rooms prepared for us: the house is plain, but American, and therefore more home-like. Retired at 8.30, very much worn out.

Sabbath, Dec. 28.—Rose at 9.15, having passed a very restless night with my cough. After dinner suffered from indigestion. Towards dusk sat on the porch and enjoyed the cool of the evening. Had a long talk with our Consul, Mr. C., from whom I obtained a good deal of information in regard to Cuba; and also heard from him the interesting narration of his arrest and subsequent release from Rebeldom. Retired at 10. *Fleas very bad.*

Monday, Dec. 29.—Weather quite warm. Stayed in the house all morning. Read in the "Marble Fawn." Afternoon, had a delightful ride with M. along the seashore.

Tuesday, Dec. 30.—Rose at 6.30, and after a hurried breakfast, started with a party for the plantation of Mr. Jenks. Our party consisted of eight, four in volantes and four on horseback. The road over which we went was fearful and execrable, being nothing but huge masses of rock, over which no vehicle but a Spanish volante would ever dare to venture, except to certain destruction. Upward we thus toiled for an hour, when suddenly we came to a level spot; and looking out, the beautiful valley of the Tumuri lay at our feet—the first piece of tropical scenery we had seen. It certainly was very lovely as it lay there, its sides clothed with palm trees and richly wooded cliffs. After gazing a while at its beauties, the rest of the party, who had lagged behind, rode up, and in a few moments we drove into the plantation. The sugar-making process is very simple; but as it was new to us, we were much interested. Our blood ran cold to see the fearful treatment the poor horses that were working the crushing-mill received from the negroes and coolies who were driving them; and then, I thought, why blame them, ignorant creatures! they know not what mercy is, as they receive but little better treatment from their masters.

All Cuba is one vast den of oppression, extortion, and cruelty. Only the other day we saw a chicken being picked alive; and when we called the attention of a Spaniard to it, he laughed and said, "That was common enough." The patient oxen are driven with a long pole, at the end of which is an iron goad several inches in length, which is frequently driven into them till the blood spirts out, and they fairly moan with pain. Such are the Spaniards!

Wednesday, Dec. 31.—Rose at 6.30, after a painfully sleepless night. Wrote home. Seized with a violent fit of coughing which caused intense pain. Evening, sat with M. in the parlour—heard some fine music from a Cuban gentleman educated in Philadelphia. Would like much to stay up and see the old year out, but am too tired.

Friday, Jan. 2, 1863.—Rose at 4.30, and after a hurried cup of coffee drove to the Guinas R. Road, from whence we started at 6.15 for Havana. Arrived at 8.30, in ample time for breakfast. Uncle D. went to see about the steamer *Ocean Bird*, to sail for Santa Cruz; and I, taking Don John in a volante, did some shopping and looked after our passports. Returned to the hotel about 1, feeling better than any day since I left home. Afternoon, sat in our room with M., not feeling as bright as in the morning.

After all uncle's trouble about the *Ocean Bird*, she is not going to sail at all—so we must take the *Conway*, (an inferior vessel). So much for Spanish truth and Spanish punctuality!

Saturday, Jan. 3.—Rose at 8.30, after a very restless, sleepless night. M. suffering much from a sore throat: she can hardly swallow. My stomach very sore from last night's coughing. Did not go out, but slept an hour or two in the rocking-chair.

[This is the last entry Willie ever made in his Diary, owing to increased debility.]

EXTRACTS

FROM

LETTERS TO M——.

LETTERS TO M.

THE Extracts which follow are made from a long correspondence with the lady whom William subsequently married.

---

419 SPRUCE STREET, *November* 8, 1856.

I will be unable to see you this afternoon, and probably for some time to come. Our dear Frank was taken very ill last night, and we fear he will not live. All the morning he had violent spasms, but he is a little easier now. God knoweth what is best: He will do all things well. To think that yesterday he was as well as any of us—now stricken down. . . . .

December 2, 1856.

. . . . . On Sabbath afternoon we had, instead of Sabbath school, a prayer-meeting preparatory to communion. Rev. Mr. T. of the Baptist Church made a beautiful address, showing how it was the first impulse of the

Christian, having found Christ himself, to go immediately to his nearest friend or relative, and say, "I have found the Messiah; come and see." During the whole address I thought of you, dear M. Now that I have found Christ, I would desire to lead you to Him also. He is a loving Saviour. He has accepted me, though a poor sinner; and He will receive you, if you come now. "Now is the accepted time." "Those that seek me *early shall* find me." It is a choice which I know you will never, no never regret.

In the evening we had another prayer-meeting, which was addressed by Rev. Messrs. F. and W. It seemed indeed to be a sweet foretaste of that eternity we shall spend around the throne of God, where I hope to meet you, and sing His praises throughout all eternity.

---

419 SPRUCE STREET, *December* 9, 1856.

On my return from the house of God this evening I opened your precious note, and words would fail to express the feelings of my inmost soul on reading those sentiments of your heart. I feel that God is indeed answering my earnest, importunate petitions on your behalf.

You mention as a reason for not coming to Christ, *Ridicule.* Oh, I hope, indeed I am sure, you will not allow so trifling a thing as this to influence your eternal welfare! A few sneers of the ungodly to bar you from eternity! Oh, no! They are only means by which God wishes to test your faith. Press onward! He has said, "Come unto me, all ye that labour and are heavy laden, and I will give you rest"—"I love them that love me; and they that seek me *early shall* find me." With such precious promises as these, how, how can you stay away from your Friend, who "sticketh closer than a brother!" Angels would rejoice, and bear aloft with shouts of joy the news of your salvation. Could you refuse to come to a Saviour who counted not His life dear for you? Pray earnestly: pour forth the inmost petitions of your soul; and God from His high throne will bend and hear the prayer of the humblest sinner. Think of this, and put not off for a moment the seeking of salvation for your soul. Come, trusting in the merits of the blood of Calvary; come humbly; come with all confidence in a loving, forgiving Saviour, and you will in no wise be cast out.

I will not cease to make you a subject of special prayer to Almighty God, that He would pour out His Spirit upon you in copious showers, and bring you early to Himself. Give the dew of your youth unto the Lord. Pray for me.

December 10, 1856.

I received your sweet note a few moments ago, and hasten to return an answer. How rejoiced am I to see that you are beginning to come to Christ! Oh, press onward! The only way to be saved is first to feel the weight of your sins, your inability to save yourself, and consequently your need of a Saviour.

Oh, M., as I walk along the streets, or go to college, and see hundreds (I would almost say) of young men rushing on to their destruction, my heart fairly bleeds for them. They all must die—sooner or later appear before the judgment-seat of a righteous God. It makes me fairly shudder to think what the fate of many of them must be, unless the hand of Mercy is stretched out to save them.

Pray for me, oh, pray for *me*, that God would give me grace to resist the many temptations which daily and hourly assail me at every step; and I will pray for you, earnestly and imploringly, that God would bring you to Himself. Yes, even before leaving my room this afternoon I will go to the throne of grace and mercy, and plead with God on your behalf. . . . . .

December 13, 1856. 11.30 P.M.

Although so near Sabbath morning, I cannot refrain from dropping you a few lines. To-night I am perfectly miserable with my head; it feels as if melted lead were running from one side to the other. I suppose you have been feasting on Thalberg, Gottschalk, and D'Angri this evening. I envy you.

When I spoke to you about joining the Church at the approaching communion, you said, "Not this time." Oh, if you do not feel prepared this time, do not defer it longer than the next. Do not, as Felix did, wait for "a more convenient season;" but rather come as you are, a humble, penitent sinner, and throwing yourself at the foot of the cross, say, "Here am I, Lord, a helpless sinner; do with me what Thou wilt." Then will He look down upon you with compassion and tender mercy, and incline your heart unto Himself. How I would rejoice to see you taking this step! "Choose this day whom ye will serve." "Fear not; I am with you." With such blessed words as these addressed to you by a loving Saviour, how can you hold back any longer from doing His commands? . . . . .

December 19, 1856.

Ere this reaches you, you will have witnessed that most solemn sacrament, the Lord's Supper; and I fondly hope that there you confirmed the resolution I doubt not you have heretofore prayerfully and carefully made, that when another communion season shall have come round, you would sit down at your Saviour's table. You have been much in my thoughts lately, and again and again at the throne of grace have I laid your case, and implored a divine and enriching blessing to descend upon you. Be earnest, be steadfast: never despair, but trust in the rich promises of a covenant-keeping God, and He will reward you plentifully.

PHILAD., *January* 1, 1857.

. . . . . So another year is gone! Another precious gem of youth lost in the ocean of eternity! . . . . .

Just before the clock struck 12 last night, I arose from my bed and poured forth a burdened soul to God, as the old year departed and a new one was ushered in; and you had a foremost place. Yes, earnestly did I plead with God to bring you early into His fold and make you His own.

Saturday morning, 2 o'clock, January 17, 1857.

Although so late, I cannot refrain from writing you. You cannot imagine how my heart leaped with joy this afternoon, when you said, "I will *try*." There is magic in the word: how often has it raised the spirits of some wretched one struggling to maintain an existence, and inspired him to new hopes of success! I could see yesterday afternoon that Satan was struggling hard in your breast. Drive him out once effectually, and by the grace of God he will never return. "Look to Jesus." . . . . . I have searched out a few texts of Scripture, which I would like you to read.

1. *A Rule for Prayer.*—1 Thess. v. 17; Phil. iv. 6.

2. *Promises.*—Deut. iv. 29; Ps. cxlv. 18, 19; Luke xi. 10; Jer. xxix. 12; 2 Cor. xii. 9.

3. *Benefit of confessing Sins.*—1 John i. 9.

Read these, and tell me this afternoon what you think. . . . . .

January 26, 1857. 8 A.M.

. . . . . Last evening I was by the death-bed of one of our Sabbath scholars. Although not regularly in my class, I have occasionally taught him, and felt a deep interest in his spiritual welfare. Had you heard what that little boy said to me, the message he sent to his class, you would have felt more powerfully than human words could utter, the power of Christ—that at the hour of death He is a "Friend that sticketh closer than a brother." . . . . . [After joyous answers to some previous questions,] I asked, Are you not afraid to die, and be laid in the cold and silent grave? "No," he replied; "Jesus was there before me, and made it soft as downy pillows. He is my own dear Saviour: He will be with me." And then turning to his brother, who is a bad boy, he said, "Brother! brother! come to Jesus: let me carry the news to heaven that you are going to love Christ. Go back to the Sabbath school, go back to church; and then, dear brother, I will die happy!" I have *read* of triumphal, peaceful death-beds, but never did I *see* any equal to that little boy, only thirteen years of age. "Be *ye also ready*, for in such an hour as ye think not, the Son of man cometh." "Watch and pray." . . . . .

Sabbath evening, February 1, 1857.

I have just returned from the death-bed of that little boy. Oh that you had been there! He offered such a prayer as I never expected to hear on earth.

In your last note you said you "had succeeded in drowning your thoughts, but the cloud was still there." Yes, and it will remain there. Go where you will, your guilty conscience will still reprove you. Your only rest, only safety, only hope, only salvation, is by going to Jesus, casting yourself a guilty sinner at His feet, and crying, "Lord, save me, I perish." . . . . . Try not to sear conscience, but listen to its reproofs: it is the voice of God warning you. God says, "Him that cometh to me I will in *no wise* cast out." What a promise! Oh, embrace it ere it be too late. That the blessed Jesus, the Lamb of Calvary, may come and dwell in your heart, is ever my earnest prayer.

February, 3, 1857.

. . . . . I begin to feel more resigned now. After much prayer, I feel that God will do with me what He thinks best; and I will place everything in His hands.* He has been with His people since the creation, and He will not forsake me. He will hear my prayer for you. Write me soon and tell me if you are still trying to come to Jesus—still knocking at the gate of heaven.

——— ———

February 7, 1857.

. . . . . I was so glad this evening when you promised me you would try and serve Christ. The promise to me was trifling compared with the promise to your Saviour. I beg of you do not break it. I entreat you, as you value your own soul, and eternal happiness, to hold on to it. Could you look into heaven this evening you would see angels rejoicing that you had resolved to cease to be a votary of this fleeting, deceitful world, and to look to Jesus as your only hope. . . . . .

Do you think about connecting yourself with the Church? It is an important step. Come, and Christ will receive you, though you were the greatest sinner. Do not desire the fashions and gaieties of this world: they may please for a time, but the dregs of the cup are bitter—even death spiritual. . . . . .

* His settled convictions were that his life would be short.

——— ———

February 21, 1857.

. . . . . All He asks of you is to give Him your heart. Satan is also applying; but how different the rewards they offer! Christ offers heaven and eternal happiness: Satan, hell and eternal misery. One or the other you must choose. Oh let it be Jesus: throw yourself upon His mercy, and He will not be unfaithful to His charge. I know it will be a little hard at first; but oh make the sacrifice. Christ says of those who are his children, that they shall "shine forth as the sun in the kingdom of their Father;" and so they shall "ever be with the Lord." "All things are theirs," whether "the world, or life, or death, or things present, or things to come; all are theirs, and they are Christ's, and Christ is God's." Here are promises, among the thousands with which the word of God is teeming: grasp them; they were intended for you. . . . . .

In serving Christ, a fountain of real, pure pleasure, heretofore unknown, will be opened, by forming your heart for the enjoyment of delights far superior to those of sense. In communion with God, in meditation upon the divine promises and love, the Christian has pleasures which he would not exchange for all the pleasures of the world. Even your tears of penitential grief would afford you more real pleasure than the world finds in noisy mirth. . . . . .

February 28, 1857.

. . . . . You say "your heart is not fit to love Jesus—you cannot love Him." So much the more necessity that you should have that heart regenerated as quickly as possible. Do not go to Him proudly and haughtily, or placing any confidence in your own good deeds. If you do, you will never find Him—no, never. You must come humbly, earnestly, devotedly, and prayerfully. Let yourself have no peace until you have made secure the salvation of your immortal soul. Just imagine the worth of a soul! The Bible says, "What profit hath a man if he gain the whole world, and lose his own soul? or what would he give in exchange for his soul?" Here, you see, God values a soul more than all this world. When you are laid upon a bed of death will not all your care be to save your soul? Even angels, those pure and holy beings, take a deep interest in your salvation. "There is joy in heaven over one sinner that repenteth." Consider, that for your neglected soul the great God, in the person of His Son, descended to this earth, endured all manner of pain and suffering, even the agonizing death of the cross; all to save, not your body—that was not worth it, but to save your soul; yes, *your soul.* If Jesus Christ thought your soul so precious, why do *you* slight it? You are studying hard to get knowledge: the time is near at hand when you must leave all: you are fast hastening to the judgment-seat of God—your soul is hurrying to Heaven or Hell. Some time is no time. Remember, the longer you put off attending to the interests of your soul, the harder it becomes. . . . . .

March 19, 1857.

. . . . . I have been head and ears into the chemistry ever since Monday, working till one or two every morning: and I have succeeded very well so far—met with no accidents worth naming; the sum total of damages has been a coat and a pair of pants ruined. I find it a most delightful study, not only in practice, but also in the theoretical or scientific part.

March 24, 1857.

. . . . . The pleasures of this world may, and do please for a while; but would you have real happiness, true peace of mind, nowhere will you find it but in Jesus—in being a Christian. Christ will be a friend to you everywhere. When all is dark around, with the eagle eye of faith you can pierce the clouds, and see Him smiling on you. That will send a thrill of joy through your soul, such as you never can experience while you live in the world. Why, then, why will you any longer reject your Saviour? Why will you not come and throw yourself at His feet? He will receive and purify your now sinful heart. Think of that woman who died at the opera. She went there as well as you. She died! You are spared! It *might have been you.* I *beg* of you to come to Christ.

April 10, 1857.

. . . . . But then, have I not the promises of God that He will care for His children? Am I one of them? Professedly, I am. *Truly*, I trust I am. God often sends trouble on His children for their good, to try their faith; and by His grace I will continue in His faith, steadfast unto the end. I would sooner lay my head upon the block than forsake Jesus. Won't you live for Him too? He *will* love you.

True friends are worth more than all the rest of the world. The world's friends are like the bubbles on a lake—stay near you for a while—the least disturbance, they vanish. . . . . .

April 29, 1857.

After much trouble I have obtained some splendid specimens of gold, silver, and copper. I had to heat them for fourteen hours in a white hot furnace, nearly roasting the people in the house.

May 1, 1857.

. . . . . I was looking over "Alone" for a little while. There is something melancholy to me in that word *alone.* But M., you need never be alone. Christ offers to be to you a friend. I pray earnestly to God that you may never be alone—that when all is dark and dreary in the outward world, you may look above and within, and find a Friend. I have very few friends—*real* friends; but I trust I have Jesus as mine. He has promised to do for us even more than we ask: I have asked Him to make you His *own;* and I am sure He will do it.

May 15, 1857. 2.30 A.M.

. . . . . I cannot go to sleep. My mind has been working itself up for the last two or three days, until now it has reached the very pitch—I must say it—of torture. My brain fairly burns. The thought that I have lived so long and done almost nothing, and that God will call me to account, makes me shudder. I know He loves me. I know I am one of His children. Would that I were what I ought to be! Would that *you* were a lamb of God! I feel as though the Devil himself were trying to take possession of my heart; but with the help of God I will resist him.

June 1, 1857.

Here I am in my sanctum all alone. With my window open, looking across that lovely garden, my thoughts have been wandering far away from earth toward that blessed home prepared, I trust, for *you* and *me* in heaven. As I look upon those stars that twinkle in the ebon vault of heaven; as I watch that pale moon as she wanders through the misty clouds; as I feel that cooling breeze wafting sweet odours from nature's own inexhaustible storehouse, that line of Bishop Heber's,

"And only man is vile,"

comes to me with redoubled force. Man, for whom all these beauteous things were made—and can it be that he has fallen? Alas! too true.

SPRING BROOK, *August* 30, 1857.

I have just returned from a walk alone in the woods, and rarely, if ever, have I felt such a desire to leave this world, and go to that which is far better. Everything around showed me the hand of a loving God. Every thing at work. Nature's vast laboratory never at rest. The unwearied sun starting from his chamber in the east, and rejoicing to run his race; the busy swarm of insect life; the birds exuberant in flight and song, pouring forth their hymn of praise to the great Creator—all at work, and all happy. They all seemed to say to me, "What are you doing? What are you living for?" It opened an unexplored avenue of thought in my mind, and touched a new chord in my heart. What am I living for? If all these inferior beings have an end in view; if they all labour, how much greater must be the end, and how much greater the labour, destined for me! God did not place me in the world for nothing. We have each one a great work to perform. Our reward is eternal life. We must work. The glorious Creator, who never slumbers or sleeps, gives us an example of the dignity of labour. Labour is noble and holy. We must labour to win souls to Jesus. I feel within me that part of my labour is to show *you* the way of salvation. . . . . .

1313 SPRUCE STREET, *December* 7, 1857.

. . . . . Although yesterday was so unfavourable, still I opened my little school with eighteen; which number was increased to twenty-five in the afternoon. I am well satisfied; indeed I feel assured that God will prosper it, if I work well my part. To Him, and to Him alone, must I look for success in this important enterprise. As our afternoon sessions were closing I was waited upon by several men and women, who came to ask us if we would not have a prayer-meeting in the evening. We agreed to do so. And although the rain came down in torrents, what was my surprise, on going there, to find nearly fifty men and women, old and young, waiting for us! Our room was too small to hold them, as many were obliged to go away. We had a delightful meeting. I spoke to them for about half an hour, and I never before felt what I said as I did then. May God bless us. This is the kind of missionary operations that I like; beginning at home, in our own city, endeavouring to exalt a race as good by nature as we are, but who have been trodden down and oppressed by their fellow-creatures. . . . .

1313 SPRUCE STREET, *December* 22, 1857.

. . . . . I feel quite anxious to know how you succeeded in Sabbath-school teaching yesterday. Remember, a solemn and important duty rests upon you. To you are committed those immortal souls, to train them up for eternity! I hope you have entered the work trusting, not in your own strength, but in that of promised grace. You might, in view of all this, be inclined, as I was, to say, "I am not fit to engage in so important a work." Yes, you are. God has said, "My grace shall be sufficient for thee." Place all your confidence in Him. If you ever expect to succeed, you must make your class the subject of constant, earnest prayer; and if you do this, God will reward you bountifully. Go on, then, in this great work, and may God grant you His grace "never to weary in well-doing."

I had fifty-five children yesterday; and in the evening, as usual, my room was crowded. Two gentlemen, who had promised me to address the meeting, disappointed me, so that I had to do all the talking; and never do I feel the Spirit of God with as much power as I do then. I feel as though the salvation of a soul depended upon my feeble efforts; and gladly would I thus devote my life-time of Sabbaths, if I could be the means of turning one sinner from the error of his ways—of leading one soul to seek for an interest in Jesus. . . . . .

1313 SPRUCE STREET, *December* 31, 1857.

. . . . . Before you and I meet again, another year will have been numbered with eternity. And what account will it bear of us to the throne of God? How many of its Sabbaths have we mis-spent! How many of its privileges have we neglected! If we could live over 1857, how much better would we do it! But we cannot. Time, ever rolling onward, is like a mighty scroll ever unfolding and refolding. But if we cannot begin again the present year, we can do better in 1858; and let such be our determination—that by the help of God we will in the coming year live a life of more zeal and more earnestness in the cause of our Divine Saviour. We have done nothing to what we ought to have done; and were God to summon us to our final account, what answer could we make for all that we have enjoyed? . . . . .

February 1, 1858.

. . . . . I feel very strangely to-night—all out of sorts, and angry with myself. My brain burns, and my nervous system is all unstrung. Why? I cannot tell.

As I look abroad over the sea of life, and see those who started in life with prospects as bright as any I have before me, tossed about, their hopes and fortunes lost, and themselves a still more melancholy wreck—I often say to myself, Where at length shall this poor mortal frame rest in peace? What difficulties are in store for me? How shall this aching heart be torn and shattered, or what anguish and bitterness shall this mind undergo? When I think of all this, my soul shrinks within me, and says, "Let me go now, and flee from all this." And then I hear the Spirit of my God saying, "Fear not, for I am with thee;"—then would my soul leap forth, and press eagerly to the conflict.

1313 SPRUCE STREET, *March* 16, 1858.
Sabbath evening.

Although I do not think it exactly proper to write letters on this evening, yet I cannot refrain from writing you before retiring. What I write you now has been pressing on my mind for several days past.

Whilst I have attended the daily prayer-meetings with great pleasure, and have heard with delight that many have been turned from the error of their ways to the knowledge and service of God; and whilst I joy in believing that God has made me one of His own, still there is one thing that weighs upon my soul and makes me sad—it is the thought, alas, I fear too true, that you are not of the fold of Christ—that you are a stranger to that peace and joy which surpass all understanding—that while God is pouring out His Holy Spirit in refreshing showers upon the souls of many, you remain untouched, still indifferent in regard to your soul. Whilst I hear that this one and that one has been rescued from sin, shall I not hear the welcome news that *you* are among the redeemed, and have chosen that better part which cannot be taken from you? Then would I feel happy in the thought that you are a participator of the same precious promises with myself, and that my many and earnest prayers have been answered.

As I was listening this morning to a sermon from the text, "Am I my brother's keeper?" and as the speaker went on to show how every man is our brother, I thought to myself, Have I done my duty towards M.? Have I done all I ought and am able to do to lead her to Christ? My conscience reproved me, and told me I had fallen short in my duty. . . . . .

Why are you out of the fold of Christ? and why are you a stranger to His people? Has heaven and its eternal happiness no attractions for you? Has Christianity no beauty which you can admire and love? Has Jesus, who died for you, taken such little hold upon your heart that you are unwilling to devote yourself to His service? Has temporal and eternal misery no hatred from you? Have the communion of the saints on earth, and the still more blessed happiness of the redeemed in glory, no attraction for you? Why then do you remain any longer on the side of Satan? Why will you refuse the offer of salvation? The time is fast approaching when you will regret your folly—when you will be in anguish to think of the many offers you have slighted. Come, and no longer delay, while the door of mercy is open and the lamp of hope is burning brightly. Come, as you value your temporal and eternal happiness. I entreat you take Him to be your God, and all will be well for time and eternity.

1313 SPRUCE STREET, *March* 22, 1858.

I have just returned from my Sabbath-school evening prayer-meeting, which was large and intensely interesting. I never before spoke with such interest as I did this evening. Sometimes I could hardly restrain the tears from gushing down my cheeks. My subject was the three banners—"Jehovah-jireh," "Jehovah-nissi," and "Jehovah-shalom;"—"The Lord will provide," "The Lord is our banner," and "The Lord send peace." Who can tell what great things God may accomplish by our humble instrumentality? Eternity alone will reveal the results.

How rejoiced was I yesterday when you told me you would come out upon the Lord's side, to be for Him, and not for another! I feel that God is answering my prayers. For a year and a half have I earnestly pled with God on your behalf; and I knew He would hear me. I knew it, for He is the hearer of prayer. Often, when I have desired to speak with you in regard to your soul, my tongue has refused to give utterance; but what I could not do in talking I did in praying. God, I believe, has heard me; and from my inmost soul I thank and praise Him for it—that you, who are as dear to me as my own life, have been brought to see the error of your ways, and have turned unto God. Do not, then, any longer delay, but come at once and dedicate yourself to God: come out, and be not ashamed of Jesus, your crucified but now risen Redeemer; and then when we are separated,* if in the providence of God we should never meet on earth again, we may meet around the throne of God on high, never to be severed.

Let me entreat you to read a portion of your Bible every morning and evening: the value which this will be to you cannot be estimated. I have carried it out with great success. And may God by His Holy Spirit give you "joy and peace in believing." May you have that "peace which passeth all understanding:" "And I pray God that your whole spirit, and soul, and body, be preserved blameless unto the coming of our Lord Jesus Christ."

Enclosed I send you a copy, or rather form of Self-dedication. I have read it over carefully and prayerfully, and have this day, in an act of writing, given myself away to God. I would advise you to follow the same plan. It is admirable. Copy it, and affix your name to the document; then when you are tempted to evil you can go to this and say, "I cannot sin, for here is the agreement in which I have given myself away."....

[The form of Dedication (by Philip Doddridge, D.D.) alluded to in the foregoing letter, and adopted by William, was found after his death, among his carefully-preserved papers, beautifully written out, and signed in his bold, dashing handwriting, as though resolution to keep his vow was marked on every letter of his name. For the benefit of any of his young friends who may feel it a duty

* M. and her sister were making their preparations for a two years tour through Europe.

to make a similar act of self-consecration, and who may not find it convenient to procure a copy, it is inserted here.]

DEDICATION.

Eternal and ever-blessed God, I desire to present myself before Thee with the deepest humiliation and abasement of soul, sensible how unworthy such a sinful worm is to appear before the holy Majesty of heaven, the King of kings, and Lord of lords; and especially upon such an occasion as this, even to dedicate myself, without reserve, to Thee. But the scheme and plan is Thine own. Thine infinite condescension hath offered it by Thy Son, and Thy grace hath inclined my heart to accept it.

I come, therefore, acknowledging myself to have been a great offender—smiting upon my breast, and saying with the humble publican, "God be merciful to me, a sinner." I come, invited by the name of Thy Son, and wholly trusting in His perfect righteousness, entreating that, for His sake, Thou wilt be merciful to my unrighteousness, and wilt no more remember my sins.

Receive, I beseech Thee, Thy revolted creature, who is now convinced of Thy right to him, and desires nothing so much as that he may be Thine.

This day do I, with the utmost solemnity, surrender myself to Thee.

I renounce all former lords who have had dominion over me; and I consecrate to Thee all that I am, and all that I have; the faculties of my mind, the members of my body, my worldly possessions, my time, and my influence over others,—to be all used entirely for Thy glory, and steadfastly employed in obedience to Thy commands, as long as Thou continuest me in life; with an ardent desire and humble resolution to continue Thine through the endless ages of eternity, ever holding myself in an attentive posture to observe the first intimations of Thy will, and ready to spring forward with zeal and joy to the immediate execution of it.

To Thy direction also I resign myself, and all I am and have, to be disposed of by Thee in such a manner as Thou shalt in Thine infinite wisdom judge most subservient to the purposes of Thy glory.

To Thee I leave the management of all events, and say, without reserve, "Not my will, but Thine be done;" rejoicing with a loyal heart in Thine unlimited government, as what ought to be the delight of the whole rational creation.

Use me, O Lord, I beseech Thee, as an instrument of Thy service. Number me among Thy peculiar people. Let me be washed in the blood of Thy dear Son. Let me be clothed with His righteousness. Let me be sanctified by His Spirit. Transform me more and more into His image. Impart to me, through Him, all needful influences of Thy purifying, cheering, and consoling Spirit. And let my life be spent under those influences, and in the light of Thy gracious countenance, as my Father and my God.

And when the solemn hour of death comes, may I remember Thy Covenant, "well ordered in all things, and sure, as all my salvation and all my desire" (2 Sam. xxiii. 5), though every hope and enjoyment is perishing; and do Thou, O Lord, remember it too.

Look down with pity, O my heavenly Father, on thy languishing, dying child. Embrace me in Thine everlasting arms. Put strength and confidence into my departing spirit, and receive it to the abode of them that sleep in Jesus, peacefully and joyfully to wait the accomplishment of Thy great promise to all Thy people, even that of a glorious resurrection, and of eternal happiness in Thy heavenly presence.

And if any surviving friend should, when I am in dust, meet with this memorial of my solemn transactions with Thee, may he make the engagement his own; and do Thou graciously admit him to partake in all the blessedness of Thy covenant, through Jesus, the great Mediator of it, to whom, with Thee, O Father, and Thy Holy Spirit, be everlasting praises. *Amen.*

(Signed) WM. D. STUART.

March 22, 1858.

March 24, 1858.

. . . . . You have made me feel very happy in the sentiments you have expressed—that you desire to become a child of God, and to be enlisted among his people. Be assured that if you seek, you *shall* find; God has promised us that we shall not seek His face in vain. No! He bids us come. He invites us to partake of His mercy, and offers us freely His salvation. He commands us to serve Him; and He holds out to us a great reward, which is nothing less than heaven with all its eternal blessings. Fear not, then, that God will leave you in your sins. All you are required to do is to have faith—to come unto Him with child-like confidence and simplicity, casting all your care upon Him; and He will say to you, as to her of old, "Daughter, thy sins are forgiven thee." But you must pray. Prayer is the great channel through which our wants are made known to God. Earnestly make known all your requests unto God, and expect an answer. Let your prayers proceed from your inmost soul, and they will reach unto the ears of the Lord of sabaoth.

Oh, how thrice precious is the hallowed name of Jesus! The thought that He descended from His heavenly home, and suffered and died for me!

> "Love so amazing, so divine,
> Demands my soul, my life, my all."

That I should have been the object of His love—that for me He was reviled and mocked—all for *me!* On whom could I, then, cast myself with more reliance than on Him? In Him I place all my trust.

> "I know that safe with Him remains,
> Protected by His power,
> What I've committed to His trust,
> Till the decisive hour."

And He did all this for *you.* Press on, then, in your Christian course, and my most earnest prayers go with you. Though you may be many miles away—though oceans may roll between us—yet the separation will but fasten the ties of love with which we are bound more firmly, and bind you closer to my heart. And if, in God's providence, either of us should be called to heaven, we will meet beyond the swellings of Jordan, upon that happy shore

> "Where death-divided friends at last,
> Shall meet to part no more."

There is a verse of Scripture which to me is one of peculiar consolation. It is this—"Fear thou not; for I am with thee: be not dismayed; for I am thy God: I will strengthen thee; yea, I will help thee; yea, I will uphold thee with the right hand of my righteousness" (Isa. xli. 10). Could anything be more consoling than this? From whom, but from God, could or would such a soothing command come? Make up your mind, carefully and with much prayer, that when another communion season shall have arrived, you will profess publicly the name of Jesus: but first profess him in your own heart, and ask for grace and strength to adorn your profession; and then all will be well with you for this life and eternity. Though the clouds of trouble and affliction may gather around you ever so heavily, and threaten to crush you, you will hear the voice of Jesus in the midst of the storm calling to you in accents full of tenderness and compassion, "Fear not; it is I." Then will your soul rise triumphantly over all earthly calamities, and enjoy a sweet foretaste of the Sabbath of rest prepared for believers in glory.

I am very glad you have adopted the plan of the

Dedication. I am sure it will be of service to you. My heart is so full that I cannot empty it in writing—full of love to God, of zeal in his service, and of a determination to live a better life.

"Oh for a closer walk with God."

April 19, 1858.

. . . . . Be steadfast. Never allow the flame of divine love to burn low on the altar of your heart. Never grow indifferent in God's service, but rather let every day of your life witness increased devotion and earnestness in His cause. Continually subject yourself to self-examination. Let the Bible be your constant study; and often be found bending the knee at the throne of grace. Oh, if a day in God's house, an hour at his table, is so lovely, what will eternity be? What will it be when we enter into that joy, and bathe in those rivers of eternal pleasure? Let our souls, then, pant for those fountains whence issue these refreshing streams—that ocean of eternal love into which they all flow. . . . .

May 11, 1858.

. . . . . I trust that by this time you have succeeded, at least in a measure, in ridding your mind of those doubts and difficulties with which you have had to contend. They are the hand of God trying your faith, convincing you of your weakness, and of His all-sufficiency. Ever be looking to Jesus: keep your eye firmly fixed on Him, as does the mariner upon the magnetic needle which guides him over the troubled ocean. You want faith—confidence in God; pray that you may have it in rich abundance; and be assured that He will give it to you.

You cannot imagine the happiness which your decision has given me. It has increased my faith to think that God has answered my prayers on your behalf. I do not now feel that going abroad will be hurtful to you. God will go with and guide you, and will direct your footsteps.

May 25, 1858.

.... You are about to take a very solemn step, and one which, I am sure, you have well considered. Have no confidence in yourself; trust not your own strength, but rather look unto Jesus, the author and finisher of your faith. I know that you have many doubts and trials; but you have a Friend able and ready to save. "Cast all your care upon Him;" trust Him with all: He will make the way clear; He will comfort you by His Spirit's presence, and give you all necessary grace. Confide in Him for time and for eternity. Hold often silent communion with your God, and remember me when at a throne of grace, for no one needs your prayers more than I.

SPRING BROOK, *July* 25, 1858.

Again the holy Sabbath, in all its loveliness, has returned; the busy world is at rest, and men are engaged in seeking for that treasure which is laid up in heaven: many are searching for those waters of eternal life, of which if a man drink he shall never thirst; and for that bread which cometh down from heaven.

Though we are separated * by many miles, our prayers this day have reached the ear of our common Father; and I trust a blessing has been poured down upon each of us. What our blessed Saviour promised to his disciples ere He departed from them, He has also promised to us, if we ask in faith. Oh, how distrustful, how doubting we are! Although we have the direct promise of God that asking we shall receive, yet we doubt it; or, what is worse, we do not think it worth asking.

I have not as yet felt that God has called me to be a minister of the Gospel, although I have prayed, "Lord, what wilt Thou have me to do?" and yet I feel that God has a great and important work for me to do. I cannot describe it; I cannot rid myself of the thought; it is firmly fixed in my mind. Pray for me that God would show me my course, and that in whatever capacity I may be placed, I may devote all my energies to the promotion of Christ's kingdom.

One of the great marks of the Christian is, that he works—ever about his Father's business. Christ did not say to his disciples, "Be idle," but "Go ye into all the world," &c.; and we, as well as they, must work. Christ has enemies to be conquered; we must be the soldiers; we must endure the hardships; and we shall, if we remain faithful, receive the Master's welcome, and wear the victor's crown. And to get all this, we must come back to that great stronghold, Prayer—the keystone of the Christian's success; the magic key unlocking the golden

* M. was visiting a beloved sister in a distant place, (but now in heaven,) prior to her embarkation for Europe.

casket of divine mercy; the Christian's artillery, penetrating the ear of the God of sabaoth. We do not pray as we ought. Have we an idea of prevailing prayer, before which mountains depart; of united prayer, which gathers us together to ask help from God; of practical prayer, which fulfils itself. Oh, let such prayer be understood; let our whole souls be yearning after a blessing; let our spirits but "break with longing," and our expectations will nothing be delayed. "And it shall come to pass that before they call, I will answer; and while they are yet speaking, I will hear."

SPRING BROOK, *August* 1, 1858.

. . . . . In the psalm which I read in course last evening (the 85th) the following words were the subject of my meditation as I lay in bed, "Surely His salvation is nigh them that fear Him." They impressed themselves deeply upon me. How do we know, when we think that God is not hearing our prayers, but that His salvation is very nigh unto us? Truly it is, though we may not be aware of it. God's ways are not our ways: His strength is shown forth in our great weakness: He casts down, but He raises up again: He wounds, but He heals: and it is by feeling our own weakness that we learn to bear with and console others; by it we obtain a readiness and skill which we could attain in no other way.

There is nothing that reconciles the child of God to death so much as the weariness of his warfare. Death is unwelcome to nature, but only then can our conflict cease. Then the flesh and all its attendant evils will be laid in the grave. Then the soul, having partaken of the new and heavenly birth, and being freed from every encumbrance, shall stand perfect in the Redeemer's righteousness before God in glory.

It becomes us, as children of God, to lift our eyes to heaven, and say, "Lord, what wilt thou have *me* to do?" We are under orders from heaven; let us see to it that these are executed in such a manner as shall give the Master cause to say, "Well done, thou good and faithful servant," &c. Our God is a great God, therefore he will be sought: He is a good God, therefore he will be found: He will bestow upon us far beyond our asking—even life for evermore. His delays are not denials.

Earthly beauty attracts only while it lasts; but virtue, wisdom, goodness, and real worth, like the loadstone, never lose their power. These are the true graces which are linked hand in hand, because it is by their influence that human hearts are so firmly united. Let it be your aim to become one of those of whom Solomon tells us, "their price is far above rubies." . . . . . Remember, the growth of the believer is not like a mushroom, but like an oak: many summers' suns and showers, many wintry blasts and chilling storms, sweep o'er it, ere it comes to perfection; but when it has attained its strength, it is the beauty and king of the forest. So is it with the Christian: many trials and afflictions must pass over him before he can be brought into perfect submission, and be a faithful servant of Christ.

Keep ever near to a throne of grace: let your prayers be brief, often, and fervent: hold frequent communion with your God and my God: be a praying Christian, remembering that those are the safest who are most in their closets, praying not to be seen of men, but heard of God. . . . .

SPRING BROOK, *August* 17, 1858.

All the family have gone to church and left me alone with my little brothers. I have spent an hour talking with them about Jesus and singing hymns; and now that they have gone to bed, I am here in my room to talk with you. I have suffered intense pain all day from neuralgia, which made me rather afraid to go out this evening. . . . .

Monday evening.—Was not that a delightful prayer-meeting to-day? Truly God was in that place, and as I went from it I said in my soul, "It was good for me to be here." An hour spent in such a place seems to make all the rest of the day go well. As the regulator to the watch, so does it seem to be to our daily actions. Within the past few days I have felt, as it were, a great burden lifted from my soul. I am beginning, I trust, to feel my own weakness and insufficiency; and as I feel it more and more, I begin to experience the all-sufficiency of Jesus. Oh, how true, pure religion humbles a man in the very dust before God: how it makes him feel his own nothingness and God's greatness! . . . .

September 3, 1858.

Grandmother (or Nanna, as I always call her) is becoming quite well again, and beginning to look like herself. For a long time I feared she was fast sinking into the grave, and my very heart bled at the thought of being separated from her who has watched over me from my first breath with a mother's care; who early dedicated me to God; who taught my infant lips first to lisp a Saviour's name; who led me often to a throne of grace, praying by day and by night that I might be saved; and who, I trust, has seen her "darling boy" born again. Yes, the very thought of being separated from her was agony to me. But thanks be to God it has been warded off, and we have the prospect that she will be spared to us yet many years.

During the coming winter I am going to take a course of Mineralogy with Prof. G——, and hope to make myself sufficiently acquainted with the science in one year to pursue the study alone with pleasure and profit.

To-morrow I spend in town, to re-organize my Sabbath school for the winter campaign. I look forward to a glorious work, and pray that many souls may be born there. Our school was founded, built up, and will, I trust, be carried on, in prayer; and you know God's promise to them that call upon His name.

September 13, 1858.

..... Just before I began this letter I thought that at least you had reached the end of your ocean voyage,* and had, for the first time, set your foot on foreign soil. If your feelings were at all similar to mine, they were strange indeed: strange sights, strange people, everything strange—even their sky is unlike our own. It is only when we are in such a situation that we feel "there's no

* M. sailed for Europe on the 1st September, 1858.

place like home." And to us, who love God, and serve Him with a pure and loving heart, there is no place like our heavenly home: there, if we really love Jesus, all our hopes and affections will be fixed. . . . .

College began on last Wednesday. I have settled in for a winter of very hard work. . . . . In addition to my other studies I hope to gain a very considerable knowledge of chemistry and mineralogy, practically, which some day may be of service to me, and always will be a pleasure.

On yesterday (Sabbath) week I opened my mission school for the winter campaign. The attendance was good; and there seemed to be manifested, both by teachers and pupils, a desire to do his and her share to promote the kingdom of Christ. . . . .

September 22, 1858.

On waking this morning, the first thought that entered my mind was, "This is M.'s birth-day." And so you are seventeen—almost a woman. This day should be to you one of great moment. You should earnestly thank your heavenly Father that you have been so long spared in health and strength, and that so many blessings have been bestowed upon you. And how should you bless and praise Him in that He has, since your last birth-day, brought you from death unto life, and from the knowledge of sin and Satan unto that blessed and glorious hope that maketh wise unto salvation! Truly, God hath done great things for us, which should cause us from our inmost soul to exclaim, "Bless the Lord, O my soul; and all that is within me bless His holy name." "His banner over us hath been love." Examine carefully your past life, and see wherein you have come short of the divine law. Seek more of the divine grace to assist you to walk an humble, devoted Christian, aiming not to be seen of men, and approved of by them, but to please God. Determine that from this time henceforth you will live more, not in the world, but above it, remembering that this is not your resting-place, but that you look for a city whose builder and maker is the Lord. Take no earthly standard of Christian piety, but rather, "looking unto Jesus," strive to walk as He walked. How often do we feel discouraged and cast down because we think we are not living as we ought! we feel that we do not love Jesus as we should, and begin to think that God has cast us off. Such have often been my feelings, and many an hour of anguish have they cost me; but I am consoled and comforted by that beautiful sentence, "My grace is sufficient for thee." What a balm for a wounded spirit is there! what consolation to hear our dear Redeemer offering such a support for our sin-weakened souls! He indeed is the "chief among ten thousand, and altogether lovely." Precious Jesus! what would I be were it not for Thee? These hidings of our Father's face are but to try our faith: we must bear with them, remembering that this "our light affliction, which is but for a moment, worketh for us a far more exceeding, even an eternal weight of glory."

And again let me say, as often I have said before, be not forgetful of prayer. I know that a person when travelling is very prone to be careless or hurried in their religious duties. In whatever else you may be hurried, never, I beg of you, let it be in your prayers. Go often, go earnestly to a throne of grace. Prayer is ever profitable: it is our covering by night and our armour by day: it sanctifies all our actions, and enrolls us under the standard of the Almighty. Fill up the void spaces of your time with prayer and meditation, remembering they are the safest who are most in their closets. An old divine tells us, "They that spend their days in faith and prayer shall end their days in peace and comfort." Be, then, ever earnest in prayer. . . . .

Sept. 24.—I am swaying to and fro between two pursuits—that of a chemist and a merchant. A great deal is to be said on both sides. For the former I have a very great liking, and I think I would excel in it in course of time: on the other hand, the mercantile life offers in one way very great inducements to me—a house long established and doing a very large business—my father's name and custom—everything prepared for me; all these things are not trifling, and ought not to be overlooked. . . . . I have prayed to God for direction, for in nothing does a young man more require Divine assistance than in choosing his occupation for life. God has promised that all things shall work together for His children's good; and shall we not trust Him, who is both able and willing to do all things for us?

Sept. 27.— . . . . I have to communicate to you the joyful news that my dear friend Phil. has at last renounced the world, and on next Sabbath will publicly profess his faith in Christ, in sitting down at that blessed table which our Lord has spread, at which His children commemorate His death. My heart is filled with joy, and nothing save your own and your dear sister's profession has caused me more real happiness. You know that I have ever looked upon him as a very dear friend, and my only regret heretofore has been that he was not a Christian. Now my joy is full. I never had the courage, I am sorry to say, to speak much with him in regard to his soul; but, as you know, I have ever made him the subject of earnest, heartfelt, importunate prayer; and now God has answered me. He answered my prayers for you, and now He has answered them for him. What an encouragement should this be to me to go on and pray yet more and more sincerely, and to ask more than I ever have before; for truly God has told me in this that no request is too great for Him to grant. Let us both pray for Phil. that God will give him grace and strength to press on in the Christian course, and that he may ever be an humble, devoted, earnest Christian. May our names not only be written in the records of God's Church on earth, but in the Lamb's book of life. . . . .

PHILADELPHIA, *January* 31, 1859.

. . . . . The work of God is going on gloriously. Everywhere are to be seen the Master's stately steppings in His sanctuary. The great news is—

"The work's reviving all around,

and everywhere sinners are calling upon the name of the Lord.

Last Thursday afternoon I presided at the Diligent prayer-meeting, and the room was crowded. There was but one spirit upon us, and that was the spirit of earnest, heartfelt prayer. Many of the profane and ungodly members were present, and seemed much impressed. I presented an anonymous request for ——, and I feel sure that the prayers, the pleadings with God on his behalf, will be answered.

On Saturday I presided at the noon prayer-meeting. The room was crowded; and during our meeting we breathed not the atmosphere of earth, but of heaven. How careful should we be to improve these precious opportunities, for each additional one makes our accountability the greater! The chairman of the Diligent meeting desired me pressingly to lead and address their meeting on to-morrow (Sabbath) evening. I hesitated; and yet I felt within me a power urging me to do it, as my privilege and duty. I felt unequal to the task, but I knelt before my God and prayed that He would put words, and thoughts, and desires into me, that I might speak, not *at*, but *to* the souls of my hearers. I addressed them from the words, "God is love;" and for upwards of half an hour did I attempt to tell them of this love. We are too much accustomed to look upon God as a Being of stern, unbending justice: true, if we view Him through any other glass than Jesus Christ, He is such; but we are only to look upon Him through Jesus. The Bible says not God is justice, God is mercy—but, "God is love." Love is the law of heaven, the essence of Divinity. Deprive God of this, and we deprive Him of Himself. Love binds spirits to angels, angels to archangels, archangels to cherubim, cherubim to seraphim—all to God. Surely, He who implanted love so deeply in our hearts should Himself be full of it. There is no theme so grand, so glorious as this! When the angels saw the exemplification of it in the sending of His Son, they strung their harps to a higher, more harmonious melody, and burst forth in that song which broke upon the shepherds' ears—"Glory to God in the highest, peace on earth, and good-will toward men." Let us dwell upon this love—eternity cannot exhaust it: let it be our evening and morning thought. The wonder is, not that we love God, but that He first loved us. Were the mother to tear from her breast her darling babe, it would not be half so wonderful. Some lakes never freeze, because of their great depth; and so, deep, fathomless, is the love of God to us, if we are His children. The springs of God's love are never dried by summer's sun, nor bound by winter's chilling blast. The fires of God's love are never quenched, because they are unquenchable. God's love is eternal; whom he loveth, he loveth to the end: it is like the bush that was burning, but never consumed.

My mission school goes on as usual, increasing daily. We are greatly encouraged, and have reason to say that our labours have not been in vain in the Lord. . . . .

February 13, 1859.

I have just returned from a very solemn sight; from a scene through which we must all, sooner or later, pass—I mean a bed of death. At the close of school this afternoon I was requested to visit the step-father of one of my scholars, who was dying. Though quite unwell, I felt it my duty to go. One of my co-workers accompanied me. We found him in a little frame building in Bedford Street, in a room about twelve feet square. His disease was pleurisy; and I saw clearly that his end was fast approaching. His mind was well-nigh gone; but when my friend asked him what were his prospects for another world, his reason returned, and the truth flashed across his mind, "I am not saved." How strange that on that all-important subject, and on that only, he should be sensible! "What shall I do for you?" I said. The quick reply was, "Oh, pray for me—that's what I want!" Never before have I so felt the almighty power of prayer as when seeing that strong man, struggling with sickness and death, feeling that his only support and hope lay in prayer. We did pray, long and earnestly, that the blessing might come down upon him even while we spoke. I left that house revolving in my mind the power and absolute necessity of secret prayer, not only at stated times, but very often.

I have often thought that Christians are, in regard to prayer, as a man who has committed to his care some mighty machine possessed of wondrous power: he does not know its strength, because he is afraid to test it. . . . .

The tide of salvation which has been sweeping over our land for the past year is daily rising. On Saturday last I attended the noon meeting, and the room was so full that we were obliged to organize a second meeting down stairs.

The afternoon meetings at the Diligent are crowded daily. One young man, (among many who are anxious about their souls,) was brought to inquire the way of salvation by the question propounded by his little daughter to her mother, namely, "Mother, does father pray?" It stung him to the heart; and though for many months he has been struggling against the Spirit, yet it got the mastery, and he is now living, we trust, a life of holiness. . . . . .

As I gradually approach the time when I must go forth into the world, I become more and more concerned as to what shall be my course. I have almost determined to follow my father's business; yet I feel as it were an invisible arm holding me back. Shall I plunge into the busy maze of mercantile life, and bid farewell to History and Science, in which I take such delight? Shall I turn back from the very threshold of Nature's vast laboratory, when the glimpses I have gotten of her wondrous laws and almighty working have only quickened my desire to penetrate more deeply, and know more of her now hidden mysteries? Shall I throw aside the scroll of History, which I have just begun to unfold, and hide from myself those scenes stamped indelibly on her page, in which I have taken such delight? Shall I no longer hold converse with her mighty dead, and learn lessons of wisdom from their sad experience? . . . . .

Wherever duty lies, there will I go. May God guide me in that path. . . . . .

March 15, 1859.

. . . . . I have had much pleasure, profit, and pain of late, in reading Lamb's "Essays of Elia." They are running over with wit, covered with the brightest sunshine; and yet, here and there through a rift in the clouds, you get an insight into the true heart and feelings of the writer; and you can see that although there is a show of gaiety and joyousness without, within there is a heart racked and torn by remorse, and struggling in vain against the cup whose dregs are eternal death.

SPRING BROOK, *May* 29, 1859.

. . . . . An every-day remark struck me this morning in quite a new light. I said to a friend, "I will go and get ready for church;"— meaning, of course, that I would dress myself. As I went out of the room the remark seemed to cling to me, "Get ready for church." Ah! I thought, how carefully do we prepare the body—the external man—for the house of God, but how little the soul—that for whose benefit the church was intended! How much time, precious, irredeemable time, do we waste upon the mouldering casket, while the immortal, undying jewel is left untouched! So is it ever with man's perverse nature: he cares much for that which can never serve him, and naught for that which alone can render him happy for ever. Death, judgment, and eternity, stare him in the face; and yet, like the foolish boy, he plays on, heedless of them all. When will we be wise? Never, until the grace of God snatches us as brands from the burning, and instils into us his Holy Spirit.

I am so much impressed with the importance of the position in which I am now placed, as regards the choosing my course for life, that I propose making my next birth-day, August 10, a day of special prayer to God for His guidance, that whatever course I may choose may be the best for His glory and for my own good. . . . . .

On next Wednesday morning I start on my long western trip, to be gone perhaps three or four months. I will start alone, but will be joined out there by uncle D. . . . . .

I had a long talk with —— the other day. He is a very clever business man, but, I fear, cares little for those heavenly treasures which make a man rich indeed. His motto seems to be, "A short life and a merry one." How fearful the thought! a short, godless life, and what then?—judgment and eternal damnation. Oh that men were wise! that they would bestow some thought on the never-dying soul! Down, down, down they go, heedlessly, carelessly, rushing to eternal ruin. . . . . .

MILWAUKIE, (WIS.,) *July* 11, 1859.

. . . . . Need I say our first visit was to Minnehaha, novel-renowned, far-famed, Hiawathaized Minnehaha—the Laughing Water. I asked to be alone. Winding down a narrow path along the edge of the rock, the Fall in all its beauty, in all that watery drapery with which dame Nature with lavish hand has decked it, burst upon my enchanted vision. I stood transfixed. And is this Minnehaha, of which I have heard so much? I am repaid, thrice repaid, for all my journey, with such an enchanting sight. I wonder not that here the Indian loved to sit; that here he plighted his faith; that here the old warrior sat when the bloody day was o'er, and soothed the heaving, angry soul within, till all was calm, peaceful and happy as the Laughing Water, which leaping from the rocks against which it fell, kissed his burning cheek and hurried on its way; that here the youthful warrior stood, and swore to his blushing bride that she should be gay, and happy, even as yon Laughing Water. I wonder not that the poor harmless Indian, when called to give up his hunting grounds as a home for the white man, prays that he may be allowed undisturbed to visit this lovely spot, and, though no longer his own, gaze upon those waters, hastening away—fit emblem of himself. After spending a long time in looking on this gem of Nature's choicest workmanship, the darkening shadows warned me to return. Farewell, Minnehaha—farewell Laughing Water, with your bending birch and towering tamarack, your mossy banks and rocky bed—all, farewell! generations, when I am dust, will gaze with delight, as I have done, upon your restless beauty; yet, on you roll, until that appointed time when this earth and all therein shall have been melted with a fervent heat; then your waters will cease to flow, while I but begin to live. . . . . .

On the afternoon of the 5th I went in search of fossils, and being the first who had attempted to creep along the bank of the river since the Flood, I was sanguine of success. After clambering along the bank for some miles, losing my foot-hold and falling some distance down the rocks—which latter did not at all tend to increase my agility—I arrived at the spot, and in an instant my eye was greeted with an orthocera, three feet long, the finest specimen I have seen. This animal is a shell-fish, belonging to the same genus but not the same class as the nautilus, being straight instead of curved, and having, like the nautilus, many compartments, which are joined together by a delicate ligament, answering the same purpose as the spine in the human being: it gets its name from two Greek words (meaning "like a horn"): it is a Pre-Adamite, and fine specimens of such a size are very rare. I worked a long time exhuming it from the rock, and at last was fortunate enough to get it out without damage, and shouldering it I started for the hotel. Its weight is 90 pounds, breadth 6 inches across the back, and about 5 inches high. I intend presenting it either to the University or the Academy of Natural Sciences.

The next day we started off to fish on a lake about fifteen miles from Minneapolis: the thermometer stood about 99°, and we in an open boat out on the lake! Whew! it was hot—my feet blistered through my boots; true, I caught 70 pounds of fish, but that was poor pay for the exposure. On getting home, I concluded that fishing on hot days don't pay. . . . . .

MICHILIMACKINAC, STRAITS OF MACKINAW,
July 24, 1859.

. . . . . The other day as I was sitting in a boat and watching each succeeding wave as it brought us nearer shore, I thought, What an emblem of ourselves, tossed in this stormy sea of Time; yet every wave of sorrow, of affliction, or of joy, as it rolls by, lessens the distance between us and the haven which we seek, even the haven of eternal rest. The land is not far ahead; should we not, as does the sailor, have everything ready to land the moment the keel of our vessel grates on the shining sands? Let us be ready, for we know not when the Son of man cometh.

I have often thought that one of the perfections of the Christian religion is to bring it to bear on the matters and occurrences of every-day life, to unite business with religion, and to keep the soul free from distraction and debasement whilst transacting the affairs of daily life. It is very easy for us to entertain holy and solemn thoughts in the church, in the prayer-meeting, and in the closet; but to carry these same feelings into the counting-house, the manufactory, or the harvest field, requires great watchfulness on the part of him who would adhere to his Christian profession. The atmosphere of the street and of the world is not that of the communion table: the one is debasing, the other exalting; the one drags the soul deep into sin, the other bears it aloft to heaven; the one shuts out the idea of eternity and future happiness, the other opens it out in all its sublimity and excellence. To pass from one to the other is like going from the equator to the poles; and just as well might you imagine the rare exotic, blooming and growing beneath a tropical sun, to survive beneath a chilling polar night, as to expect the soul, warmed and nourished at a communion table, to grow and flourish when exposed to the chilling influence of the cold world without. So difficult is the task, so seemingly impossible to some, that but few undertake it, and fewer succeed in its accomplishment.

Too many are prone to say, Let sermons, and church, and all that pertains to religion, be for Sabbath; and let all the week be for business and pleasure. Religion is made a suit of fine clothes, to be carefully put on on the Sabbath, and as carefully laid aside when the day is done.

If it were true that business and religion could not accord, what sane man would hesitate, monk-like, to shut himself from the world, and devote his time to the preparation of his soul for eternity? Life here is but for a moment; life hereafter is for ever. But God assures us that we can do both;—I mean not that we can serve God and Mammon, but that we can be *in* the world, and yet not *of* the world; and He enjoins us to be "Not slothful in business; fervent in spirit; serving the Lord." The great, the momentous question with us is, How can we attain this summit of Christian character here on earth? The answer is, By prayer;—in a moment, quicker than the electric spark, the thrill of aspiration flashes from man to God. When you are in sorrow, when you are in affliction, when you are tempted, flee to your closet, hold close communion with your God; and when you come forth your spirit will be calm and unclouded as the noonday sun. With this potent aid, with the Holy Spirit to direct the soul, you can with ease and joy bring religion into every walk of life, and instead of being a burden, make it a joy and rejoicing.

Let it be our great aim to carry our religious principle with us into the world; bring it to bear on worldly affairs and every-day actions, and the life of the Christian becomes nobler than that of the philosopher or physicist—everything done by principle, and that the noblest of all principles. Religion does more than lament and mourn over the instability of earthly things: it diligently seeks for and finds in them the seeds of immortality. Let religion be intimately associated with your worldly affairs, and you will take from this world all that is worth keeping. Every kind word, and every self-sacrificing act done for Jesus' sake, will impress itself indelibly on the soul, and will pass on with it to comfort and rejoice it in eternity. . . . .

July 15, 1859.

. . . . . It would have gratified me more than I can express to have been with you in Jerusalem, to tread those narrow streets rendered sacred by the footsteps of Jesus and his beloved disciples; to wander over that mountain hallowed by his prayers. What spot on earth could be more sacred than that where Jesus prayed? How sublime the thought—the Son of God supplicating for sinful man! It is natural for the human mind to love more dearly those persons and places in which it has a peculiar, personal interest; and so I think these hallowed spots will be rendered doubly dear to us when we think of them, not in connection with the Saviour of the world, but with *our* Saviour; not that on Olivet He prayed for a dying world only, but for *us;* not that in Gethsemane He suffered such mental agony that His sweat was as great drops of blood, that all the world might be saved, but that *we* might be brought from death unto life—that at last He died on Calvary, that you and I might have eternal life. To me this adds a double chain of love and interest to the scenes of the Saviour's life. And should it not increase our love now, to think that He suffered all for *us*, unworthy, ungrateful sinners? . . . . .

PHILADELPHIA, *August* 10, 1859.

Home again. Found every one in perfect health. My birth-day, the day which must decide my course for life. I feel deeply its solemn importance; whether I shall enter the ranks of the Gospel ministry, or serve my Master in the humble capacity of a layman.

September 5, 1859.

. . . . . To-day I enter the store, after much prayer and thought. In view of all the circumstances of the case, I have concluded that it will be best. When I study I have not good health; and of what service can a man be unless he has this blessing, which is primarily essential to his usefulness in any sphere. There is no position more respectable, or more honoured in any community, than that of the Christian merchant. His sphere of usefulness is much more widely spread than that of the minister; the latter, as a general thing, can only promote the cause of Christ by his personal efforts; the former can serve his Master, not only by his own personal labours, but also by using his means in such a way as the kingdom of Christ may be greatly advanced. It is in this latter calling that I conscientiously feel that I can be most useful. I pray God that I may be "diligent in business, fervent in spirit, serving the Lord;" that I may never, for the sake of gain, do anything that will defraud my neighbour, or cause me any remorse of conscience; and that if God should prosper me in business, I may remember that riches are the gift of God intrusted to me, and are to be used in the advancement of His kingdom. . . . . .

October 22, 1859.

. . . . . After much consideration, I have moved my mission school—permanently, I trust—to St. Mary Street, where I have secured the lecture-room of a church, and began last Sabbath with sixty scholars. We have prayer-meetings, also, every Wednesday and Sabbath evening. We trust that the mission will result in much good to the neighbourhood. It is very wicked, and there is much need of religious influences. God grant that we may be successful.

Last Tuesday evening Dr. Scudder delivered a lecture on behalf of my mission. He is the eminent missionary from India; and truly the lecture was worthy of the man. Every one who was present was delighted; and very many have pressed me to have it repeated—which I have concluded to do. The proceeds are to clothe and feed the poor of St. Mary Street during the winter.

Next Sabbath will be our communion, and then I will again have the blessed privilege of celebrating my dear Redeemer's death and resurrection. It is nearly three years since I joined the Church; and, oh, how little advance I have made; how weak my faith; what a babe in Christ I am. Yet I have great reason to thank God that I am even that; to thank Him that He ever put it into my mind to become a Christian—to seek not these fleeting, earthly things, but the enduring, lasting treasures of eternity. . . . . .

December 8, 1859.

. . . . . Since I last wrote, our country has been called to mourn the death of one who did much to impress fading Nature on the living page—to snatch the noble monuments of bygone days from oblivion, and hand them down clad in fresh vigour and beauty to succeeding generations, and who has rendered "Sleepy Hollow" world-known by his genial humour and wit. Washington Irving is no more. Another of America's noblest sons is laid low in the dust, and in vain we look for one to fill his place. His remains were laid in the village church-yard, near his much-loved home, and close to the old wooden bridge on which he often musingly stood, and which has been so inimitably described in the "Legend." I trust he had that better glory and hope laid up for him in his Father's house, without which the praise and adulation of the world is worse than nothing, for it only leaves an aching void, which cannot be filled by anything earthly. . . . . .

Sabbath evening, February 13, 1860.

. . . . . This morning I had a severe attack of neuralgia, and even questioned whether I should go to my mission school. Duty conquered. I went, and right glad was I that I did. It was a precious day to myself, and also, I trust, to many of the poor outcasts whom I visited, telling them in their own wretched hovels of the love of Jesus, which passeth all understanding. My resolution was, and is, "If they will not come to the Bible, I will take it to them; if they will not come and be told of Jesus, I will go and tell them of Him in their own homes." I believe that one at least has, by God's grace and through my humble instrumentality, been awakened, and I trust will soon find Jesus precious unto her soul.

Is not this a glorious work—these missions among the degraded outcasts of our city? If we are faithful, God will abundantly bless us, and give us many souls as seals to our labours. We must not glory, save in the cross of Christ. In that, and in that only, we may boast. On next Wednesday evening I am to have in our meeting some twenty or twenty-five persons, many of whom never were in a church, and know nothing of Jesus. They are coming, as they say, to see how they like it; and I feel a very solemn responsibility resting upon me in that I must address these perishing souls. I must address them in such a manner as will interest them and win their attention, so that they will come again; nay more, I must say what will touch their hearts. I am not equal to such a task. May God give me grace and utterance to speak the word of truth with boldness and earnestness, and that every word I utter may come from a heart warmed with love to Jesus, and a desire for the conversion of my fellow-men. . . . . .

February 27, 1860.

. . . . You have lost a dearly beloved sister;* I have lost a very dear friend. The Church militant has lost one of its brightest and most Christ-like members, and the Church triumphant has added to its ranks a devoted follower of the Lord Jesus. Another star has faded from this earthly firmament, to be rekindled with a brighter, purer, holier light, in the firmament above. Safe at last in her Father's house! safe in the bosom of that God and Saviour to honour and serve whom was her highest privilege and greatest joy! The storm at last is over, and she sweetly sleeps. At last she has reached

* Mrs. Sarah M. Wylie, wife of Rev. W. T. Wylie of Milton, Pa., after a protracted and painful illness.

the haven of eternal rest, where pain and suffering are unknown. Now she walks the streets of the New Jerusalem, and has heard the voice of her Saviour saying unto her, "Come, ye blessed of my Father, inherit the kingdom prepared for you from the foundation of the world." Now she mingles her voice with the redeemed of every age in singing the song of Moses and the Lamb. She sees unfolded to her wondering eyes the fulness of the love of God. I almost think I see her looking down upon us from heaven, and in her own winning voice saying, "Come up hither."

Your little household is one less on earth—one more in heaven. Be not sad. She is not dead, but sleepeth. God is a loving God: He doeth all things well. Think of her, not as a lifeless corpse, but as a glorified saint in heaven. Dry your tears, and rather rejoice in her happy change; and when you look into that grave where soon the remains of your dear sister will be laid, remember that "this mortal must put on immortality," that "this corruptible must put on incorruption;" look not at that coffin as containing the one whom you love, but look up and see that ransomed soul, having burst the bonds of its chrysalis, soaring aloft to the presence of *her* Father and *our* Father, of *her* God and *our* God. Would you be comforted? There is a balm in Gilead. . . . . .

Sabbath evening, March 26, 1860.

. . . . . To-day has been a very encouraging one to me. My Sabbath school attendance was better, and my teachers seemed more earnest in their work. The attendance at my Bible class numbered twenty: is not that encouraging for the third Sabbath? How my inmost soul goes up in gratitude to God for ever putting it into my heart to engage in this work, and for giving me such delight and success! My lesson was the temptation of Christ; and when I got into my subject, the hour and a half flew rapidly by. As we closed, some came to me, and with the tears almost starting in their eyes, told me how much they enjoyed the instructions, and begged that I would enter their names upon my roll. My plan is to speak very plainly, simply, and understandingly; and I pray that God will bless it to the conversion of their souls. . . . . .

To make us cheerful and happy Christians, we need more activity in our Master's work. It is spiritual exercise that keeps the soul in health. *Now* is the time to do good. There will be no Sabbath schools or Bible classes in heaven; no careless to warn; no ignorant to instruct. Would we exercise our zeal, courage, labour and patience? we must do it now. Let us hasten, for time is flying. Work! work! while it is day, for the night cometh—the long, long, weary night of death, in which no man can work. Let us bring out the Bible more when we talk together; there are in it pearls of inestimable value, if we will but seek them out. Let us speak oftener of the eternal home to which we travel: children, as the holidays draw near, love to talk of home; and why should not we talk of that home where we expect to dwell for ever? Let us commune together more, and as the Saviour revealed Himself to the disciples on the way to Emmaus, so He will reveal Himself to us. The spiritual flame within us needs stirring as well as feeding to keep it up. The weakest may sharpen the strongest, as the whetstone does the scythe. If we seek to water the souls of others, our own shall be abundantly watered. Death will soon be among us: let us all be prepared: let us beware of a spirit of slumber and formality, especially in private reading and prayer: let our path to the fountain be worn with daily journeys, and let our key to the treasury of grace be bright with constant use. . . . . .

Sabbath evening, April 16, 1860.

I have just come in from my mission school prayer-meeting, completely worn out—weary, not *of* my Master's work, but *in it.* To-day has been another precious Sabbath to me. My school, morning and afternoon, was good; then came my delightful Bible class; and then a very encouraging prayer-meeting this evening. How joyful I felt for my own, but inestimably more for my Master's sake, to see that at last we have been enabled to make an impression upon these poor degraded ones, and persuade them to come up to the house of God! I feel there are glorious things in store for our little mission. There I hope to labour as long as God shall spare my poor life; and I want no other monument than that—a monument each stone of which is an immortal soul, which God has enabled by His grace and Spirit's assistance to be snatched from death and made an heir of eternal life. . . . . .

Sabbath evening, May 13, 1860.

. . . . . God says, "I will cause you to pass under the rod, and I will bring you into the bond of the covenant." Sweet rod, that drives the soul to such a precious resting-place! blessed affliction, that makes us more confident in God! One of the resolutions made by Jonathan Edwards, when starting out in life, is worthy of such a noble and gifted mind—"*Resolved*, To improve afflictions to the *uttermost*." If we do thus, we will do well.

You have now no earthly father* to lean upon and look to for comfort and guidance; but there is one upon whom you can lean—upon "the Beloved." Be found coming up out of the wilderness of natural sin "leaning upon the Beloved." If you are thus found, then every hour that strikes is an hour less between you and glory. An hour with Christ will make up for all the pain and grief that we may have endured here;—"half an hour with God will make us forget a lifetime of agony." Do you want love?—He is the everlasting fountain of love.

June 16, 1860.

. . . . . Marriage was meant to double man's happiness, and when contracted in the fear of God it accomplishes its purpose;—on other terms, the misery is insupportable. The man who dares venture here without the guidance of "the Wonderful, the Counsellor," is gambling with a stake which may be to him eternal death; for who has such an

* M.'s father departed this life on the 26th April 1860, after a few days illness.

influence for good or evil over a man as his wife? If we leave God out of view in the beginning, the downward course is easy and rapid; the results are not for time, —they are for eternity.

We must, then, have the grace, the truth of God in *our hearts.* If it is there, it will well up. You may attempt to repress the gushing spring, but it will rise at another place, spreading life and fertility wherever it goes: so with truth in our own souls; if it is there, it will be seen and felt by ourselves, and by those around us. . . . . Religion is the crown and glory of man's life: without it he is a pitiful wreck, tossed about upon a boundless sea. Man in his natural condition knows nothing higher or nobler than earthly pleasure; and when religion comes and drives this away, he fears he is about to lose his all: but when his bonds are broken, and the scales drop from his eyes, then he bows before the majesty and rejoices in the love of God. That heart is happiest whose godliness is greatest; that home the most blessed where it is most on the ascendant; that work-shop the best conditioned where it is most felt; that nation the safest and most prosperous where the lamp of life sheds light upon the path.

Religion is the *director* of the Christian's life. Can we ever have a wiser guide than the all-wise God? Can we ever find a safer or more pleasant path than that into which the Eternal leads us? Can we select a better standard, a better aim, than that which God provides for us? Like the ship upon the ocean, we may be beaten and tossed by the storm until hope seems to have for ever faded from us; but then *One* comes to us over the angry waves, and we hear His voice far above the howling winds, saying, "It is I; fear not;" and His presence makes a calm. The chart which has been given us to guide us through life is divine, bearing the impress of an eternal, unalterable, inflexible mind, and consequently never can be changed.

We cannot bring our religion *to* the Bible; we must get it *from* it. Man cannot judge the Word of God—it judges him; it is the director of his steps and the sun of his soul. Guided by it, he walks under the direction of the Father of lights, with whom there is no variableness neither shadow of turning, to that abode where the glory of God is manifested to all, and the Lamb is the light thereof. That Director, in his all-wise providence, leads us through devious ways to our rest—many he leads through paths of bereavement and sorrow, as he has you; but soon all will merge into the full sunlight and glory of the Father's presence. Is it not a joyous thought, after a long absence in a foreign land, where no familiar face smiled upon us, to know that on turning homeward, "there is an eye will mark our coming, and look brighter when we come?" How much more gladdening that Word of God which irradiates the Christian's path—a pillar of cloud by day and of fire by night!

But godliness is the *ornament* and *glory* of life, as well as its director. What makes the soul beautiful? All God's works are surpassingly lovely. Look at the modest flower as it lifts its dewy cup to greet the morning sun, and see what beauty beams upon us there. Contemplate the firmament above us—fitting type of Jehovah's immensity—and mark the beauty there. Now, if these ephemeral things are clad in loveliness by God, may we not expect more exquisite beauty in the immortal soul of man? It was once in the image of God—it is capable of wearing that image again. In what is the beauty of the soul? In its *holiness;* and this holiness is developed by the sorrows, and sufferings, and persecutions of the soul. Were it not for the clouds and the rain, the gorgeous tints of the rainbow would never gild our sky; and were it not for the trials sent by the Spirit, the beauties of holiness would never shine so brightly in the Christian's soul. Like the fabled dragon, the Christian rises refreshed and strengthened from every blow, even though the dearest heart-string has been severed. It is holiness, then, that is the ornament of life: without it no transcendent talents or rare acquirements can give beauty to the spirit in the eye of God. Knowledge is power, but it is the power of evil: acquirements may be extensive, but they are like gaudy trappings on a hearse, unless truth in the heart become holiness in the life. But let this truth be implanted in the soul of man, and it becomes his joy as well as his director and ornament. Christianity introduces us to the highest joy of earth or heaven—even joy in the Holy Ghost; and without this, man is, of all objects in the universe, the most pitiable. Man's heart was made to be happy in God, and without Him eternity cannot fill up the void. We may seek joy in human affections, but death comes, strikes down the object of our love, and hides it from our sight. It is impossible that any object whose root is in the dust can gladden the soul of man, apart from the God who made it. Has God, then, left us without joy? No. Even in this sinful world there is a joy; and the knowledge, love, and fear of God are its fountain-head. In reconciliation to God, in growing holiness, in greater love to Jesus, the man of God finds the streams of his joy. Is the land of his fathers a source of joy to the returning exile? Are the green fields and bright heavens a source of gladness to him who has long been immured in a dungeon? Far more is a sense of God's favour to a soul which has returned from its wanderings to seek rest and repose on the bosom of its God.

Lastly, truth in the heart—holiness—is a prelude of the life that is to come. It is a sad thing to stand by an open grave and see dust returning to dust—one, perhaps, with whom we have taken sweet counsel, on whose arm we have often leaned, whose soul has touched our own, and in which the inmost secrets of our own heart are entombed. The cold earth must hide them; and even affection must hasten to bury them out of our sight. But that very body thus consigned to dust must come forth a glorious body, when "death shall be swallowed up in life." That which is sown in dishonour is to grow in glory, if united to Him who is the resurrection and the life, who has abolished death, and brought life and immortality to light in the Gospel. And thus we look upon the work of God's Spirit in the soul as the crown and consummation of life." . . . .

SPRING BROOK, *Sabbath, August* 26, 1860.

. . . . . In just half a year from this day God has, in his all-wise providence, seen fit to remove from you two loved ones—objects around which your dearest affections earnestly clung—a father and a sister. In the hour when affliction first comes upon us we are crushed, and cannot, in the depth of our sorrow, see that any good thing can come out of a bereavement. But when the grave has closed over the loved ones, and we sit down to sober reflection, then we see the lesson God intended to teach, and wonder why we have not seen it before. Surely God had some important end in view in thus snatching away two of his creatures in the prime and vigour of life. Have you as yet learned that lesson? Have you seen what God intended to teach you? It may have been that your spirit was rebellious, and this was sent to teach you patience and submission to your heavenly Father's will. Perhaps you leaned too much upon earthly support, and He took that away in order to make you look to and lean only upon Him. Try and see what this lesson is; and having seen it, profit by it. I believe it is our duty, when we are afflicted, to pray for guidance, in order that we may see the lesson intended to be taught us. These afflictions are the salt cast into the Marah fountain of our hearts, bitter with sin, in order that the water may be made sweet. Yea, even though the furnace of our affliction be seven times heated, yet the Refiner sits by: his desire is to purify, not to consume. The spices in the Temple were bruised spices. We need not expect to reach heaven except through much tribulation. It will a thousand-fold add to our enjoyment there, to think of what we have passed through to reach it. . . . . Let our voice be, "Not my will, but Thine be done." Let us seek greater nearness to God, striving at all times to be like Jesus. . . . .

At Sea—Steamship "City of Baltimore,"
Sabbath, May 19, 1861.

..... Last evening was lovely. The moon shone out calmly and beautifully upon us, and reflected from the fading hills of Rhode Island, seemed to bid us God-speed. As I walked the deck and looked toward my native land, a thousand memories rushed upon me, which found utterance in my exclamation to a Scotch lady returning to her fatherland—"Would that I, like you, were returning to my home again!"

After a fine night's sleep I awoke this morning much refreshed. To-day is lovely. We had a service in the cabin at 10.30, conducted by Captain Petrie. The saloon was crowded, and the service solemn and impressive. How hard it is to keep Sabbath on board ship! ....

I am much pleased with our vessel. The accommodations are very good, and the table excellent. Our captain is a jolly good fellow, and both he and the purser have shown me much attention already. ....

Monday evening.—Another delightful day, though now the clouds are black and angry, and threaten a storm. I fear my friends at home have wasted a good deal of sympathy upon me in regard to sea-sickness. I never was better in my life, and can eat my four meals per diem with unexampled regularity. When I came on board, father put me in charge of the captain and purser, as one who had been "*very sick*, and needed a great deal of attention." Yesterday morning the captain and I had a good laugh about it when he saw me enjoying my breakfast, remarking that he thought "I'd do." This morning we were summoned to see the crew put through their exercises. All the officers, crew, and waiters, are portioned off to the several boats, and every few days they are drilled in clearing them away, so that in case of accident there may be no confusion, but by each one knowing his place, and being skilled in his work, many lives may be saved which otherwise would be lost. . . . .

Tuesday evening.—Rolling! pitching! tossing! How can I write? As we apprehended, the heavy clouds which gathered around us last evening brought us a storm. When I went on deck this morning I found a heavy sea running, and the wind dead ahead, blowing a perfect gale. Though the decks were wet with spray, in company with two or three others I walked for a long time, until at length we were driven below by the rain. It was an amusing sight our dinner-table to-day: hardly had the soup been removed when about thirty made a bolt for the scuppers—among whom were my travelling companions. When the substantials came, hardly twenty-five of our one hundred and fifty passengers were left at the table—the rest not caring to dine. For myself, thus far I have been exempt. I am very well, and my appetite increases. All afternoon I sat on the smoke-stack enjoying the grand scene before me. The ship was under full sail and dashed through the water in right gallant style. . . . .

[After describing at length some of his fellow-passengers, he proceeds:—]

My travelling companions are both very clever, and in company with two other young men, one from California and the other from Switzerland, there is no lack of sport. We have with us another notability. You may remember the advertisements which have appeared for several years past, and have caused a great deal of merriment, reading somewhat thus:—"A retired physician, whose sands of life are nearly run out, whilst travelling through India with an only daughter who was dying of consumption, discovered (or fell in with) a preparation which perfectly cured her; and being desirous of serving in some way his fellow-men, he will send the recipe to any one who will enclose him three postage stamps." His dodge was as follows:—he would by return of mail send the recipe, adding at the bottom, "that if the heat in boiling was a little too great, it would become a deadly poison." Of course, no one would dare to try it. Sure of the effect of his warning, he would say, by way of *Nota Bene*, that "he had a small quantity on hand prepared by a skilful chemist, which he would be happy to supply at $2 per bottle." This retired physician, whose sands of life have been running out for a few years past, is a hale, hearty young Yankee, of about thirty-five, whose sands, from all appearances, will run a long time yet. He has made over $90,000 by his quackery, and is now going to Europe to travel and open his trade in London. . . . .

Thursday evening.—Yesterday I was unable to write owing to the storm. We ran all day through a dense fog, at full speed, with all sail set. It was a terribly grand sight. We passed several icebergs—one of them very large—coming uncomfortably close. I am still very well, and have been able to act as nurse to several of my sea-sick friends. Not only am I well, but I am enjoying myself. A gentleman told me this morning, "You seem to be the happiest one on board." Externally I may be; but he did not know how my heart was yearning for the loved ones at home—how I sit behind the wheel-house, where undisturbed I may look back toward that loved land momentarily becoming more distant.....

When I arose this morning I found the fog gone and a clear western wind blowing, which hastens us on our course. The sea has been heavy, and the ship rolls considerably. All morning I lay on the deck reading "John Halifax, Gentleman," by Miss Muloch: if you have not read it, I heartily recommend it as one of the most natural, well-written tales I have read.....

Friday evening.—Another rather gloomy day. Every now and then the sun would peep out upon us from behind a bank of clouds, and then quickly hiding himself again, a smart shower of rain would drive us within;—long heavy swells would come rolling in from the west, causing our vessel to perambulate rather extensively around her centre of gravity. For a couple of hours I sat in the "Fiddle," (as we have dubbed the main hatchway,) with the captain and Bayard Taylor: the former is really one of the cleverest (I mean English clever) men I have met—a gentleman full of fun and anecdote, and withal a splendid seaman. I picked up a good deal of information from the captain and Mr. Taylor in regard to travelling in Germany, France, &c.; both of them having been there very often.

Saturday evening.—A lovely day. Although now and

then a smart shower would drive us in, yet withal the scene was surpassingly lovely;—the dark-green billows, crested with foam, broke upon our stern and hurried our vessel on her eastern course. . . . .

Sabbath.—Morning service is over, and my thoughts turn, as ever, to home. . . . . What a wretched place this is to keep the Sabbath in! If there were only some place, except my dark state-room, where I could be alone, or at least have only such company as I chose. On deck it is too cold to read, and in the cabin it is out of the question. I feel indeed that my two Sabbaths on board have been misspent. . . . .

Monday evening.—To-day has been charming—clear, yet the sky has not the deep blue it has in America. . . . . As I look round the cabin I see many busy in getting ready for the morning mail. Our voyage is nearly done. We have had a safe and speedy passage almost across the Atlantic. My health is much improved, and although still weak, I feel that I am rapidly becoming myself again. . . . . I soon shall land among strangers. Strange scenes are before me—temptations, perhaps, that I know not of; much pleasure and knowledge. Pray that I may avoid the wrong, and use to the best advantage the right; that I may never forget who and what I am; that, be the temptation ever so strong, I may have a high, pure bond of restraint—a bond above all that is earthly and mercenary—love to my blessed Saviour. And may this influence be such, as, filling my heart with noblest and holiest desires, I may appear to others as one who is indeed a child of God. . . . .

Tuesday morning.—At 4 this morning we were roused by the cry of "Land ahead!" On going on deck I could, away in the distance, see the mountains of Ireland looming up. A nearer approach showed it to be the "Skittles," a group of rocks at the entrance of Bantry Bay. We have just passed Cape Clear—the last point of land seen by outward bound vessels. Would that I could only see them fading in the distance, and myself homeward bound! I was much amused at an Irishman we have on board. On going on deck this morning, and seeing his native isle once more, he reverently doffed his hat, with the exclamation, "Good-morning to your ladyship; how are ye now?" The day is perfect; the water is smooth as glass, and a large flock of sea-gulls are following astern, much to the amusement of the youngsters, who are feeding them with crackers......

BIRKENHEAD, "CLAUGHTON FIRS,"
May 31, 1861.

Here I am, after a delightful passage, safely ensconced in my uncle's house at Birkenhead.

..... We arrived off Cork the same day I wrote you, about 3 o'clock. The afternoon was calm and clear, and all were very happy in view of a speedy termination of the voyage. After tea a party of us gathered round the smoke-stack, and sat from 8 to 2 o'clock talking and hearing the captain tell stories. When we retired, the half moon was slowly rising over the mountains of Wales. Rising early, and coming on deck, I found that we were just opposite the fatal rocks on which the *Royal Charter* was dashed to pieces. You may remember the circumstances. I could not help thinking about it as we left Queenstown. Their passage had been as pleasant as ours; they had telegraphed to their friends of their safe arrival—and yet were lost. Long after I went to my bed I thought about it, until the very thought put me to sleep. At 8 o'clock the pilot came on board; and at 1 o'clock we arrived off the Huskisson Dock. Soon after, the tug came alongside, on the deck of which I recognized my cousin A. S., as well as my uncle D. We came ashore in the tug; our baggage was examined; took a cab; crossed the Woodside Ferry, and soon arrived at Claughton Firs.

. . . . . All evening my tongue was kept busy answering questions in regard to American politics, in which I find people take a much deeper interest than I had any idea of. . . . . .

At noon, J. S. having heard of my arrival, came down from Manchester. I was rejoiced to see him, and soon we were as of old. After dinner we started out to drive over the hills towards Chester. I enjoyed the ride very much; and between us four cousins fun was not wanting. Along the road the yellow and scarlet hawthorn was growing luxuriantly, while the chirping of the sparrows, the antiquated tower peeping through the trees, and the old windmill lazily turning on the hill, all told me unmistakably that I was in Old England, and not in Young America. After tea we went for a walk in Birkenhead Park. What an advantage the English have over us in their long twilights! After all work is done there are two or three hours of twilight, when those who have been cooped up all day can go out and enjoy themselves.

The Green presented a beautiful sight last evening: here a father was playing with his little ones; there a club playing cricket; further on, youngsters enjoying themselves hugely with a game of tag, whilst little knots scattered here and there over the grass seemed in the very hey-day of enjoyment. England far surpasses us in her parks. I do not suppose that in all America we have such an one as this. . . . . .

MANCHESTER, "THE ELMS," *June* 6, 1861.

. . . . . After tea, in company with J. and J., walked over Kensall Moor. The view was beautiful from the top of the hills skirting the moor, through which the Irwell winds very sluggishly. On the opposite side we could see the little cottages built upon the rising hill, with their lights flickering through the trees; while away in the distance were the hills known as the Back Bone of Old England, behind which the sun had just set. J. and I were very happy in meeting again. On returning, we found H., an artist of much celebrity here, had dropped in; and gathering round the fire, a round of stories, and songs, and conundrums began, which did not end until near the small hours. . . . . .

Aunt J. says that I am improved so much since I landed, that no one would know me to be the same person. I feel well, though my strength is coming to me slowly. . . . . .

June 7, 1861.—A clear sunshiny morning. Left

Manchester at 9.45 in the mail-coach for Buxton. The air was clear and bracing, and at full speed we hastened toward the blue hills of Derbyshire looming up in the distance. Our road was one of those smooth, level turnpikes, for which England is justly famous. Long rows of hawthorn hedges lined it, save where here and there the little country inn modestly peeped from out the surrounding trees. Many of these have queer, and some pompous names, such as, "The Royal Arms"—"The Dial," having for a motto, "Go about your business"—"The Old Grey Horse," &c. A ride of an hour brought us to Stockport, noticeable only for smoke and dirt. From this place we began to ascend the hills skirting Derbyshire. The scene on either hand was truly enchanting—fields clad in the richest green skirting the mountain-sides, relieved here and there by a little village, whose old gray church-tower, nearly hidden by the clinging ivy, told of days gone by, and of generations now mingled with their kindred dust.

We continued to ascend by a winding road until we had reached an elevation of 1,300 feet above the level of the sea. Here a sudden turn in the road brought us in full view of the celebrated watering-place of Buxton, chiefly celebrated for its tepid baths, the discovery of which dates back to the Roman invasion. . . . . .

Back of the town rises a high rock known as the Chee Tor, and from its top a view of great beauty may be obtained.

At Fairfield, lying at the base of the Tor, there is to be seen the following epitaph:—

"Beneath this stone here lie two children dear,
The one at Stony Middleton, the other here."

Took a drag for Castleton, 12 or 14 miles distant. On ascending the hills beyond Buxton we had a fine view of the surrounding country. The ground is not well fitted for vegetation, being very limy—a fact that is well attested to by the large number of lime-kilns to be seen in every direction. The country folk are principally engaged in sheep-raising, and in working the lead mines. The latter are neither rich nor deep: they are worked by what is termed "surface-mining," and while they give a sufficient subsistence to the individual miner, are not of sufficient extent to pay profitably a large company. About two miles from Buxton we pass the hamlet of Peak Forest, which until within a year or so past enjoyed the same privileges as Gretna Green, and was extensively patronized by runaway lovers. The situation is very picturesque, and the old keeper (quite a curiosity in his way) will for a pittance tell many a strange story whose scene lies within these walls.

A few miles further on we come to the ebbing and flowing well. It is considered one of the wonders of Derbyshire. The water flows for five minutes, at intervals of every ten, and the quantity thrown up at each flow is about 120 hogsheads. The water was flowing out when we reached; yet, though we sat on the bank for fifteen or twenty minutes, we were not favoured with a sight of the sudden flow—probably owing to the long drought.

About 7 in the evening we came in sight of Mam Tor, or "the Shivering Mountain," one of the highest in the Peak, having an altitude of 2,000 feet above the level of the sea.

At the top of the Mam Tor is the entrance to the famous Blue John Mine. Dismounting from our vehicle, we sent it on to the town, and tried to obtain admission to the little hut guarding the mouth of the cavern. We were too late, and were obliged to turn our footsteps toward the hotel. Following a sheep path which leads around the mountain, again the valley burst upon us, more extensive and more beautiful than before. The sun was still bright upon the steep rugged summit of the Tor, while over the valley the subdued twilight was stealing rapidly. Soon regaining the road, a few steps brought us to Castleton, a little old English town where coaching days are still a thing of the present. Its houses of old gray stone half hidden by the clinging vines—their snow-white stoops attesting to the cleanliness of the inhabitants, the long narrow lanes, and the old church with its weather-beaten towers, all convey to the mind an idea of true happiness and enjoyment.

At the "Nag's Head" we found clean and comfortable quarters. Immediately after tea we started out to hunt the guides, in order that if possible we might at once see the mines. By dint of a little Yankee perseverance we found the son of the keeper of the Blue John, who kindly offered us *freely* his services. He joined us after finding the guide to the Speedwell, and off we started. Half way up the hill, between the top of which and the Mam Tor the turnpike is cut, we came to the entrance to the Speedwell. This is an artificial opening made in search of lead. The work was commenced upwards of eighty years ago by a party of adventurers from Staffordshire, who, after eleven years labour, gave up in despair. To enter the mine you descend 106 stone steps, at the bottom of which is the level, cut for 700 feet through the solid rock: this is about 7 feet in height, and through it a stream of pure water passes, about 3 feet deep. . . . . At the foot of the steps we entered a boat, and each, with candle in hand, impelled ourselves along by staples fastened in the rock. At intervals of 50 or 60 yards we stuck candles in the wall, the effect of which was very fine. The level terminates in a cavern, not unaptly termed the "Bottomless Pit," for its height and depth have never as yet been measured. Although 40,000 tons of rock, obtained in blasting, have been thrown into this gulf, no effect has been produced upon it, for still the fathoming-line shows no bottom: although a rocket has been shot up to the height of 450 feet, no top could be seen--nothing but blackness and darkness. Across the gulf an arch has been thrown, so that visitors can leave the boat and gaze into the darkness. Our guide climbed up the side of the cavern to the height of about 100 feet, and there ignited a blue light. The effect was grand: the huge masses of rock, that never saw the light of the sun, looming out from the darkness and casting their black shadows on the walls behind, rising higher and higher until lost in impenetrable gloom—all this produced upon us a strange, indescribable effect. To be thus far in the bowels of the earth, witnessing the stupendous, silent workings of nature, it made us feel somewhat of the greatness and wondrous power of Him who is nature's God.

Returning again to our boat, we looked far down the stream, and there we could see the lights which we had left, sparkling like jewel-drops upon the water. We made ourselves merry with songs, and the cavern echoed and re-echoed with the notes of the "Star Spangled Banner," "Nelly was a Lady," &c.

Leaving the Speedwell, we started for the Blue John, through the "Winnats," or Wind Gates. This is a deep ravine about a mile in length, leading from Castleton to the top of the mountain opposite the Mam Tor, and is wild and rugged beyond description. It derives its name from the howling made by the wind as it sweeps through it. On either side the pass are precipices rising to a great height, dark, rugged, and steep;—they seem the very embodiment of all that is forbidding and stern. Yet they are not devoid of beauty, for among their crags may be found lichens and mosses of rare form and beauty; and these, mingling with the more gaudy colouring of the surrounding flowers, seem to bring out in still bolder relief the huge cliffs to which they are attached.

After a weary walk we reached the entrance of the Blue John Mine—the only place in the world where any quantity of this beautiful mineral is found. It is a fluate of lime, not exactly the same as fluor spar, the latter being crystallized, and not having the same colour as the former.

Having lit our lamps we descended into the mine, first down a number of steps into a small cavern, then along a narrow passage lined with beautiful sparkling stalactites, then down winding steps 100 feet more, when we stood in Lord Mulgrave's Dining-Room. . . . . Passing on, we came to a large cavern where our guide lit a Bengola light—the effect was grand, the stalactites and stalagmites being coloured. We then retraced our steps and stopped at a spring where we drank Adam's ale, pure and cold, trickling from the rock. . . . . We then passed into the end of the workings, to see the Blue John in its natural state, after which we ascended to the upper air. Registering our names, and having procured some splendid specimens of the Blue John, we returned to town at midnight. Not a light was seen or sound to be heard; so, weary with the labour of the day, we slipped away to bed.

June 8—CASTLETON.—Rose at 7, and before breakfast walked to see the Peak Cavern. The entrance to this is through a deep gorge in the Peak, whose summit is crowned by the famous castle, once one of the most powerful strongholds in Britain. . . . . The little winding path leading up to the mouth of the cavern is eminently picturesque. On one side the rock is fringed with shrubbery and stunted pines, while the other rises a barren rugged steep, from the crevices of which flocks of jackdaws fly forth at the slightest sound, and fill the air with their harsh screams. The mouth of the cave, which is almost a perfect archway, is 45 feet high, 120 feet wide, and about 50 feet deep. This part of the cavern is used as a rope and twine factory, and the burr of the machinery, the sharp voices of the cord-winders, together with the little cottage half hidden among the rocks, give to the scenery a wild effect, as though this were the home of some unnatural beings. . . . .

The castle on the summit is one of the oldest and most interesting of Norman fortresses. A venerable wreck of other days, "it is the silent monument of days when 'might made right,' and its history tells of a time when the passions of men ruled over truth and justice." . . . . .

After breakfast we took a fly for Edensor. A very pleasant ride of 11 miles brought us to the door of the "Castle Hotel," at one of the entrances to Chatsworth. Having ordered a dinner to be ready for us on our return, we set off to see this mansion fit for a king. Crossing the Derwent by a substantial stone bridge, we soon found ourselves confronting the gilded iron gate surmounted by two rampant stags. The hour of opening not having arrived, we strolled through the stables; and with them I must say I was greatly disappointed: true, they are large, and are built of stone, but I have seen in our own country stables cleaner, better arranged, and much more substantially and elegantly fitted up. . . . . Returning to the entrance, we were conducted to the house by an old man in livery, whose red nose and livid cheeks led us strongly to believe that he had these many years enjoyed the good things of this life. At the house we were put in charge of the housekeeper, who put us through with lightning speed. No time was allowed for anything. When we came to the room where the minerals and malachite vases were, I wanted to stop; but no, we must pass on, as another party was waiting. . . . . The Picture Galleries are miserably arranged—so narrow that one cannot get at a proper distance to enjoy a picture; and very poorly lighted—instead of having an open exposure, the light comes in through a court. One painting in the gallery struck me as very fine—it was called "Monks at Prayer." The double light from the setting sun and swinging lamps produced a marvellous effect. The drawing was good, each monk's face being a study in itself.

In the Billiard Room is Landseer's celebrated picture, entitled "Bolton Abbey in the Olden Time." I have long been familiar with the spirited engraving taken from this picture, but it falls far below the original. The happy look of the old prior as he surveys the good things spread out before him, the stag whose body seems almost to quiver with departing life, and the sparkling fish—all are masterpieces of art. . . . .

The walls of the Sculpture Gallery are of polished gritstone, which forms a very effective background for the statuary. We first noticed Canova's celebrated statue of "Napoleon's Mother." There was something about it so subdued;—the position is not tragic, there is nothing grand, but that quiet, dignified air of repose which so well becomes such a subject. I was better pleased with it than with anything else in the room. . . . . A bust of "Petrarch's Laura," by Canova, is also well worth attention, and though small, and in rather an obscure position, is one of the gems of the collection . . . . .

Passing from the Gallery we enter the Orangery. Most of the plants in this collection were the property of Josephine when at Malmaison. Here we leave the house, rather disappointed at having been hurried through, —still, not less impressed with its splendour. Taking another guide, we proceed to the Grand Conservatory. This mountain of glass covers an acre of ground. No more enchanting sight can greet the eye than the one presented on entering this crystal structure. Stately palms, gracefully waving acacias, and the slender sugar-cane, luxuriate in their own soil, and in the temperature best suited to their growth and perfection.

Leaving this, we pass along by the waterfall and fountains, thence round by the front of the house, and emerge at the gate parallel to the one at which we entered.

From Chatsworth we drove to Haddon Hall. . . . . This

is situated on a natural limestone elevation on the left bank of the river Wye. The first glimpse which we caught of it was eminently picturesque. Its embattled turrets and castellated form rising from a grove of noble trees impressed us deeply. Arriving in front of the building, a narrow lane led to the ancient bridge across the Wye; a few steps more and we stood at the castle gate. How old it looks!—the wood rotted away from the massive bolts, and whole framework seeming just ready to fall to the ground.

MATLOCK, BATH, DERBYSHIRE,
June 9, 1861.

..... We arrived at this delightful place last evening from Chatsworth and dear old Haddon Hall (or, as the natives say, "dear hold Addon All"), and are now very comfortably quartered in the "New Bath Hotel"—the nicest English house that I have as yet met with. Everything is so clean and neat—attentive servants, an agreeable landlady, and capital cooking. .....

This afternoon I am going to visit Lea Hurst, the home of Florence Nightingale. I regret that she is at present absent, as a gentleman here, a friend of hers and mine, would take me to call on her were she at home.

I have a poor opinion of many of the English people. Many who call themselves ladies and gentlemen have, according to my ideas, very little politeness. On several occasions, when they have found that I was an American, they have made the most insulting remarks in regard to my country, which, at the present time, are both unchristian and unfeeling. I always try never to lower myself by saying anything ungentlemanly, but I give them back in their own coin. Yesterday, to one who had been taunting me in a most sarcastic manner for two days, I gave a few home thrusts which made his ears tingle. It is not every one who acts thus, but the snobocracy, the "would-be-woulds," monied toad-stools, that have sprung suddenly upon some wave of fortune, and take upon themselves airs as though William the Conqueror were their father and they had a universal license to patronize and snub whom they please. . . . . . You cannot make the English understand America. Their perceptions are not quick, and I have talked in vain, for hours, trying to explain, as well as I could, our Federal institutions. They are a solid, substantial, noble-hearted people; but, oh, how self-righteous! England and her deeds are the Alpha and Omega of all they know. Were it not for England, the world would go helter skelter through space, and no power could stop it. . . . .

"THE ELMS," MANCHESTER,
June 16, 1861.

This is the twilight hour. The sun is just setting gloriously, and my blinds are rustling with a delicious breeze—grateful indeed, after so warm a day. The weather has been perfect, though a shade too warm for almost a week. I am hoping for a cool continuance while I visit London. This morning I heard Rev. Mr. M'Caw. His text was, "For our God is a consuming fire." The sermon was extemporaneous, and very good; the more so because his words came from the heart. After tea I took my little Union Hymn Book and refreshed myself with some of its sweet familiar hymns. A little while ago I was walking round Kensall Moor: the scene was calm and lovely. Looking toward the city, the chimneys were silent, the busy hum of machinery was hushed, the heavy rumbling of carts was unheard—all was rest, quiet Sabbath rest. Thought I, Is my soul thus at rest? and then again, Happy that it is not; for woe be to him whose soul dwells at ease, and is lulled in peaceful security! Though we are not at rest, tossed about on this troubled sea of life, buffeted by sorrow and sin, yet "there remaineth a rest for the people of God." How the soul leaps with joy at this blessed declaration! how it spurs us on to be faithful unto the end, that there is a rest! Not always shall it be thus;—not always shall it be that every joy has its proportionate sorrow, that every pleasure has its pain. No, no; there is a *rest!* rest, eternal, perfect rest, for the souls of God's children. How I love to think about it! How I love to let my soul soar away to those realms of bliss, and feast itself upon visions of heavenly rest! . . . . .

You say rightly, that "literary pursuits, love of poetry, &c., may be carried to such an extent as to utterly unfit us for every-day life." The poetical mind is rarely the practical mind; it dwells on the ideal, the unreal, and rarely descends, and never with pleasure, to those simple matter-of-fact things of which man's life is made up, and upon which so much of his happiness depends.

Tuesday evening.—Here I am at last in London, and

alone. It was bad enough when I had company; but now it is a thousand-fold worse. I felt it so much after I arrived;—sitting down to my dinner alone, all strangers about me; walking up and down the thronged streets without meeting one single familiar face; and at last coming up here to my little room without speaking one familiar word to anybody. Is it a wonder that it makes me home-sick, and that I long to be back again with those who love me? There may be pleasure in travelling when one has congenial company, but there is none to me when I have none. . . . . To-morrow I intend consulting Dr. Quain, said to be very skilful in diseases of the chest. Although I feel quite well, I would like to have his opinion. I shall stay here a week or so, and then go to Cumberland. . . . . .

LONDON, *June 22*, 1861.

. . . . . On Wednesday I went to St. James's Park to see the Queen pass to the Drawing Room. As this was her first public appearance since her mother's death, all London was agog, and never did I see such a collection of finery and toggery as was then and there presented. For at least two hours a continuous stream of magnificent equipages rolled up to the Palace door. At about 2 o'clock music was heard, and, preceded by the Royal Life Guards, Her Majesty came from Buckingham Palace. I had a capital view of her, and I assure you she is just the image of the little photograph which I have shown you. She was dressed in black, with a head-dress of black feathers —no jewels were to be seen. I had also a good look at the Princess Alice. She is very pretty, and I really feel sorry that she is to be married to the Prince of Hesse. A poor thing royalty is, that a man cannot choose his own wife, nor a woman her husband.

LONDON, *June* 23, 1861.

Another Sabbath evening. Yesterday uncle J. arrived, so that to-day I had company. This morning, shortly after breakfast, we started out to Surrey Chapel to hear Newman Hall. It is an octagonal building, one story high, and having a very shabby appearance. It is, nevertheless, a sacred spot, for its walls have re-echoed with the eloquence of Rowland Hill, of Sherman, and last, but by no means least, of Newman Hall. It is of the Independents, but Mr. Hall being one of the Countess of Huntingdon's Connexion, a part of the Church of England service is also read. After the service Mr. Hall entered the pulpit. Imagine a tall, rather thin man, having a long, pale face, with black side whiskers, partially bald, and with a deep set black eye. The very moment he opens his mouth you are riveted, and he carries you with him whithersoever he will; nor is the charm broken until he ceases to speak. It seemed to me as though the mantle of the sainted Hill, whose bust is immediately behind the pulpit, had indeed descended upon him with all its freshness and power. His text was Col. iii. 12, 13, and such a sermon I have rarely listened to—such grappling with error—such brilliant showing forth of the truth and power of God's word—such argumentation; all coupled with the deepest tenderness and love for the souls of his hearers, and with most earnest pleading that they would look unto Jesus and be saved. . . . .

There is one thing to which I cannot reconcile myself here;—it is the common practice of going from place to place in omnibuses on the Sabbath. I know it must be done, as the distances are so great; still, it seems to me unlike the Sabbath. At this hotel, "Castle and Falcon," they are very strict: when I went down to the coffee-room this morning I found all the newspapers removed, and good religious books scattered along the tables, and the waiters who were disengaged reading their Bibles. Where in America would we see such a sight as this? . . . .

Monday evening.—You will see by the papers which I send you that London has, within the past forty-eight hours, met with two severe losses;—one in the very sudden death of the Lord Chancellor; and the other, the great fire, which broke out on Saturday afternoon and is still raging. On Sabbath morning the Superintendent of the Fire Brigade was crushed by the falling walls He was an elder in Dr. Cumming's church, and beloved by all who knew him. I was told this morning by a gentleman connected with the Phoenix, the oldest and best insurance company in London, that the loss thus far is £3,000,000 sterling. The river is covered with tallow from the vaults. And this evening another of the warehouses took fire, and is now burning: it contains 18,000 barrels of tallow. . . . . I spent most of this afternoon at Smith, Beck and Beck's, the great microscope makers, where I fairly revelled in beautiful microscopic preparations; nor did I come away without my trophies—the temptations were too strong to resist. . . . .

LONDON, *June* 28, 1861.

. . . . . I passed the whole afternoon just looking through the British Museum. It is indeed a wonderful place, and far surpassed my highest expectation. . . . .

I was not particularly struck with the Elgin Marbles. It may be a great want of refined taste in me to say so; but I think if the laudations of most people were sifted to the bottom, they would come to the same conclusion. They may be interesting to the antiquarian, but I do not see where the lines of beauty are in those crumbling stumps. Suppose the figures were perfect, the marble is always rough and crumbling on the surface, and they look just like a statue before it is cut out or polished.

There is some beautiful statuary in the Grand Hall and in the Lycian Room. Many of the Assyrian Remains were very interesting, more on account of their antiquity than anything else.

From the Statuary I went to the Library. Here I was perfectly amazed at the vastness of the collection. Nothing is to me a more pleasing sight than a fine collection of books. With the Autographs I was fascinated, and spent a long time in trying to decipher some of them. Think of gazing upon words penned by Luther and Calvin, Erasmus and Huss; of seeing the very Prayer Book written by Lady Jane Grey, upon which her eyes were last fixed ere they were closed in death; the Will of Mary Queen of Scots, and the Magna Charta to which King John in anger affixed his name; pages too of Childe Harold with Byron's own corrections;—all these are indeed treasures. Here are the workings of mind; and, after all, mind triumphs over matter, for a letter of Rubens will bring more in proportion than one of his paintings.

On Thursday morning I called at the American Legation to procure a ticket for the House of Commons. The gentlemen of the Legation were dressing for the Drawing Room, to which I could have gone, but these hard times I would not spend almost $150 for the sake of an hour's pleasure.

I visited the Victoria Cross Gallery, paintings by M. De Sourges of noble deeds of British soldiers in the Crimea, Baltic, and India, for which they have received the V. C. The collection is very good. M. De S. excels in the freeness of his drawing, together with the rich tone which he gives to his pictures.

From thence I went to the Water-Colour Exhibition, Pall Mall. With these pictures I was delighted. There was a beautiful painting of the Acropolis, taken at deep sunset: the whole front of the building is one blaze of light, while far back of the building the moon is rising, and its rays are seen stealing across that part of the porch which is screened from the more powerful rays of the sun. There were many other gems, of which I have not time to speak now. One I noticed particularly—a view of Coblentz just after sunset. I never saw a picture in which subdued, perfect rest was embodied as in this. . . . .

BLACKPOOL, *July* 7, 1861.

A very severe attack of neuralgia in my face has prevented me from going to church this morning. It began yesterday morning, kept me awake nearly all night, and is not much better to-day. Were it not for this I would report myself as perfectly well. Yesterday I bathed in the sea, and enjoyed it greatly. To-day is perfect;—the sea breeze is just enough to be pleasant, neither chilly nor warm. Here, as I sit upon the Cliff and look towards the West, my thoughts fly to that far off land where my loved ones dwell. How my heart is yearning to be with them! Often I wonder—and the thought for the moment brings with it a painful anxiety—Are they well? I shudder to think that the hand of sickness, yes, and the cold, damp hand of death, might be laid upon some one of them, and I would not know it. Yes, the grave might have hid them for ever from my sight, and I would still be looking forward to meeting them again upon earth. The very thought of this fills my heart with the deepest sadness, and causes tears of regret that I ever left them. Yet the happy thought comes, and all is well, "Say unto the righteous that it shall be well with him." Though I would be far from saying that I deserve such a name, still I cannot but think that I have an interest in this precious promise. My Father cares for you all. I know it. To His care, in earnest prayer, have I commended you; and I know that He will do with you all as seemeth good in His sight, ordering all things so that it shall be well with us in life, and that in the life to come we shall drink of rivers of pleasure for evermore.

What cause I have for deep gratitude to God this day! He has in His wonderful goodness brought me back almost from the very gates of death, and I am again perfectly well and strong. Disease has not left its fell mark upon me. I am again myself, and the world is bright before me. As Dr. Quain told me, "Blessed with a good constitution, you have every prospect of a long and healthful life," what a responsibility rests upon me to work for Christ! Although much precious time has been wasted, still it is not all gone; the opportunities have not all fled; there is yet time to work, and there is much work to be done. You remember the reason Nehemiah gave for the rapid manner in which the temple was built—"The people had a mind for the work." What we all need is a mind to work for Christ. We have mind enough for the pleasures and pursuits of time, but little enough for the concerns of eternity. . . . . .

What Sabbath desecration there is here! You do not see one or two persons engaged in some violent profanation of God's holy day, such as swearing, billiard-playing, &c., but nearly every one seems so listless. But few attend church. I heard an old Presbyterian elder saying, "It is too warm to go to church this morning," (the thermometer not more than 70° or 75°;) yet he can walk in the sun up and down the cliffs the whole morning. And so it is—multitudes lolling about on the grass, or strolling along the sands, seeming as though they thought if they committed no actual sin they were keeping the Sabbath properly. I really must say, that as far as I have seen, the English by no means keep the Sabbath as well as we do in America. . . . . . At the dinner-table my neuralgia became so excruciating, that in a fit of desperation I took chloroform. It put me asleep, removed the pain, and I have been but a short time up from its effects. It is now 9 o'clock; the sun has just set, and the long, soft, English twilight has set in. The Promenade is crowded, and from my little window I now look down and see them passing and repassing along the Cliff; yet though I am alone, I am sure that none of them is happier than I. . . . . .

There often comes over me an indescribable feeling of loneliness. The only place I feel at home is at the mercy-seat. There I do feel that I am not at least a stranger. Although very far from what I should be, I feel that I am welcome, and can tell all my cares and thoughts to One who can be touched with a feeling of my infirmity—to One who can enter fully into all my feelings, and can give me that assistance and grace which I so much need. May that mercy-seat ever be to us the happiest, most welcome spot upon earth; may we ever go to it with joyous hearts, and say when leaving, Truly "it was good for me to be there:" there may we find a well of purest joy and peace, from which we may drink to the satisfying of our souls. . . . . .

I often think of my own little brothers and yours. The world is before them, and they are rapidly advancing toward its temptations and trials. God grant that their every talent may be entirely devoted to His fear and service; that Wisdom's ways may be their ways, and that their footsteps may be directed in her paths. My own sisters, too, I often think of. My heart's desire and prayer for them is that they may be saved. Oh, that God in His infinite goodness and mercy would lead them seriously to consider the things that pertain to their peace before they shall be for ever hidden from their eyes. . . . . .

July 9.—Although the morning was cloudy and the waves dashed angrily against the rocks as though foreboding a storm, we did not give up our intention of spending the day at Furness Abbey. So after a substantial breakfast we took the train for Fleetwood, and soon found ourselves at the end of the long pier jutting out into Morecambe Bay. As the tide here has a rise and fall of 25 feet, the pier is necessarily very long and high, so that the steamers can land their passengers at all hours. As it was, the tide was running out very rapidly, and the waters of the river Wye, as they rushed past, reminded us somewhat of the lower rapids at Niagara. Soon we were on board the steam yacht *Helvellyn*, and a more beautiful little vessel I never saw—sharp as an arrow, and fitted up with great comfort and elegance. Precisely at noon we cast off, and the rapid stream swung us round the light-house and out into the open bay. Looking up the bay, we could see in the distance the old county town of Lancaster; while in the foreground were the famous Lancaster Sands, now a thoroughfare, but over which in the course of a few hours the water will be flowing 15 or 20 feet deep.

The scenery of Morecambe Bay has by some been said to surpass that of the far-famed Bay of Naples. Not having seen the latter we cannot express an opinion. To us it was an object of great beauty, as when half way across the sun burst through the clouds, and away in the distance we saw the gray tops of Helvellyn and Langdale Rikes, while on either side the hills were lined with ripening grain.

Soon the grim black walls of Peel Castle confront us, and we are again at shore. This castle was built by the Abbot of Furness in 1327, for the purpose of guarding the adjacent shore, from which the abbey is but a mile or so distant. It was used as a depository for the treasures of the abbey, and the whole colony betook themselves thither as a place of retreat from hostile incursions. . . . . .

The castle consists of a large tower or keep strongly built, with two outer walls and a deep moat, which at high tide was filled with water to the depth of 20 feet. . . . . . The walls are pierced with holes for the purpose of pouring down melted lead upon the unbidden visitors. Arquebuse and culverin were not scarce, as the many remnants testify; and as this was, in the days of Queen Bess, the only port between Milford Haven and Scotland, its being securely held was of the utmost importance.

But we stay too long—the train is waiting, the guard has shouted for the third time, "Gentlemen, *please* take your seats"—so we must be off. Along the narrow causeway, beside the green fields, and through a long dark tunnel, and the train suddenly stops at a beautiful little station, and we are at Furness.

Think of it! the Vale of Deadly Nightshade has been disturbed by a railway; it runs within a few yards of where the old Baron of Kendal had hoped to sleep undisturbed; it whirls along in the very sight of the high altar, and the nave re-echoes the shriek of the engine, where before was heard the *Jubilate Deo* or the solemn requiem for the dead. The abbot's lodge has been rebuilt for a railway station, and a pretty one it is with its flying buttresses and antique chimneys, almost leading one to watch for the grave old dignitary himself, coming forth in cowl and cassock to meet his guests.

Having ordered dinner we sally forth. . . . . And now we enter the little iron gate and the north front of the abbey is before us;—there are the great choir and nave, where many a time the long processions of monks walked at midnight swinging their golden lamps; and there the carved sedilia, where often the old abbot sat in the far back times and listened to the solemn notes of the *De Profundis* chanted by twice a hundred voices.

The stone is a red sandstone, and the architecture the severe Norman, in accordance with the rules of the Order. . . . . On entering, our attention was first directed to the chancel. It extends some 60 or 70 feet to the eastward of the body of the church. It is 20 feet broad, and its walls are 60 feet high. The great east window was 50 feet high; and the painted window, judging from the parts still preserved in Bowness Church, must have been very magnificent. . . . . In the centre of the chancel lies the figure of a knight in armour, cross-legged. In the south wall are the sedilia. These are canopied stalls, adorned in Gothic style; in them the officiating priest sat at intervals during the service of high mass. Those beautiful ornaments have been completely disfigured by the villanous attempts of visitors to hand their names down to posterity by scribbling and scratching them upon the seats and sides. . . . . In the corner are two monuments, supposed to be of two knights of the Lancaster family known to be buried here.

From the chancel we pass into the chapter-house. Here the Order sat in solemn conclave to try cases of misdemeanour and receive applicants for admission to the Order. This is the only building marked with any of the elegance of Gothic sculpture. It has been a noble room, 60 × 45. The roof was vaulted, formed of 12 ribbed arches, and supported by a double row of pillars six in each, the capitals of which were either plain or foliated. . . .

Over this chapter-house was the scriptorium, where the monks illuminated manuscripts.

Passing from this and ascending the hill side, we have a good view of the Vale of Deadly Nightshade, and here we would sit down upon this grassy knoll and contemplate the lovely scene. We have had quite enough of knocking our heads against arches lower now than they once were, and of cracking our shins against broken staircases that lead to nothing. To our left the grand old western tower stands out against a bed of green; and there through its broken arch you may see the avenue lined with the ash, through which came visitors, knights and nobles, to enjoy the abbot's hospitality. Here are the lakes well stocked with fish, and the orchards with fruit; further on are the little cells where the monks often retired to meditate and *pray*.

By far the finest view we got of the ruin was from the east side, when sitting upon the tombstone of some old abbot we looked through the vast, shattered, ruined frame of the once gorgeous window, and saw in perspective the choir and distant arches, the remains of the nave closed in by the woods.

One of the great beauties of Furness consists in the luxuriance of the parasitic foliage, which everywhere is to be found clinging to the walls. Over the arches, around the broken columns of the chapter-house, and in and out the vacant windows clusters the thick ivy; and from innumerable cracks and crannies, from nooks once adorned with the effigy of saint or angel, droops the graceful fern, while moss and lichen conceal the tombs of knights and prelates; and through all, Nature has spread a luxuriant carpet of high green grass, and save in one little room there is no roof but hers.

Ding-a-ling—ding-a-ling—ding-a-ling suddenly broke our reverie, and we were called from the dead to the living, from contemplation of the past to a consideration of the present.

After a very good dinner, and an hour's rest by way of digestion, we resumed our seats in the cars and soon were back at Peel. Here our little steamer was awaiting us, and soon had recrossed Morecambe Bay. Just as the sun was setting we found ourselves back at the hotel, feeling richly repaid by a day spent at Furness Abbey.

WAST DALE HEAD, HEAD OF WAST WATER,
FOOT OF SCAW FELL, *July* 27, 1861.

In this little secluded hamlet, far from civilization, I sit down to write. The people here are in about the 17th century—no post-office, no roads, no newspapers, no anything. All is primitive, and as ignorant as you could well imagine; indeed, from personal observation, I do not think that one in ten can tell how old he is. Here in this little valley, not more than two miles square, they have lived as their fathers and grandfathers did before them, and many of them have reached manhood and never saw the outer world except from the mountain-top when hunting lost sheep. . . . .

The reason why I have time to write here is, that the rest of my party, consisting of my two cousins and a clever young gentleman from Liverpool whom we met yesterday, have gone on to the top of Scaw Fell Pike (3,160 feet), while I, poor city boy, had to give out. I became so nervous and so dizzy that I concluded prudence would be much the better part of valour. I had got to the top of Ling Mell (1,500 feet), almost perpendicular, when my heart began to beat so violently, and I became so giddy as to have to lie down for some time. Finding it quite impossible for me to go on although the tug was over, I requested the party to go forward, intending to come down alone. Coming down was harder than going up, the grass being so wet and the stones so loose as that many times I would slip twenty or thirty feet before I would get my footing. After getting back to our little farm-house I took my glass and walked down to the head of the lake to get a view of Scaw Fell, and a grand one I did get. Just as I arrived at the best place, the misty curtain was lifted from the top of the Pikes, and then I saw them, gray and barren, in bold relief against the deep blue sky. After looking for about ten minutes, Mr. Scaw Fell, thinking I had seen quite enough, and being perhaps rather modest, put on his night-cap and retired. I have got many mosses and ferns upon the hill and crags, which I am pressing in a book. Could my friends see me I am sure they would be amused—a pair of treble thick soled boots, breeches to the knees, satchel on my back, my little cap adorned with stag moss, and to crown all, a good shillelah to assist my pedestrianisms. . . . .

EDINBURGH, *July* 31, 1861.

Here I am in this beautiful old town of eleven-storied houses and bare-legged soldiers—this city of Knox and Chalmers; and where, above all other places, they talk so much and know so little about America. The Messrs. Nelson have received me with the greatest cordiality: to-day I dine with them: they have invited me to spend a week at their country house in the island of Arran—an invitation I am inclined to accept, as I know I will have a pleasant time. . . . .

From my window I have a fine view of the city;—to the right is the old Castle, with its huge Mons Meg pointing towards me; in front is the Old Town, with its Cowgate and Grassmarket—the silent witnesses to the persecutions of those of whom it is said that

> "—— persecution dragged them into fame,
> And chased them up to heaven."

Between the Old and the New Town there is a deep ravine, which has been turned into a beautiful promenade, beneath which the railroad runs; a little to my left is the magnificent monument erected to Sir Walter Scott; while further on is the Calton Hill, crowned with a monument to Nelson. In the background are Arthur's Seat and Salisbury Crags, at whose foot may be seen the ancient towers of Holyrood, where the beautiful Mary once reigned supreme, and where her favourite Rizzio met a bloody death. . . . .

The residence of my friends the Nelsons is at the foot of Arthur's Seat and Salisbury Crags, and from their drawing-room windows there is a splendid view of the neighbouring loch, the fields of Preston, and the ruins of Craigmillar Castle, once a residence of Queen Mary. On opening the door I was greeted by the word "Salve," inscribed in the tiled vestibule; and I assure you it was no empty word—it was welcome indeed, as hearty from the ladies as it had been from the gentlemen of the family. After dinner, in company with Messrs. William and Thomas Nelson, I drove to the Grange Cemetery to visit the grave of Dr. Chalmers. It was just at dusk, and the gates were shut, but we obtained admission from the keeper. We walked slowly up that gravel walk along which once moved a sorrow-stricken city to do their last homage at the grave of him who was the noble champion of their religious liberty. Almost at the end of the walk we came to the spot where, marked by a massive slab, repose the remains of Thomas Chalmers. Turning round, attracted by a familiar name, I stood beside the grave of your former co-pastor Mr. Dickinson; and from his grave I plucked a few flowers, which I am pressing and will bring home to Mrs. D., as I am sure she will value them. A little further on I was again attracted by a slab of Aberdeen granite, on which was chiselled the name Hugh Miller: here again I involuntarily stopped, and thought of that gigantic mind, overwrought and over-tasked, which perished ere its rich treasures were fully given to the world. . . . .

This morning, while pressing the flowers collected last evening, my friend M'Farlane made his appearance. I was delighted to see one so fresh from home, and we had a long talk, after which we ascended Sir Walter Scott's beautiful monument. From thence we went to Edinburgh Castle, where we spent some time in wandering about and inspecting the famous Crown jewels, dating back to King Robert Bruce; we also saw Mary Queen of Scots' room, in which James First of England was born. Returning down High Street, along which many a martyr has been hurried, we entered Grey Friars' Churchyard, where our covenanting forefathers signed the testimony with their blood, and where is the monument erected to the memory of those who fell martyrs in the cause of "Christ's crown and covenant." Here we saw also the monument to Alexander Henderson, the great Reformer. . . . .

Edinburgh is a charming city; and when in the Old Town it requires but little stretch of imagination to fancy one's self living two or three centuries ago. . . . .

LAMLASH, ISLAND OF ARRAN, FIRTH OF CLYDE.
August 11, 1861.

. . . . . I cannot realize that in years I am a man; so gradually has the change stolen upon me, that now when it has come I know it not. I trust I feel what a solemn and important thing it is to set out *right*—to make a proper beginning in the world, for very much of a man's future happiness and success depends upon this. How many a bitter hour and saddening thought it spares him; and what delight he has in thinking that from the beginning all has been well! . . . .

I am enjoying myself exceedingly. All day long I am out sailing, fishing, or walking; so that now I am as brown as a berry; but what difference does that make, when one's health is good.

My plan for Switzerland is now pretty well matured. I shall leave here on Thursday night, and reach Liverpool early on Friday morning, where we will make our necessary purchases. On Saturday morning we will all start for London, and spend the Sabbath either there or in Paris—probably in London. We will then push on to

Switzerland, visiting Geneva, Lucerne, Chamouni, St. Bernard, and in fact everything of interest on the way. I am trying to arrange matters so as to be in Geneva when the Evangelical Alliance meets; and on my way back I will stop in Paris and London. . . . .

LAMLASH, ISLAND OF ARRAN, *August* 18, 1861.

Again the Sabbath has returned. All night long a fearful storm has been raging, and to-day is as wild as you could possibly imagine. The wind is not sighing, but howling down the glen; and the waves are breaking angrily along the shore. . . . . I feel myself daily taking greater delight in prayer and meditation; and yet I hardly dare say this lest I fall into temptation, and become in a measure satisfied with my condition. Oh, how Satan does tempt me!—whenever a sweet sense of my Saviour's presence comes to me, whenever I am thinking with delight on the goodness of God, then Satan comes with some evil thoughts and disturbs my peace. But why this? Do I forget that in this world there is no peace, no rest for the weary, no comfort? All must be a continued, continuing struggle, until we reach that higher, nobler, happier world, where *all is peace.* There the Christian soldier shall at last find rest; there, coming from the dust and heat of the conflict, shall he unbuckle his armour, take off his helmet, lay down his sword, and being clad in the emblem of peace, even the robe of his Redeemer's righteousness, join in the everlasting hymn of praise to a glorified Redeemer, and add another voice to the angelic choir, singing, "Glory, honour, praise and power, to Him that sitteth on the throne, and to the Lamb for ever and ever!"

Sabbath evening.—The storm is over; the angry sea is at rest; the wind has died away, and everything has that peaceful look which seems so especially fitting for the evening of this holy day. Oh, rest, rest, rest! "that I might fly away and be at rest!" This has all day long been the burden of my thoughts. Still, I fondly hope, indeed I may say with a full assurance of truth, that we are daily approaching this rest; that we can take up the words of the beautiful hymn, and sing from the depths of a happy soul,—

"Here in this body pent,
Absent from Thee I roam;
Yet nightly pitch my moving tent
A day's march nearer home."

I have often thought what a blessed thing it would be for ourselves if we could enter heaven together. To be together in life, together in death, to begin together our eternal life in glory, would indeed be happiness. . . . .

Wednesday morning.—I shall remain here perhaps till Monday; then, in company with Mr. Nelson, go to Oban, and make that a central point from which to visit Staffa, Iona, and the Western Highlands. My cousin Andrew, through some misunderstanding, went to Switzerland without me. I am, however, going in September so as to be in Geneva at the Conference, which opens on the 3rd. Indeed I am very glad I am not on the Continent now; the weather is so intensely hot that no one can travel, or even walk, in the middle of the day, and I am sure such weather would do me no good.

I often wish, when I see these Scotch girls how they walk and bear exposure without injury, that our sweet lassies were just like them. The fatigue and exposure which the ladies of our party have undergone in the past ten days would, I was going to say, almost kill the majority of American girls. Although the young ladies here have neither the delicacy of form nor feature which characterizes our own, still they have a fresh bloom of health upon their cheek, even when well up in years, which I should much like to see exchanged for the too often pale look of our American ladies. . . . .

LAMLASH, *August* 26, 1861.

. . . . . I have given up the idea of going to the Evangelical Alliance, and instead will attend the meeting of the British Association at Manchester, which opens on Wednesday first. . . . .

You would be amused could you look in here almost any day and hear the battling I do for America. Sometimes I have as many as a dozen at me at once; and although I cannot, and would not, attempt to deny or excuse much that they say on the Slavery question, still I answer by suggesting to them, by way of remembrance, a few of their own vile sins: they all, however, do me the credit of saying that I am the warmest advocate of what is right in America that they have yet seen. Be sure that whatever may be the tone of the English press, or the action of the English Government, we have the heartfelt sympathy of the great mass of the Scotch people: all they want is a little more decision on the part of the North in regard to the question of Slavery. Nor can I think them wrong; for I know full well that this question was carefully and sedulously excluded from all the prayers and addresses in the Union meetings during the late revival. . . . .

Sad news again from our beloved America. Yet I have not a shadow of a doubt as to the issue. These reverses have gained us a sympathy here that success never would have done. . . . .

BADEN-BADEN, *September* 22, 1861.

. . . . . To-day as I walked through the town and saw every shop open, heard the band playing in front of the Keusall, and everything going on in utter disregard of the Lord's Day, I felt that indeed I was a stranger here. No Sabbath! "There is no God," written on the face of everything. Unhappy country!—poor, miserable people! I could not refrain from lifting up my heart in thanksgivings that my lot was not cast in this place, but in America, among a Sabbath-keeping people;—a land with the Bible; a land, though it may have many faults, I love with my whole heart, and out of which I would not live though a palace were the reward. If there is one thing that I desire to return home for, in addition to my desire to be with my loved ones, it is that I may again enjoy my Sabbath privileges. I long for my Sabbath school, and for our delightful prayer-meetings—for sweet communion with God's children, and for the regular means of grace. I am weary of this ever-changing scene, this bustle of travel, and I long for the quiet of my own native city.

I was reading to-day an exposition of the text, "Thou wilt keep him in perfect peace whose mind is stayed on thee." Notice it. *Perfect peace;* what a promise for the poor, doubting, trembling believer! what a rock on which to build one's struggling hopes! *Perfect peace;* not a peace whose joy is marred by sorrow or remorse; not restless, like the midnight tossings of him whose fevered frame longs for the morning light; not peace to-day and trouble to-morrow. No, no! God will *keep* his dear ones in *perfect peace.* This promise is to us: we have a deep interest in it: it has much to do with our happiness. Have we this peace? Let us examine ourselves, and see whether we have that within us which, when all is dark and black around us, will still keep our souls in *perfect peace*, enabling us to look above and beyond this vale of tears to something brighter and better beyond the skies. . . . .

PHILADELPHIA, *November* 25, 1861.

. . . . . To-night grandmother has left me,* and I feel her loss deeply. No longer is she under the same roof with me: I can no longer go up to her room and tell her my cares and troubles: to see her now I must go to another house, and I cannot be with her as much as formerly. She has been a very good grandmother to me, and much, oh, how much, I owe her! . . . .

* On the death of her son-in-law, John Rumsey, Esq., Mrs. Dennison felt it her duty to live with her widowed daughter.

Sabbath evening, January 12, 1862.

My day's work is just completed. . . . . It has been a great pleasure—more even than ordinary—to wait in the courts of the Lord's house. I felt, and feel as never before, the solemn import of the work in which I am engaged; and am resolved, by God's grace, to be more faithful in my duties. Last night I was reading in your sainted sister's Memoir, and came to those resolutions she penned for her guidance and direction. One of them fixed itself deeply upon me: it was, "To *do* everything as if worth *doing*"—"Make a business of everything that I undertake." I trust that she, being dead, may yet speak to me in this, and that it may inspire me to a more upward earnestness and zeal for my Saviour's cause: He is a precious Saviour, and is worthy of our noblest efforts.

I feel very much encouraged with my mission school. Never had a superintendent a more faithful band of teachers—instant in season and out of season—labouring most faithfully to satisfy both the eternal and temporal wants of their respective little flocks. I feel that my position is a very important and responsible one. Oh that God would give me grace to be faithful. Our work widens and deepens on our hands: to-day we devised still more extended plans of usefulness, which, if we are faithful, God will bless. . . . .

1313 SPRUCE STREET,
Sabbath evening, March 23, 1862.

A rather weary, because idle day, has passed. . . . . It has seemed strange to me to be in the city, not sick, and yet not at my work. It reminded me forcibly of one of those long, weary Sabbaths last spring, when I longed so much to be out, and yet could not be. . . . .

Oh, could I only be what I want to be! I sometimes do despair, when I think of my cold-heartedness, my indifference to the momentous concerns of eternity. To think that at any moment we may be summoned before God! whether waking or sleeping, it matters not. What must we be made of, to live on satisfied in such neglect?

I do not mean that we are not God's children, for I humbly trust that we are; but this should only be a more urgent reason for greater wakefulness and watchfulness. We must be ever ready, with our lamps trimmed, and waiting for our Master. . . . . .

"CLAUGHTON FIRS," BIRKENHEAD,
May 17, 1862.

Here I am, safe in Liverpool; and as I sit in this dining-room I cannot but think of my dreaming the last night I slept at Lansdowne of my being here, and exclaiming to myself, "What a fool I am, to be away thus from my home again!" Now indeed it is reality, and the broad Atlantic rolls between us. We left Queenstown yesterday at 3, and arrived at the anchorage at 12. The confusion in examining the baggage of so many passengers was necessarily great, so that it was nearly 3 o'clock before I left Liverpool. Mr. Caldwell has gone up to Manchester, where I will meet him on Monday. Uncle David says that father wrote him saying that I would remain over all summer;—to which I gave an emphatic denial, and told him that I would not stay later than 7th July.

. . . . . When I look back at our voyage, and think what it might have been, I cannot but think how God has favoured us;—no storms, no fogs, no danger of any kind—all bright, clear, and prosperous. There are few indeed who have as many prayers as I have daily offered for their welfare: I know it, I feel it, and I trust it may but stimulate me to greater fervency before the throne of grace. I was thinking to-day, as I left the ship, how in a few hours we would all be scattered, and never meet again until we stand before God's judgment-seat. I trust that I did nothing to dishonour the name of my Saviour: I am not conscious of anything; but that is not the question. Did I do anything for His cause—anything to honour His name? I trust my example was not all for nought; and yet, how do we every day come far short of our duty, and do nothing as we should for our blessed Saviour, who died that we might live. The delight, the joy of doing good! how the heart thrills with pleasure at the thought of doing that which pleases Him who did so much for us! . . . .

MANCHESTER, *May* 22, 1862.

. . . . . In my reading last night I was much struck with the following verse (Job xv. 11), "Are the consolations of God *small* with thee?" How much there is in that question to one who is a professed follower of the Lord Jesus! on a moment's thought, with what force and power does it come home to the mind! To me, at the time, peculiarly so. I was sitting in my room in the

"Queen's Hotel" alone, about midnight. Sad thoughts filled my mind. I felt the tear starting in my eye, and looking down at the Bible which lay open on my knee before me, my eye fell upon the words, "Are the consolations of God small with thee?" What comfort they brought! sadness vanished like a flash. How, thought I, could they be small with one who has enjoyed so much;—and, with a heart overflowing with thankfulness and joy, I knelt at the mercy-seat, and committed all to the care of Him who has promised that it shall be well with the righteous. Now my fears are all gone, and I dwell with increased delight upon those precious words. Lay them up in your heart, and let them lead you to ask more and expect more from God; let them increase your faith in Him who has failed in not one thing that He has promised.

LONDON, *May* 24, 1862.

I left Manchester last evening at 5, and came up here, arriving at 11. I am at my old quarters, the "Castle and Falcon," where I am well taken care of. I had a pleasant trip coming up, barring the gentlemen talked too much when I wanted to be quiet. Can you imagine it!—three *sociable* Englishmen, and all in favour of the North! Such a spectacle I never saw before, never expected to see, and may never see again. I suggest that, for the character of the nation, they be cased, and added to the list of trophies in the Exhibition.

To-morrow I shall try and hear Rev. Dr. Hamilton; and in the evening, either Spurgeon or Newman Hall.

Since I commenced gargling with salt I find my throat is much better, and I hope to find from it permanent relief. . . . .

LONDON, *May* 25, 1862.

It is almost midnight, and I have sought the retirement of my little chamber to write. Another Sabbath is almost gone, and what have I done to improve it? Not feeling very bright I have stayed in the hotel all day—the most of the time in my room, reading, praying, and meditating. Under the circumstances, I thoroughly enjoyed the day. The sermon which I read was one which peculiarly pleased me, and suited my circumstances: it was one of Dr. Addison Alexander's, entitled "Intercessory Prayer," from 1 Thess. v. 25, "Brethren, pray for us." You have the book; read this sermon: I think you will like it. It exhibits God's manifold rich grace most beautifully; showing how little God might have done for us, compared with what He has, and yet have saved us. Of these blessings, the privilege of praying for others is dwelt upon with great force and beauty. We can appreciate these words: we know, when far separated, how it has gladdened our hearts to be able to meet at the throne of grace, and to feel that we can plead for one another. This is a blessed gift of God. Though we cannot save others, though we cannot stand for them in judgment, still we *can* pray for them, and we have been promised that "the prayer of faith availeth much." Let us try and realize this more—look upon it more as a gift of God than as a matter of course; and may this lead us to value the privilege more highly. . . . . How fervent our petitions are for the objects dearest to our hearts! What desolation would it be were this denied us, and we could only pray for ourselves! Do not fail to read this sermon, and notice how beautiful it is, especially the conclusion.

Monday, May 26.—All day long I have been at the International Exhibition; and now that I sit down to say something about it, I know not where to begin or what to write. Paintings and machinery, bronzes and china, light-houses, Armstrong guns and jewellery, are all in one confused mass in my brain, and I hardly know how to separate them. Perhaps I had better tell you what I saw as I went along; and first, as to the building. It is in Kensington, adjoining the grounds of the South Kensington Museum and the Royal Horticultural Society: being more intended for permanence than the Palace of 1851, its walls are of stone and brick, and its roof of wood and glass: it is not, as the other was, a "Crystal Palace;" nor has it that beauty of form nor convenience of internal arrangement which (as I recollect it) characterized the building of 1851. There are too many "annexes," as they are called, running out from the main building, utterly bewildering the visitor in his endeavours to see everything. At either end of the nave there are domes, one greater and one lesser. The internal decorations are much superior to the other building: the painting is simple, but in good taste; and the harmony of colour is striking throughout. Around the circle of the dome and along the lower edges of the roof and the facings of the galleries, are painted, in antique letter, texts of Scripture, or the sayings of great men, all tending to give God the glory for everything. The display (except from the United States) is, as might be expected, far superior to anything in former years; the English people seem to have laboured hard to make this the greatest of all Exhibitions, and I believe they have fully succeeded.

The first thing which strikes the eye of the visitor is a beautiful fountain in encaustic tile-work; the subject is mythological, and as that is a branch in which I am not posted, especially the mythology of Britain, I cannot speak of the subject, but merely say that the effect is beautiful: around it, filling the four corners, are cases of magnificent oxydized silver-work; between these are beautiful bronze figures, large as life. Looking down the nave you see the entrance to the various courts faced by bronze and iron gates of great beauty. Gun trophies and cannon trophies, fur trophies and jewel trophies—all of them composed of the most valuable and perfect specimens of their kind, and each a gem in itself.

The collection of Paintings is by far the finest I have seen. It is said that for general pictures (I mean leaving out such as the Immaculate Conception, than which there are a thousand here I would rather have,) it is the finest collection ever brought together. The Queen and the Emperor, all the galleries of England and Europe, have lent their choicest gems. There is a likeness of Eugenie by Winterhalter, just finished, to which I would be almost tempted to apply the term angelic: also, a picture of the Princess Royal and her children, by the same artist, which is very fine. All the gems of Hogarth, Landseer, Cooper, Eddy, Lawrence, &c., are here collected, and you can study them from their first attempt to their master-pieces.

The collection of Statuary is fine, though by no means to be compared with the Paintings.

The display of Gobelins Tapestry and Sevres China is superb; and indeed, in bronzes, jewellery, and all that is beautiful and ornamental, France carries the palm. She exhibits likewise considerable machinery, which is very ingenious.

The Machinery department is very fine. It occupies a room 500 × 1200 feet; and there you may see in active operation, either full size or in miniature, all the appliances of steam — engines, pumps, cotton-spinning, weaving, cloth-making, coining, diamond-cutting, &c.

But I weary you with my detail. It is, in short, a World's Fair, in every sense of the word. There you see people and their works from every clime and nation; and I could not but think, as I came away, What a wonderful creature man is! Who could have made him but an infinite God! What an overwhelming argument, I thought, is this against those who call man the production of chance, or the improvement of a lower being! The only way of accounting for such versatile and profound genius is to be found in these words, " *God* breathed into man the breath of life, and he became a *living soul.* . . . .

I feel every day that I cannot be sufficiently thankful for what God has done for me. He has thrown around me many safeguards, and given me grace to resist many temptations; and that grace I know will ever be equal to the trial. Being, as I have been in my travels, all alone, and with an unlimited purse, many a young man in similar circumstances has strayed far from the path of virtue and righteousness, and returned to his home a wreck of his former self. God has mercifully preserved me: to Him be all the glory. . . . .

MILLTOWN, BANBRIDGE, IRELAND,
June 10, 1862.

. . . . . On Saturday I called upon several clergymen, Dr. Edgar and others, and then went out with George Weir to his father's place, Lisnabreeny, about 2½ miles from Belfast, upon the mountain side. Here I was heartily welcomed by all the family, and made to feel, as far as in their power, at home. Home, however, is where the heart is; and all attempts to make one, when absent, feel that he is at home, only serve to render the void more perceptible. Such were my felt thoughts as I gathered with this family around their fireside, and saw how happy they were.

On Sabbath morning we drove to Belfast in a jaunting-car, in a pouring rain, to hear Dr. Cooke; but, unfortunately, he was sick and could not preach. In the evening we went to the church at Castlereagh, near Mr. Weir's house, and heard an excellent sermon. On Monday I had contemplated visiting an Irish fair; but the young gentleman who was to have gone with me was suddenly called away to see a dying patient, and I did not care about going alone. To-day I left Belfast at 1, arrived at Lurgan at 2, and then drove six miles over to this place, the beautiful homestead of the Smyth family. I have no doubt but that I shall enjoy the few days that I am to remain with them, for they are very hospitable.

On my way over from Lurgan I visited Donacloney Church, where father was baptized, and where he worshipped up to the time of his going to America. In the yard beside the church my grandparents are buried, and their children have marked the place by a neat slab and railing.

The weather here is most depressing—rain, chilling rain, every day without intermission. If I had not before me the prospect of a speedy return, I would get the blues so badly as to be a most incurable case. This afternoon I have been laid hold of by my father's old pastor and some others of the congregation; and nothing will satisfy them but that I must remain here over Sabbath, and address their Sabbath school. Now you must know that in this section of the country "Stuart" is a charmed name, and is held as the synonym of something very good; and I fear very much that if I stay I would sadly remove the impressions they have of me, for, from what I can learn, some one has given them far too good an opinion of my abilities......

This night three weeks, should all go well, I will again land upon my native shores......

LITTLETON, N. H., *September* 27, 1862.

Here we are, after a long ride of 170 miles, in this painfully quiet town, where we are obliged to spend the Sabbath. We left Springfield this morning at 8 o'clock, viâ the Connecticut Valley Railroad, and arrived here at 6. The scenery is very fine. Yesterday afternoon we drove about Springfield, and among other places visited the Cemetery, and could testify of it, as the English fop did of Pompeii, "A pretty place, but sadly out of repair." Mother came home suffering a good deal from dyspepsia, and went at once to bed; and I myself, being rather stupid, retired at the premature hour of 8. Do you know, I think I am rather a spoiled child for travelling: I do not care to see sights, natural or artificial, as much as I did a year ago. To take me travelling now, as far as seeing anything goes, is just throwing the money away. I do not mean that I do not enjoy myself; but it is the enjoyment, or rather negative pleasure, produced by general change of employment and scene, and not by any particular object. We shall remain in the White Mountains the most of next week, returning to Springfield to spend the Sabbath, and then go on Monday to Albany and Niagara. . . . . . I cannot help thinking, as I sit half shivering in this little room, lit by a miserable camphene lamp, and but barely furnished, how much comfort people are willing to sacrifice for the sake of gadding about and seeing a little of the world . . . . .

Sabbath, Sept. 28.—I have just come down from the cupola, where for some hours I have been enjoying the distant view of the mountains, and the changing foliage in the valley between. . . . . . This morning we went to the Congregational Church, and heard a very excellent sermon on the temptation of Christ. The church was very cold, and I fear that my feelings rather interfered with my full enjoyment of the sermon. The minister began his sermon with a supposition from which I differed entirely; namely, that Christ's temptation was not an actual event, but a vision. He endeavoured to prove his statement by quoting the visions of Daniel, Ezekiel, and Peter, ignoring entirely the fact that we are expressly told in Holy Writ that these latter were visions. I would like to know how he would make out our Saviour's fasting forty days and nights to be a vision? If so, then he did not fast, but only dreamed that he fasted. Is not this absurd?

LETTERS TO C. H. W.

LETTERS TO C. H. W.

N collecting materials for the preparation of this volume, the author of the following letter was requested to furnish any of Willie's letters that would aid the writer in his work. Although a great disparity existed in the ages of these correspondents, yet, from a similarity in tastes and pursuits, especially in the blessed work of founding and carrying forward Mission Sabbath Schools in the outskirts of our large cities, an unusually warm and mutual attachment sprang up, which continued to increase in strength until God ended the plans and labours of his younger servant by taking him up to a higher and holier sphere of labour.

Accompanying a large package of letters Mr. Wolff writes to the author:—

CINCINNATI, *April* 5, 1864.

DEAR SIR,

Your favour of the 1st instant is before me. As requested, I hereby send you all the letters at present within my reach written by our deceased friend Wm. D. Stuart. As representative documents they will furnish you with all in my power to give. Cheerfully, too, will I give my views "of the mind, heart, and character of William."

1st. *His mind.*—Having conversed with him uninterruptedly for hours at a time, touching upon almost all topics adapted to miscellaneous conversation, and frequently attempting to solve moral problems pertaining to the happiness of man, we never parted but my memory retained certain admirable axioms that he forcibly stated, and which had been so clearly set forth as to place his mind, in my estimation, far above that of the young men of the age. Among the many pleasing themes was the one referring to the influence our acquirements here would have upon our progress in the better land. His very inmost soul would kindle at the thought of eternal progression. "Oh," said he to me on one occasion, "I have obtained a glimpse of God's wonderful creative power and goodness, through my investigations by the microscope, that I had no conception of before; and while man has been given the power thus minutely to examine the beauties of sin-cursed nature here, what will be the powers of untrammelled mind beyond the grave!"

There appeared a wonderful intuitive perception in the grasp of his mind. In many instances he would catch the meaning fully before half my sentence would be completed. Then, too, there was a sturdiness, a wholesome vigour and strength in his mind, remarkable in any one, but rare as the most precious stone in the person of a wealthy man's son.

2nd. *His heart.*—A line or two will explain all I could say. It was gentle as a woman's, noble as the most chivalrous could require, and true as the needle to the pole.

3rd. *His character.*—In our most intimate intercourse—and there were times when he would talk to me in the most confidential manner—there was a lofty sentiment, a pureness of motive and intention, an abhorrence of anything unjust or unmanly, that stamped him in my estimation the purest, noblest, best young man among the very many I have known.

4th. *His administrative powers.*—On visiting his Mission Sabbath School for the first time, it was remarkable what a change was wrought in his whole demeanour on entering the stand to open the exercises. There were among his Sabbath-school children both boys and girls, some as unruly and wicked as the purlieus of the by-ways and alleys of the most wretched part of the city could furnish. They were unused to control or discipline; and yet when he took the stand, and commanded order and silence, it was yielded at once. The quiet, firm, but gentle dignity; the commanding presence in one so young; the ease and grace with which it was accomplished, proved it to be a talent never acquired, but a gracious gift from God. Unlike others thus gifted, he seemed to be humbly unconscious of this pre-eminence to rule and control.

The whole discipline of the school was in accordance with the above.

It is needless for me to elaborate. You will have access to all that is needed to make your Biography complete. . . . . Let me, however, make a suggestion. Cannot you prepare one for the public Sabbath-school libraries? It would be invaluable as an incentive for our rich families to set apart sons and daughters to work for the Lord in the Sabbath schools. . . . . . I remain,

Dear Sir,

Truly yours,

CHAS. H. WOLFF.

PHILADELPHIA, *March* 23, 1860.

DEAR SIR,

In our express parcel from the store to-day I send you the Bible which you desired me to obtain for you. The long delay was occasioned by a difficulty in obtaining the edition you desired, and in getting a cover made; all, however, is now complete, and I trust will meet with your full approval.

Your commission I have not executed to the letter, but rather beg that you will accept of this as a token of regard from one who is a fellow-worker with you in the Christ-appointed work of bringing in the lambs of the flock, training them for usefulness in this world, and fitting them, by the grace and assistance of God, for happiness in the next. . . . .

Wishing you joy and success in all your endeavours to promote our Master's kingdom, I am

Yours faithfully,

WM. D. STUART.

PHILADELPHIA, *September* 7, 1860.

MY DEAR FRIEND,

. . . . . My mission school has resumed. Fall work with fresh vigour. As long as the warm weather lasts we have open-air services, which are very successful. Our audiences are mixed, generally of the lowest class; yet they are models of decorum and attention. On last Sabbath afternoon we held two meetings: the first at 4 o'clock, in the worst den of wickedness in the city; we continued there for three quarters of an hour, and distributing tracts, left for our second meeting, which we held among the whites in another neighbourhood. We continued in this latter place for an hour and a quarter, and again distributing tracts dismissed them until the evening. At our first meeting we had an audience of about 100; at the second about 500.

Our plan of procedure is simply this:—Three or four of us go together, and asking permission to stand upon some one's steps, we begin to sing a hymn, one of our number handing slips of paper with the hymns printed to all who come; as soon as we close the singing another immediately begins a prayer; then a few striking verses of Scripture are read and commented upon; then we sing and speak alternately, the addresses varying in length from five to ten minutes. This is taking the Gospel to their very doors, making them hear it whether they will or no; and then if they still refuse, their destruction is with themselves. This branch of our labour is new, but has made a good start. Pray for our success: we need your prayers.

I am now only awaiting a letter from Lieut. Blackmore (who has been for twenty-eight years successfully engaged in bringing back unfortunate females in London), to take measures for the initiation of a like movement in our own city. As this would injure us much, should it be a failure, we keep it entirely to ourselves for the present —thinking and praying over it *often*. . . . .

PHILADELPHIA, *October* 12, 1860.

I regret that I have so long been compelled to forego writing to you; the more so because I desired to thank you most heartily for the kind, *more than friendly*, advice which you gave me when last we met. It was to me a double assurance that I have in you a friend indeed, and words cannot express my gratitude to you for it, nor tell you how much good it has done me. I would have written you long ere this, but my eyes would not permit me to write at all. I strained them so much in preparing my Essay on "The Microscope," that I have hardly been able to use them since.

A very fortunate opening has been made for me in the store. I have entire charge of the White Goods; in addition to which I am to have four first class Linen accounts, which will keep me pretty busy. Feeling now that this department is entirely my own, it gives me an impulse such as I never felt before. Judging from my own experience, I think that there is nothing like making a young man (no matter how young) feel that there is a responsibility attached to him. I feel it now, and it acts like magic upon me, urging me on in a manner I never knew before.

I am very busy preparing for Gough's lecture at the Academy of Music, for the benefit of our mission. We expect to realize enough to support a missionary next winter and supply a Dorcas society.

Our school is filling up rapidly. We average about seventy-five, with a corps of eight teachers. We consider this a good year's work, in a neighbourhood where before an attendance of five could only be got after seven years labour. Our third Anniversary will be held on the first Sabbath of December, in the afternoon. I wish you could be with us. Nothing would give me greater pleasure than to hear a word from you. Enclosed find a tract which I prepared for our Out-Door Mission.* . . . .

PHILADELPHIA, *November* 28, 1860.

. . . . . Since I wrote you, Mr. Gough has delivered two lectures for the benefit of my mission school, in the Academy of Music, to large and brilliant audiences. We cleared about $1100—a good fund to work on during the winter. Last evening we established our Dorcas society, and everything bids fair for great success.

All the time I could spare from the store I have been devoting to studying out an apparatus to give microscopic exhibitions with an artificial light, so that they

* See p. 333.

may be given at night. Thus far we have succeeded perfectly, and I hope to be able to give an exhibition early in January.....

Business is stagnated completely. Most of our manufactories are working on half time. I fear there will be much suffering this winter. Yet, truth and right are mighty, and will prevail. I believe that a glorious future is before our country. The blackest storm precedes the clearest weather; and when these Fire Eaters are brought to their right mind, and the people wake up, as I think they are doing, to see the necessity of putting honest, yes, and God-fearing men in power, then all will roll on well. We are in the hands of a good and gracious God: let us but trust Him as we should, and all will be well.

PHILADELPHIA, *January* 22, 1861.

..... Since I wrote you, our Sabbath School Anniversaries, Festivals, and Annual Meetings have taken place. On last evening our Sabbath School Association met, and the Reports of our Mission Schools were presented: they were of the most interesting and cheering character. My own school never was better: we have 117 children on the roll, and about 75 in regular attendance. Our Dorcas Society has clothed and provided for over 60 families, and our children are now comfortable and neat. Our Report shows a distribution of over 14,000 pages of tracts, and over 700 persons conversed with upon the subject of their soul's salvation. There is an increased and growing interest in our city in the cause of Sabbath schools, and especially mission schools. Christians are beginning to wake up to the fact that something must be done for the children going to our public schools, where they are denied the privilege of reading or studying God's Holy Word, in order that they may not grow up and go out into the world with a Christless and Godless education.

Our noon-day prayer-meetings continue crowded, and with unabated interest.

I have just finished reading a book of great interest—"Motley's History of the Dutch Republic:" if you have not read it, and have the time, I would heartily recommend it to your perusal. I think that the character of William of Orange should be familiarly known to every Christian.

I see by the London periodicals that there is a great movement among the working men. Twice a week they hold prayer-meetings, not in the day time, for they must be at their work, but from eleven at night until six in the morning: they meet for prayer, conversation, and the devising of plans wherewith the better to reach those of their companions who are careless and indifferent: after breakfasting together they separate to their different work places. I firmly believe that the present year will witness greater and more momentous events than any previous. . . . .

PHILADELPHIA, *April* 17, 1861.

. . . . . Since your delightful visit to me I have been improving rapidly, owing to a continuation of fine weather, which enabled me to take a great deal of exercise. My breast is still quite sore, but it is gradually healing, and I am enabled to hold myself tolerably straight. A gentleman who had not seen me since I was taken sick, met me in the street the other day: throwing up his arms in perfect amazement, he exclaimed, "Why, William, I am very sorry to see you looking so badly;" and then, after a few moments' conversation, he gravely asked me, "Has your physician any hopes at all of your recovery?" Consolation, at any rate. I laughed, and told him I was getting quite well; at which he seemed greatly astonished. ..... I suppose that, comparatively removed as you are from the scene of action, your city is hardly so excited as ours in regard to war. Over 8,000 men have been enlisted since Monday, and all our well-drilled volunteer corps are ready to move at a moment's notice...... Large bodies of troops are constantly passing through to Washington; and from every public building, newspaper office, and many private dwellings, the Stars and Stripes are waving. The old Keystone State is aroused, and she will again prove herself as gallant and as brave as upon the plains of Mexico.....

I cannot but think and ponder over the present condition of affairs—a portion of our Confederation striving by every means which Satan has placed within their power to tear down and trample upon the noblest and freest Government the world ever saw—the heritage committed to us in sacred trust by those who bled that it might live; and to establish upon a firmer and more enduring basis the vilest, most fiendish, and most Satanic system of oppression and degradation, both of body and soul.

We have might and right on our side, and I believe

that the God of armies will fight for us as He did for our forefathers when they strove to drive oppression from the land. And now that the struggle has begun, my voice is, Let it go on until that fearful evil shall be once and for ever driven from among us—when the oppressed shall go free, and the slave shall no more hear the voice of his master! . . . . .

PHILADELPHIA, *May* 15, 1861.

. . . . . I have just made up my mind to go to Europe. I sail on Saturday in the *City of Baltimore.* G. W. is going out in her; and as several physicians have advised me that the best thing I could do would be to take this trip, I have concluded to go at once, while I am sure of good Christian company. My stay is very indefinite—certainly not longer than six months. I feel quite well now, but am still very weak.

And now farewell. May God bless you and yours—watch over and keep you in health and happiness—pour out upon you abundantly His richest blessings, and make you all His own dear children. May I not ask you in your prayers to remember the wanderer (as for the time being I shall be). Pray for him that he may be kept very near to his Saviour; that his conduct not only may be such as becometh the Gospel of Christ, but that he may be beautiful *within*—one who may be every whit a Christian, that is, Christ-like. . . . . .

PHILADELPHIA, *November* 13, 1861.

Unless you have heard of my return from some other source, you will, I think, be rather surprised to find me writing you once more from my own home......

They tell me that I am quite altered, having grown much stouter and browner than when I went away. I am sure I never enjoyed such perfect health before; and the next thing for me to do is to keep it. I found all well at home, and looking as before; but there was a sadness attending that reunion—one loved face was missing*—one dear one was absent from that family circle, never to return. I could not but contrast our condition half a year since—he in perfect health, and I much wasted by disease. Now he has been taken, whilst I have been fully restored, and re-invigorated for my duties.

Poor aunt F. is a perfect wreck, wasted almost to a shadow. It is indeed sad for her to be left so lonely after thirty-three years of as happy a life as ever any woman enjoyed and that is saying a great deal.

I find my mission school prosperous. We have about 150 scholars, and 10 teachers. I notice much improvement in the children, and am greatly cheered in my work......

PHILADELPHIA, *January* 15, 1862.

.....Our congregation has done me the honour to make me a trustee and their treasurer; so that between the duties of the latter and my mission school I have but

* John Rumsey, Esq., died September 18, 1861.

little leisure. I have adopted the plan which I believe to be a good one—namely, never to seek an office, but if chosen to one, accept, if you can give its duties their full and proper attention, and you feel you can do good.

With my mission school I am greatly encouraged. Never had superintendent a more faithful, self-denying band of teachers, so unceasing in their efforts for both the spiritual and temporal good of their scholars. I have good reason to think that they are all men and women of prayer; and you well know that with such a power success cannot but follow. We held our fourth Anniversary on the first Sabbath of December, and a Festival on New Year's Day; both of which were occasions of great interest.....

PHILADELPHIA, *November* 7, 1862.

..... Only a day or two ago I was thinking how much of my life and energy has left me; and I almost forget how "very well" feels. I do not mean by this to murmur, for I know that I am in His hands who "doeth *all* things well," and who surely knows what is best for me.

I am much ashamed of myself in not having long ere this thanked you for having planned such a visit for me to your own home—a visit which would have given me so much pleasure, and which would have left behind it such pleasant memories.

And now to a little fact which, I am sure, for my sake you will be glad to hear. My physicians have advised me to spend the winter in the West Indies; and I will sail from New York on December 9. But before that I intend to do as you have often advised me—get married. You know, my dear friend, what great pleasure it would give me to have you present on that occasion. . . . . . In these expressions the bride-elect joins with me most cordially. . . . . The wedding will be on Tuesday, 25th instant. . . . . .

PHILADELPHIA, *November* 18, 1862.

I wrote you last week in regard to my approaching marriage. In view of my continued sickness, it has been deferred ten days. . . . . .

GOD'S THREATENINGS.

[The subject of this Memoir, while engaged in his mission work, was in the habit of distributing the following paper as a Tract. It has been ascertained that he was himself the author of it. See p. 324.]

"E is faithful that promised," are words of sweet consolation and comfort to the child of God. When surrounded by enemies, temporal and spiritual; when the heavens are dark, and no kindly ray of light gleams through to lighten and cheer the saddened soul—even in that hour the child of God clings in earnest faith to these precious words, "He is faithful that promised." Yes, faithful to the end. But as "He is faithful that promised," so is He equally faithful that threatened. Mark these solemn words, "He will by no means clear the guilty," uttered as they were amid the thunderings and lightnings of Sinai, when God in his glory appeared unto Moses, and proclaimed himself a God "forgiving iniquity and transgression and sin." He devised a glorious plan for the salvation of fallen man; but when that has been set aside and rejected, there is no means, not even with God, with whom all things are, by which the guilty sinner can be saved. God's justice, his honour, his integrity, demand that the guilty sinner shall suffer the penalty due to him for sin.

Reader! are you clinging to any hope of future mercy for salvation. Do you hope that God is so full of compassionate tender love, that when he sees you going down to eternal punishment He will in pitying mercy devise some way whereby you yet may be saved? Be not deceived! God's love is infinite and unchangeable: so is His justice. Those whom He loves, and who obey His commands, He will love to the end; and those who reject the offers of his mercy He will punish to the uttermost. God "is not slack concerning his promises:" neither is he slack concerning his threatenings. The wrath of man time will wear away and appease; but not so with the eternal God. He is "a jealous God." No one who rejects the offer of his Son—his "only-begotten and well-beloved Son"—shall pass on unpunished.

There is no cleft in all Sinai where you can escape the vengeance of the coming storm. You may cry,—

"Hide me, O my Saviour, hide!

but that Saviour will have become your accuser, and your judge.

Sinner! are you yet suffering your precious and immortal soul to be tossed upon the ocean of uncertainty? Are you yet trusting to that which is the most impossible thing under heaven—God's changeableness. Heaven and earth may change, but God cannot. Unalterable as Himself, His precepts and His threatenings have stood, and will stand for ever. Trust to no future mercy, which cannot be, but take God at His word, and come to Him now; or else that same voice, which now, in tender, loving accents, invites you, pleads with you to come and find rest in Jesus, will be heard in stern tones bidding your condemned and guilty soul—"Depart into everlasting fire, prepared for the devil and his angels."

"Time's sun is fast setting, its twilight is nigh,
Its evening is falling in clouds o'er the sky,
Its shadows are stretching in ominous gloom,
Its midnight approaches—the midnight of doom!
Then haste, sinner, haste, there is mercy for thee;
And wrath is preparing—flee, lingerer, flee."

LETTERS TO PHIL.

LETTERS TO PHIL.

THE following extracts are from a correspondence with his most intimate friend, nearly of his own age. While a playful vein of humour pervades the entire correspondence, the subject nearest the writer's heart—the religion of Christ—is prominently uppermost.

SPRING BROOK, *September* 29, 1858.

DEAR PHIL.,

It was with no ordinary feelings of pleasure that I learned on last Saturday evening that you had at last determined to unite with the Church, and cast in your lot with the people of God.

I almost feel like reproaching you for not making known such an important event to me yourself; and yet I think your feelings must be somewhat similar to my own—for I never had the courage to tell my mother even when I determined to join the Church.

I feel confident, Phil., that you have fully considered the subject in your own mind, and feel the responsibility you are about to take upon you. Never of yourself can you fulfil your obligations; but seek wisdom and strength from on high. Pray earnestly to God for the outpouring of His Holy Spirit upon you, and He will give you ability to walk a holy, consistent, Christian life, letting others see that you have been with Jesus. And that God will abundantly bless you, and make you one of His own adopted children, is the prayer of

Your sincere friend,

WM. D. STUART.

[After giving some account of his visit to the mines of Wisconsin and to Chicago, he closes his letter under date of Mineral Point, June 24, 1859, thus:—]

I am very glad to hear of J. M'A. being at the prayer-meetings. I have always felt a deep interest in him, and have ever remembered him in my prayers. I cannot but think that he too will be brought into the kingdom of our blessed Saviour. God will hear and answer prayer. Influence him, dear Phil., by your prayers and example. I know there is much good in him, though, I fear, deeply hid.

Remember me to my associates in our Monday evening prayer-meetings, but especially to the Sabbath school, to the teachers, and to the little ones, for the welfare of whom I am deeply solicitous. And now, that the Shepherd of Israel, that good Shepherd of the flock, may watch over and preserve us through life, and afterwards receive us into his kingdom, is ever the earnest prayer of

Yours affectionately,

WILL.

On board Steamer "Lady Elgin,"
Straits of Mackinaw, *July* 13, 1859.

Dear Phil.,

Here I am, away upon Lake Michigan, nearly two thousand miles from home, and bound for the Copper Diggings. But perhaps you will say, "Where have you been? what have you seen since you last wrote?" Let me tell you. My last letter was, I believe, dated from Mineral Point. Having stayed there a week, we took the cars for Prairie du Chien. The same evening we went on board the splendid steamer "Itasca," *en route* for St. Paul. For an hour all went "merry as a marriage bell," when suddenly a fearful crash, and a shaking in the upper cabin (for you must know that the upper cabins of these boats are frequently blown off and float down the river, much to the dismay of those on board), warned us of danger. It was indeed a fearful night. One who has not seen it has no idea of the sublime fury of a Mississippi storm. In the midst of this we struck a large raft, which carried away our rudder and back works, crippling us completely. Fortunately, we were near an island, on which the boat was run, until damages could be repaired.

Next morning was bright and beautiful, and never did I enjoy anything more than the sail up the Mississippi. As we entered Lake Pepin, which is but a widening of the river, the first object that attracted my attention was the "Maiden's Leap," where the fair Winona, who had been wedded by her father to a noble chief, but who loved another and an humbler man, rather than marry him who was not the chosen of her heart, on the eve of her marriage cast herself from the lofty crag. The story is, as far as I can learn, true; there are Indians now living in the neighbourhood who certify to it.

With St. Paul I was much disappointed. It is a very wicked place—judging from the immense amount of gambling and number of drinking shops. Making my stay here short, I went up to Minneapolis, where I spent a week delightfully. I saw Minnehaha. The beautiful maiden, daughter of the arrow-head maker, chief of the Dacotahs, alas! she had gone. I will not attempt to describe Minnehaha: it would be like a journeyman painter attempting to copy Raphael—a stone mason to model from Michael Angelo.

Minnesota is a grand place—glorious climate—splendid scenery. Nowhere can you drive five miles without coming upon some of the beautiful lakes, ranging from 5 to 25 miles in length, and about half as wide. People never take cold. Doctors call the climate "distressingly healthy." I sat in an open boat all day, with my boots soaking wet, and never felt worse from it. We are approaching the Sault St. Marie, where this must be mailed.

I am truly yours,

WILL.

1313 SPRUCE STREET,
Monday night, January 30, 1860.

DEAR PHIL.,

Your very, very welcome note I received on Sabbath morning, and much I thank you for it. Also I thank you for your warm and kind congratulations on the return of my dear friends from their travels.* I spent

* M. and her sister had just returned from Europe, where they had been travelling for eighteen months.

about two hours with them on the morning after their arrival. They went up to Milton to see their dying sister next morning, and of course I have not seen them since. M. was to have come down to-night, and if she did I will probably see her to-morrow.

Phil., I feel very much ashamed of myself in that I have apparently neglected you so long; but I trust you know me well enough to be assured that it arises not from anything save necessity. I love you as I ever did, and ever will; and I trust God will long spare us both to become honoured and useful members of society and of His Church. You ask me if I am tired of Sabbath school? Tired! God forbid. I love it more than ever, and rather than shrink back from the work, I would fain seek out some new channel of usefulness. We haven't got long to stay in this world, Phil.—time is very short—there is a very great work to be done, and there are few to do it. God's people must work—they must be ever and always at it. There rests upon me, and upon all of us, a solemn responsibility. I feel it—feel it deeply, and I am not happy unless I am at work for Christ.

And now, Phil., it is almost midnight, and I must close. I am coming to see you some evening this week, if at all possible.

Believe me ever
Your faithful friend,
WILL.

March 7, 1860.

DEAR PHIL.,

Your welcome note I received on Monday. So you have reached the years of manhood. I suppose on the eventful morning you informed your parents "that a man got into the house last night." Accept my warm congratulations on your coming of age. Now that you are your own master, I trust—I am sure—you will feel yourself under even greater obligations to pursue the right path than when under your parents. Although we naturally think and act for ourselves for some years previous to our majority, still, when that time comes, we cannot but feel that we are then entirely dependent upon ourselves, and have not another to think and act for us—except as in a measure a "wife" can. We are exposed to many trials and temptations; but if we take God for our Father, Christ for our Saviour, and the Bible as our guide, we cannot err. Not "All's well that *ends* well," but better, All's well that *begins* well.

Drop me a line and say what evening you will come round, so that I may be at home.

Faithfully yours,

WM. D. STUART.

PHILADELPHIA, *March* 14, 1861.

DEAR PHIL.,

Your welcome letters came duly to hand, and would have been replied to long ere this, but ever since a week or so after the first of the year, when I was out of town, I have been confined to the house with a heavy cold and the usual accompaniments. I have not been in bed all the time, being able now and then to go out and take a walk in the middle of the day. This sickness has been accompanied with great nervousness, so that I could not possibly write a readable letter. To-day I feel better than I have been yet, although I suffer much from blisters on my breast. As soon as I am strong enough I will go away, most probably to my favourite haunt, Minnesota;—it is the greatest place in the world for sick people.

..... Our Mission School comes on swimmingly. We have a larger school, larger prayer-meetings, and a larger corps of teachers than ever before. On New Year's Day we had our Annual Festival: the room was crowded, not with strange children, but with those who are in regular attendance, and with our friends. The children were fed until they could eat no more, and they took the rest away in their pockets.....

Well, Phil., you have found what every young man finds when he is away from home long enough—that there is no place like home.* I knew you would be home-sick, and expected to hear of it before this. Never mind, you will soon be back, and it will make you love your home more, and value it more highly.....

Faithfully yours,

WM. D. STUART.

BLACKPOOL, *July* 4, 1861.

DEAR PHIL.,

Ever since I landed I have been trying to get time to write you, but I have been so busy that it was as much as I could do to get two letters per week written home. Now I have come to this quiet place to settle down for a couple of weeks and enjoy the sea breezes.

* Phil. was at this time in Cuba on business.

If you look on the west coast of England, between the River Ribble and Morecambe Bay, you will see Blackpool. It is a delightful watering-place, where you can be as gay or as sober, as lively or as quiet as you please. The latter suits me much the best, as my object now is health. I have been to London, and consulted with a very eminent physician there. He says I am perfectly sound, and need have no fear of weakness of the chest or lungs. He has, however, directed me to come here in order that I may have the swellings on my neck reduced; the sea atmosphere having a very beneficial effect in such cases.

You will hardly think it credible when I tell you that I have gained thirty-three pounds since I left New York; yet such is the veritable fact; and with the exception of my breast being a little tender from frequent blisterings, I am very well indeed.

You ought to be here in the evening about sunset. There is a promenade, or "Parade," as they call it, extending from the front of our hotel about two miles down the beach: at this time it is crowded with girls, very pretty, for England, and indeed some of them look very sweetly: they have fine, clear, healthy complexions, but are not so beautiful as our American girls.

To-day there is a grand dinner in London, given by Americans in honour of the 4th July. I had an invitation to be present, but declined, not being very bright, and the distance too great. . . . .

There was nothing, dear Phil., that I regretted more on leaving home than not seeing you. I looked every day for the arrival of the *Quaker City*, but was disappointed. It seemed rather hard, that after watching to see you, and expecting you day by day for two weeks, I should after all be disappointed. . . . .

Faithfully yours,

WM. D. STUART.

[Shortly after the breaking out of the Rebellion, his friend Phil. entered the Navy as an engineer. The two letters which follow were written him while attached to the Squadron of the Gulf:—]

PHILADELPHIA, *January* 31, 1862.

DEAR PHIL.,

As I see by the papers that a mail is to be made up to-morrow morning for the Gulf, per steamer *Rhode Island*, I eagerly embrace the opportunity of writing you.

Well, old fellow, how do you like the service of your uncle Samuel? Does it come up to your ideas, and have you concluded to make it a life-long service?

Everything is very quiet here. Since you left we have had our Mission School Festival and Anniversary; which passed off very well. Our school is increasing, and God is abundantly blessing our labours. It makes me feel very happy to see the fruits of our labour; and yet we have to be very careful lest we become proud and forget that it is God, and not ourselves, who has done this. I am becoming more and more impressed with the necessity of those who profess Christ doing all they can, and quickly too, for the promotion of His kingdom. . . . .

You know that I can speak from experience. Let me tell you, you cannot know what the real happiness of this world is until you have the entire love of a Christian woman—one to whom you can at all times go and be sure of sympathy, and who will be able to point you to a comfort above that which the world can give.

May God bless you, is the prayer of

Yours faithfully,

WM. D. STUART.

PHILADELPHIA, *April* 2, 1862.

DEAR PHIL.,

Gulf mails are such irregular things that I do not feel like waiting for an answer to my last, but by way of spending a pleasant half hour and curing a headache, will write again.

I have not been as well as when you saw me. The fact is I do not get enough exercise for a growing boy, and it tells upon me. I am, however, just on the eve of purchasing a "gallant steed;" daily rides upon which will, I have no doubt, make me quite my antique self again. . . . .

It is a not unfrequent query amongst us, "Where is the *Wissahickon?*"* Every arrival from Ship Island I read the news carefully, and see mentioned a dozen or two other vessels of which I never heard, but never hear of yours. I have no doubt you will turn up some fine morning, covered with glory, (at least I hope so).

Gough was here last month, lecturing for the benefit of my Mission School, and we netted the nice little sum of $900.

May God bless you, old fellow, is the earnest prayer of

Yours truly,

WM. D. STUART.

* The name of the ship on which he was serving.

[On receipt of the sad tidings of William's death, Phil. writes :—]

U. S. Steamer "Juniata,"
Fortress Munroe,
April 9, 1863.

To Mrs. Wm. D. Stuart.

My Dear Friend,

I need not tell you how shocked and grieved I was, upon reading the paper this morning, to find I had lost my most valued friend. Of his lovely and lovable disposition I will not speak, for you know that full well; nor of his many traits of character which endeared him to every one. My poor sympathy, in this hour of your distress, is all I can offer, and this I do most sincerely.

Willie was to me a brother in affection, and a true friend in counsel. How well do I remember his many pleadings with me, in years past, to turn from my evil ways to the true Light; and though for a long time I refused his advice, so affectionately urged, he never lost his interest in my spiritual welfare. And when at last I resolved to make a profession of religion, he was the first to bid me God-speed in my new career. We have not lost him, but for a season; for although removed from this earth, we know he is in the mansions of the blessed, and there awaits our coming.

May God bless you in this heavy sorrow, and bind you more closely to Himself; and may you find it true that your affliction, "which is but for a moment, worketh out a far more exceeding and an eternal weight of glory."

Sincerely your friend,
P. H. White.

APPENDIX.

APPENDIX.

ADDRESS OF REV. DR. WYLIE.

T is natural to anticipate the death of the aged. The shock of corn is gathered in its season. The leaves of autumn fall. Evening has come, and the sun sets behind the distant clouds. But here we have one taken away from us whose bright and beautiful morning was just opening upon him; whose "sun has gone down while it was yet day." His position in life; the associations with which he was connected; the near and tender ties which had so recently been established,—all these things rendered life to him most charming and desirable. He felt this. And we might consider that not only was it proper to feel it, but that it would have been sinful had he not recognized the Divine goodness, and gratefully desired that he might still have lived longer. But, while he had this desire, it was in submission to the will of his heavenly Father; and never can we forget his language, when, soon after he had been informed that all hopes of his recovery were gone, after remarking that he would like to live, yet he added, "It is all right. I would have desired to labour longer for Christ. I have felt as if there was still more work for me to do; but I trust I am ready—I hope I am ready." And ere we parted with him on that occasion, in a most tender manner he drew down our bended head to his lips and whispered to us, "Oh, pray for me, that the hope I have may be upon a sound foundation, and that it may be well with me at the last."

And now, while it is natural for us to mourn his early death, we cannot call it an untimely death. The question is not how *long* a man has lived, but, how *well* has he lived; and he had done his work—he had secured the salvation, we have every reason to believe, of his own soul, and he had done good service for the cause of God his Saviour. And therefore we may feel assured that he was ready to depart, and that he has gone now TO BE WITH JESUS.

There was very much in the character of our departed brother to render him an object of love to those with whom he was associated. Naturally he was warm-hearted, generous, frank, and ardent; and we are not surprised that he was almost idolized by those with whom he came in contact and was familiarly associated. He was a person, too, of superior talents; he was fond of the pursuits of literature and of science, and we believe that had he devoted himself to these objects he would have attained to eminence. But he had higher aspirations; and those things which to many are but recreations he aimed to render subservient to the cause and work of Jesus Christ. He devoted himself, we have every reason to believe, with an undivided heart to the service of the Saviour. For him to live was Christ. We know not, indeed, at what time he may have come under the regenerating power of the Spirit of God, but in early life the truths of religion made a deep impression on him. When scarcely fifteen years of age he became a teacher in the Sabbath school connected with the congregation to which he belonged, and afterwards the superintendent of another school—a mission school. Some might have supposed that from his extreme youth he would have proved unfit for such a responsibility; but he manifested that he was equal to its performance. I do not remember ever having heard of one so early in life occupying a position such as this. And yet he discharged its duties so faithfully and successfully, that there never was cause for anything but gratulation that he had undertaken them.

He gave himself thoroughly and fully to any work in which he was engaged, and especially to the work of instructing and benefiting the degraded and neglected ones who formed his mission Sabbath school. That Sabbath school was especially near to his heart. He mentioned, when he was about to depart, that he desired it should be most prayerfully attended to and cherished; that it was a tree he had planted with a great many prayers, and he looked for the fruit to grow. Said he, "I have felt that God was not going to take me away so soon; that he had more work for me to do. I have felt since I was a little boy that the visitation of the sick was my work." It *was* his work, and now it remains his monument.

It was about the sixteenth year of his life that he made a public profession of religion. It was a period of revival in the congregation, and in company with a large number of young persons he gave himself up to the service of the Lord Jesus Christ. And those who witnessed his daily conduct could testify that his profession was sincere and genuine; and now we feel it to be our duty to give this testimony—that he was one who adorned the doctrine of God his Saviour by a walk and conversation becoming the gospel.

It is perhaps two years since the anxious love of friends noticed that his health was declining. Once and again, and a third time, he left his native land, in order that he might be restored. But it was in vain. All that kindness and love and the best of skill could do were of no avail. He came home a few weeks ago, in order that, surrounded by those who loved him so well, where he could see their faces and hear their voices, he might say to them "FAREWELL," and give his testimony for the comfort of those who survived him;—he came home, that he might *die*.

And when we think of the circumstances connected with his departure; when we think that life was so attractive to him, and yet he was so willing to go; and when we think of his sweet composure, and solemnity, and earnestness, and freedom from perturbation and fear of every kind, and his joyful anticipations of the better life—oh! we feel as though those who have been bereaved might rather to-day rejoice than mourn.

May not these parents, whose beloved son has been called away to heaven, well say, "The Lord gave, and the Lord hath taken away; blessed be the name of the Lord?" Oh, what would their highest ambition desire for that dear child beyond, above, nay equal to that he has now attained and is now enjoying? What are the brightest crowns of earth compared with that crown of unfading glory he is wearing now? All their anxieties are relieved. All their fears for his future are dissipated. He has entered into his REST; he has obtained possession of the "inheritance incorruptible, and undefiled, and that fadeth not away, reserved in heaven for them who are kept by the power of God through faith unto salvation."

And may not those from whom a brother has been taken be resigned? Oh, we would say to them, to each one of them—"Thy brother shall live again;" nay, he *is* living *even now*, he is living as really as when he was on the earth—it is merely a change of place and condition—his existence is as actual and his enjoyment is far greater.

Oh, then, may we not give him up, when God has called upon us to make this surrender? May not that stricken one, who has been called to endure a loss so painful as this, be submissive to the will of Heaven? "Thy Maker is thine husband," says the Lord of hosts. "As thy day is, so shall thy strength be." "I will never leave thee nor forsake thee." More treasure than ever before in heaven, and therefore the heart more there also. Oh, what bright anticipations does the removal of those we love to a better land present to us, when we think that after our brief conflict on earth is terminated we shall meet with them again in heaven!

To those who were his friends and associates what a solemn lesson this providence affords! Was he not one of whom it could be said, he acted wisely when he chose that "good part" that should never be taken from him? There were influences which might have turned him in other directions; there were circumstances which might have caused him to make a different choice; but he chose the service of God his Saviour—and never had he reason to regret it. And whatever honours he might have attained, whatever position in society, whatever name among the eminent, learned, or distinguished of any kind might have been his, all these things are as nothing compared with what he now has. If there be, then, those associated with him who have not made a similar choice, I would call upon them now to act, and to act wisely, in view of the eternal world, in view of their souls' best interests. Let all be admonished how uncertain and unsatisfying our life is. Things we love most tenderly, the object of our dearest affection, may be torn away from us at any moment. Let us learn to set our affection on things above, and not on things on the earth. The voice of God speaks to you and says, "Prepare to meet thy God." It is not those who are far advanced in life, who anticipate an early removal from the world, but the youngest here, those in strongest vigour and health, should take warning and feel that they may be called away. Oh, may it be the happiness of every one of us, when *we* shall be separated from those we love, to be able to leave behind us the testimony of our dying lips to the steadfastness of our faith in Christ! May we have that Saviour to support us whose arms of love alone can uphold us as we pass through the swellings of Jordan! Let us consider that we must some time or other grapple with Death, enter into conflict with the king of terrors; and what have we to support us in that hour? Oh, if we have not a Saviour we must perish!

God grant that each of us, admonished by His word, admonished by His providence, may choose Jesus as *our* Redeemer; and we will then find that this God will be our God, and will guide us even unto death; that He will guide us by His counsel while we live, and that afterward He will receive us into His glory.

Happy will it be for *us* if such shall be our condition.

ADDRESS OF REV. DR. BOARDMAN.

I SHOULD not have ventured to add even one word to the excellent Address we have just heard, had I not been providentially present this morning at a scene of touching interest, closely connected with these solemnities. It was the gathering in yonder room of the children and adults comprising the Coloured Sunday School of our departed young friend around the remains of their beloved superintendent. Very affecting it was to witness the mute sorrow of that group of mourners. They had received too many benefits at his hands, they knew too well the unselfish kindness he had lavished upon them, not to feel keenly their great bereavement; and the single thought I have to present is this : It has been announced that the college class-mates of our friend were to attend his funeral. I take it for granted they are present; and I beg to point these young men to the scene I have described. I beg to say to you that the silent tears of these children of Africa are a nobler tribute to his character and worth than you will any of you be likely to secure amidst the mere earthly honours of the most eminent professional career. I cannot answer for those around me, but my own experience supplies no parallel to the case before us. I recall no other instance of a young man born, like William Stuart, to fortune, carefully educated, graced with the generous culture supplied by books and choice companionship and foreign travel, surrounded with all the amenities of social life, and cherished with admiring affection by a wide circle of friends—such a youth turning away from the blandishments of earth, and selecting as the sphere of his activities and his happiness a coloured mission school in a neglected neighbourhood of a great city. With such vigilance did he prosecute this work, and so deeply were his sympathies enlisted in it, that one of the last things he did, before going on board the steamer at New York which was to convey him to the West Indies, was to sit down, in his weakness and sorrow of heart, and write a long, faithful, and affectionate letter, to that most interesting charge, pointing them to the Lamb of God, and entreating them for Christ's sake to be reconciled to God. Can you wonder that they came this morning to take a sorrowing farewell of their cherished teacher and friend? Or can you wonder that I press this bright example upon you for your imitation? I speak to you, young men, "because ye are strong." Go, follow William Stuart, as he followed Christ. Dedicate your strength, your time, your honours, and your lives to the service of Jesus of Nazareth. On every side there are fields white to the harvest. Thrust in your sickles and gather the precious grain into His garner, and you, too, will hear from His lips that heavenly benediction, "Well done, good and faithful servant; enter thou into the joy of thy Lord."

PRAYER OF REV. DR. BOARDMAN.

O LORD, our God, who is like unto Thee? Thy wisdom is unsearchable, and Thy ways past finding out. Thy judgments are a great deep. We bow down before Thy righteous judgments. Thou doest Thy will in the army of heaven, and among the inhabitants of the earth; and none can stay Thine hand, or say unto Thee, What doest Thou?

It has pleased Thee to come near to this family, and sorely to afflict them. Blessed be Thy name for the consolation which Thou hast mingled with their sorrows. We praise and magnify Thy name for Thy love and mercy to Thy young servant; for all his gifts and all his graces; for the love of Christ which was shed abroad in his heart; for the fidelity, watchfulness, and zeal with which he consecrated himself to the glory of God and the good of man. We bless Thee that in Thy good providence Thou didst permit him to lead a life of great usefulness; and we pray that Thou wouldst cause that "tree" which he planted to take root and bear fruit unto eternal life; and in the last great day may he who sowed, and they who, coming after him, shall reap, rejoice together in a glorious harvest.

O Lord, our Father in heaven, Thou who hast afflicted this family, alone canst comfort them. Thou art leading them in a way that they knew not. In the midst of affluence and prosperity, of sweet companionship and all domestic blessings, Thou hast been pleased to bring upon them the shadow of a great sorrow. Enable them with humble and steadfast faith to lay hold upon Thy strength, that they may be supported. Help these beloved parents to say, Thy will be done. Enable them to give into Thy hands the son of their love, whom Thou dost love even more than they loved him. Enable them to give him back to Thee, with all his gifts and all his virtues, feeling that it is a precious sacrifice to lay upon Thine altar, and grateful to Thee for all Thy goodness and loving-kindness to him and to them. Bind up, O Lord, the hearts of this bereaved household. Bless these sisters and these youthful brothers. O that they may have the teachings of Thy Spirit; that they may be drawn to Christ by a Saviour's love. May they follow him who has gone as he followed Christ, and so be prepared for a blessed and eternal reunion with him in the presence of God and the Lamb.

And O God of pity and of grace, here is one other stricken heart before Thee, who comes with nuptial flowers to strew them upon the grave. Wilt Thou comfort her? Enable her in patient submission to bow to this afflictive stroke, rejoicing in all the love she has given and felt—rejoicing still more in the precious consolations of the Gospel of Christ. Enable her humbly and gratefully to feel that union to Christ is an immortal union. Enable her to commit herself into the hands of that Saviour who loved him who has gone with an infinite love, and provided for him in his Father's house a nobler portion than earth could furnish. May Thy everlasting arms be about her. May Thy divine love support her. And may she be enabled to take hold of the promises, which are all yea and amen in Christ Jesus. May she find *peace* in believing.

Look in mercy, we entreat Thee, upon all this family circle. Send consolation wherever Thou hast sent sorrow. Impress upon the hearts of the young men present the solemn and monitory lessons of this providence. Turn off their thoughts from this empty world. May they renounce its pomp, and pleasures, and honours, for the love, and praise, and service of God. O Lord, draw them away from the enticements of earth and sin, that they may choose that good part which shall never be taken away from them.

O God of mercy and of grace, we adore and praise Thee for the love which Thou hast manifested to our lost world. Here, in this house of sorrow; here, gathered around the dead, we praise Thee for the great love wherewith Thou hast loved us: that we have a Saviour who has triumphed over death and hell; one who is mighty to save, and to console; one who is preparing His people, by the discipline of His providence and the teachings of His Word and Spirit, for a blessed reunion in those realms of light and glory into which sin and sickness, sorrow and death, shall never enter. Here would we lay the tribute of our praise and thanksgiving at our Saviour's feet, imploring Thee of Thy mercy to prepare us all to stand at length in Thy presence, washed in the blood of the Lamb, clothed with the righteousness of the Redeemer, and accepted in the Beloved!

Have mercy upon us, and accept and save us in Christ our Saviour. Amen.

ADDRESS OF REV. ALBERT BARNES AT THE GRAVE.

AFTER a few introductory sentences, expressive of joyful triumph over the grave opened before the sad group of mourners, and of the manner of life of the departed, and of his early and complete consecration of himself to the service and glory of Christ, through whom he obtained the great victory, the Rev. Mr. Barnes proceeded to enforce the lessons of the solemn scene upon those around him.

My friends, said he, preparation for usefulness in this life, in its best sense, is preparation for heaven; and the fitness for usefulness which he had while on earth, through the grace of God in Christ Jesus, was a fitness for a higher, a heavenly sphere. That which qualified him so eminently for usefulness on earth, was, through the grace of God and the divine purposes of mercy, a qualification for an entrance among the angels, and among the redeemed of God, the spirits of just men made perfect. That which bound him to so many Christian hearts here by the ties of affection and love, was the same which now qualifies him for being united to the Redeemer in heaven, and for being made happy through everlasting ages!

I regard the very large assemblage gathered together in the house, and this large concourse around this open grave of our departed brother, as a tribute to Christianity—as an expression of the views cherished by those assembled in regard to the value of religion in a young man. Notwithstanding all that there was in his birth, his social position, his prospects in life, his relations to the world—however worthy of attention and respect—yet these would not have drawn together this assemblage on this occasion. It is because William Stuart was a Christian young man, warm-hearted, generous, full of love to God and love to man, that you have gathered here to-day, that you may express not only your interest in him, but your regard for that religion which he commended in his life and death. If we wish our friends to gather around our grave when we are dead, we must show in our lives that there is something in us that makes us worthy to be loved while living, and to be regretted when we die.

We must live for other purposes than for ourselves. We must look out upon the world, upon our suffering fellow-men, and relieve their burdens, lighten their cares, sympathize with them in their trials, if we would wish them to come around our graves, and drop a tear over us when we die.

How impressively does this open grave speak to us respecting the shortness and uncertainty of life! It will not be improper for me to say, that a few short months ago I pronounced in relation to him these words, "What God hath joined together let not man put asunder." But God has put asunder in a little while what we had joined. His hand has done it. There is consolation in the reflection that His grace is sufficient to sustain and to comfort all these stricken hearts to-day.

And how impressively does this scene speak to the Christian young men here assembled! There are not a few young men here who have, like Stuart, devoted themselves to the service of God. Behold now what is the value of religion! What else can avail now? What in life could be of value to him now in this grave? It is religion that imparts consolation to us as we weep; religion that receives our tribute here this afternoon. It is the religion of Christ that draws us here. Oh, let us cherish this religion. Let us also imitate Christ, and imitate our friend as he imitated the Saviour. As we stand here let me entreat you to remember that the grave is before you; that but few steps are left for any of us to take—but few for the bright and healthy young men around me, before they too shall lie in the cold, silent grave. What, therefore, your hands find to do, do it with your might; for there is no wisdom, nor device, nor knowledge in the grave, whither we are going. Bear in remembrance, dear young friends, that whatever may be regretted on the bed of death, you will never regret that you devoted yourselves early to the service of God; that you practised self-denial and sacrifice that you might follow that Saviour who sacrificed Himself for you, and gave His own precious blood that you might live and be useful and happy for ever.

Are there, in this large assemblage, within the reach of my voice, any who are unreconciled to God—who have no religion, no faith in Christ? Oh, let me entreat you to look at this grave, and to remember what is here done. Here, I entreat you, in the name of my

Master, and in view of the eternity before you, to give your youthful hearts to Christ. I entreat you, by all that you behold today; by the last look that you will cast upon the coffin of your dear departed friend; by all that is tender and sacred in religion; by all that is valuable in your own souls, to consecrate yourselves to the service of the Son of God. Be a Christian; live a Christian; live so that you may die a Christian, and win and wear a bright crown in the realms of eternal blessedness.

On the conclusion of Mr. Barnes' remarks, a brief and impressive prayer was offered by the Rev. Dr. Suddards, and the mourning train of sorrowing relatives and friends (though, thanks be to God, sorrowing not as those having no hope), slowly moved away from the quiet resting-place of the dead.

CHILDREN'S GATHERING.

On the afternoon of Sabbath, April 12th, succeeding the death of Willie, a meeting of the Sabbath schools of the congregation was held in the church. The place was filled by a very large and deeply attentive audience. A feeling of solemnity pervaded the entire assemblage. The teachers and children of the Coloured Mission School occupied the middle aisle. The noticeable attention given by the latter to the exercises of the occasion evidenced that they were aware of its solemn nature and import. It needed but a slight effort of memory to recall the appearance of him who had so recently been their superintendent, as on the anniversary occasions of the schools he had met in the same place with the children whom he loved, and who loved him. The comparison of the circumstances under which they had been wont to assemble, and those which now called them together, could not fail to sorrowfully suggest itself to every mind.

After appropriate devotional exercises, the following Addresses were delivered:—

REV. DR. WYLIE'S ADDRESS.

My dear Children, I need not ask you to sit very still and quiet this afternoon. Think what it is that has led to our being here. It is but a few months since these schools were assembled in this place, but under very different circumstances. One was then among the living who is now among the dead. One was then on the earth who is now, we have every reason to believe, in heaven. One then was here in regard to whom we cherished the fond expectation, at that time, that he would live to labour among the beloved children to whose welfare he had devoted himself. But he has gone away from us on earth for ever. We may apply to him the language that was used in reference to the Saviour—"He is not here; he is risen." The voice of Christ came to him saying, "Come up hither." He has left the field of his usefulness and of his service on earth, and he has gone to enter upon the rest remaining for the people of God.

We have no doubt that even in heaven he will think of this Sabbath school, which was his special charge. We have no doubt that even in heaven he will pray for it; for we believe that persons who are in heaven do pray, and we cannot see anything wrong in supposing that they pray, in submission to the will of God, for those whom they left behind them in this world.

Now, my dear children, I feel that you will all cherish with love the remembrance of that dear young man. There were no persons who knew him well who did not love him. There were so many amiable traits of character in him, that, so far as we know, he won the affection of all with whom he associated. And though he might have turned aside to the enjoyments which wealth and position in society would have given him, he chose to devote himself to the service of the Lord Jesus Christ. We have no doubt that if he did not plant the seeds of disease, at least he hastened the result by what he did for this Coloured Mission School. Think of the Wednesday evening and Sabbath evening meetings, which he attended in all kinds of weather;—no matter what might be his own condition, he was sure to be there. Think of the punctuality with which he was present in the Sabbath school; and think of the time and the toil that he devoted throughout to the welfare of that institution. And then remember that not merely did he give and labour for it, but it was the subject of his most earnest prayers. It was founded in prayer. Many a prayer he offered for it; and when he was about to leave this world that Sabbath school was among the last things that he spoke of; and he did not leave the world without making arrangements in regard to its future management, and committing it to those to whom he thought proper to confide the trust. Oh, then, surely we must feel that we ought to cherish his memory.

I will not speak much more about it, because there are others who will refer to the subject more at length; but there is another thing which I have to say this afternoon. Just before I came here I was by the bedside, probably I should say the dying bedside, of one who was for many years a teacher in our Sabbath school, and who had been William Stuart's teacher. He gave me a message for the school: "Let all of them be followers of the Lord Jesus Christ. He is all my salvation, and all my desire." He was very weak. He had just been moved in his bed, and was exceedingly exhausted, and could not say much, but he referred to William Stuart, and mentioned that he had presented many a prayer in his behalf.

And it occurs to us here to mention what encouragement there is to teachers to pray. He prayed for that pupil, and for other pupils, and observe how his prayers have been answered. So, my dear teachers, you may be confident that if you, with earnestness and sincerity, present your petitions at God's throne, you will find that God will give an answer, and you will accomplish the great end and aim at which you are striving—the conversion of the souls of the dear children who are to live for ever, either in eternal happiness or eternal woe.

And now remember, dear children, that there should be this afternoon a most solemn and earnest attention. For my own part, I do not know that I have ever been at a meeting in this church that has affected my own mind with deeper feelings of solemnity than this. Personally, I loved warmly that young man, and I respected him and admired him too, and I would have rejoiced if God had spared him for longer days and greater usefulness. But he is taken away! It is natural for us to mourn. And yet, we ought to be thankful and to rejoice that we feel he has gone to heaven, and is now with Christ, which is far better. I hope there are many in our Sabbath school who will follow his example. I hope many a little boy and many a little girl will try to follow him as he followed Christ; and that all the teachers together will imitate his fidelity and punctuality, and his diligence in every good word and work.

And oh, what a satisfaction that will be to you in a dying hour! I am sure that there was not the least regret, when he was about to leave this world, that he had sacrificed anything, that he had toiled and laboured in the cause of Christ; and though he desired to live, the reason he gave for his desire was, that he might do still more for Christ. He was not weary of the work—he rejoiced that he was permitted to engage in it.

Now sing two verses of the 23rd psalm. You all know it, my dear children, and I think it is a very suitable psalm for the occasion. Let every one sing aloud and with spirit.

Dr. Wylie now introduced the Rev. Dr. Faires to the children, who addressed them as follows :—

REV. DR. FAIRES' ADDRESS.

Dear Children and Teachers, the Lord has seen meet to call away one very dear to us from his work on earth to his reward in heaven. We have therefore met together to express our sorrow that we shall no more on earth see his face or hear his voice.

But we must mourn with submission to the will of God. If a friend has lent us a rare jewel, and permitted us to hold it in our hands and admire its brightness and beauty, when he reclaims it, and extends his hand to receive it from us, shall we strive to keep that which was only lent, and refuse to give back to the proprietor that which is his own? The friend whose early death we lament was such a jewel, beautified by the grace of God with holiness, and bright with manifold virtues. Shall we, then, repine and murmur because the King of heaven has, if we may so speak, resumed possession of his own jewel that he may set it to shine for ever in the crown of our glorious Redeemer?

There is, moreover, a consideration which should greatly alleviate our sorrow. Instability appertains to the things of earth. The most solid and costly structures crumble into ruin—the brightest colours of the most exquisite painting become faint—the grass withers—the flower fades—the rainbow, the beautiful sign of God's covenant, vanishes—the sun will in time grow dim, and the very heavens will pass away with a great noise. Instability, moreover, appertains not only to things material, but extends also to things possessed of moral qualities. Thus human character so frequently changes for the worse, that concerning those we deem the purest and best of men, we can never be certain whether they will continue such to the end of their lives. How often in our experience has the gold become dim, and the most fine gold changed! We are unable to read men's hearts, or to predict the end of their course from its beginning, or to know beforehand what is written in God's book. But when the good and pure have persevered unto the end; maintaining consistency of character; growing constantly in holiness, moral strength, and usefulness; yielding in increasing abundance and variety the fruits of the Spirit, and becoming more and more like Christ,—we know that by death they are removed beyond the reach of temptation and the possibility of sin; and that the moral excellences which they exhibited during life, purified from every taint, are enstamped indelibly upon their souls as their character for eternity.

Believing such things, should we not be comforted in our sorrow, and rather rejoice that our departed friend, freed from all imperfection and sin, and confirmed in holiness, now stands a beautiful pillar in God's heavenly temple, to go no more out?

But without dwelling longer on such topics, I proceed to the special duty assigned to me, and read in your hearing the farewell letter which he wrote to the teachers and children of the St. Mary Street Mission School, only a few hours before he embarked for a distant island seeking restoration of health :—

NEW YORK, *Dec.* 8, 1862.

MY DEAR TEACHERS AND CHILDREN,

It is a matter of the deepest regret to me that I was prevented from meeting with you on last Sabbath afternoon to say farewell. It was not because I have lost my interest in you—far from it. Ever since I was privileged to organize our little mission it has been an object lying very near my heart, and one for which I have daily prayed. Feeling that I have come far short of duty, I nevertheless do feel that whilst my health lasted I endeavoured to do it. God has seen fit, in his all-wise providence, to remove from me this blessing, and I am now about to leave my native land for the third time in search of health. It is a sore trial for me thus to be laid aside and deprived of the delightful labours of the Sabbath school. [The speaker read this sentence again, as a most suggestive one to Sabbath-school teachers.] Though absent in body I will be with you in spirit, and feel sure that while the ocean may separate us, our prayers will meet before a common mercy-seat.

To you, dear teachers, who have given yourselves to this self-denying work, what shall I say? Your work is most solemn and important. The salvation of immortal souls in a degree depends upon your efforts. Be diligent, be earnest, be prayerful. I know there will come many a dark hour, when all entrance to the sinful heart seems cut off, and you are tempted to say, "Ephraim is joined unto his idols, let him alone." Remember then the encouraging words of the Lord Jesus,—"Be thou faithful unto death, and I will give thee a crown of life." "He that turneth many to righteousness shall shine as the stars for ever and ever." Let these words cheer you in your noble work, remove every sadness, and lighten every trial. Remember that though earthly works may fade, the work done for God *it* fadeth not. May God's blessed Spirit be ever nigh unto you; and when death's short way is passed, may you every one receive from your Saviour the welcome summons, "Well done, good and faithful servant; enter thou into the joy of thy Lord."

To you, children, what shall I say? Love your teachers; be regular and punctual in your attendance upon the school; be respectful and obedient to him, and love your superintendent; but above all, learn to love Christ. For this purpose this Sabbath school was opened in your midst. For this your teachers labour and pray. For this God is waiting. As I have often told you when in your midst, all will go for nothing unless you give yourselves to Christ. Remember life is uncertain. Death, judgment, and eternity are before you. Choose, then, for yourselves that better part, which cannot be taken from you. Serve God, and he will not forget you. Love him, trust him, and he will be to you a pillar of cloud by day, and a pillar of fire by night, guiding you safely through this world's wilderness, over the Jordan of death, to that Canaan of eternal rest,

" Where the anthems of rapture unceasingly roll,
And the smile of the Lord is the feast of the soul."

And now, teachers and children, FAREWELL ! Be perfect, be of good comfort, be of one mind, live in peace ; and the God of love and peace shall be with you. And the very God of peace sanctify you ; and I pray God your whole spirit and soul and body be preserved blameless unto the coming of our Lord Jesus Christ.

Yours in Christian bonds,

WILLIAM D. STUART.

Children of the St. Mary Street Mission School, you know in what circumstances these words were written. You perceive how in his weakness and weariness, and amid the confusion and many distractions attendant upon departure from home for a long absence, your kind superintendent remembered you with tender solicitude. Will you not, then, yield to his urgent entreaty, and give your hearts to the Saviour? It was for this he established the mission school, and brought you into it. It was for this he prayed and laboured, in summer and in winter, by day and by night, in health and in sickness. It was for this he wrote the affectionate letter to which you have just been listening.

If, then, you appreciate his devoted, self-denying, and incessant labours for your good—if you remember with gratitude his many acts of kindness—if you fondly cherish his memory—if you desire to see him again—*love Christ.* Thus you will secure for yourselves the highest possible good—the salvation of your souls; thus, and only thus, you may reasonably hope to enjoy the high happiness of at last meeting in bliss and glory the redeemed and beatified spirit of your departed friend.

Teachers of the St. Mary Street Mission School, note well the remarkable sentence in the letter of your late superintendent :—

"It is a sore trial for me thus to be laid aside and deprived of the delightful labours of the Sabbath school." Catch the spirit of these memorable words; imitate the noble example of the writer; and let your labour in the Sabbath school be a delight.

And bear in mind that in your efforts to elevate the degraded, instruct the ignorant, and guide souls to the Saviour, you are imitating the still higher example of Christ, who left the glories of heaven for the humiliations of earth, that He might seek and save them that were lost. Labour, then, prayerfully, lovingly, hopefully, constantly, that you may be instrumental in saving lost souls.

The souls of your pupils, saved by God's blessing bestowed upon your faithful labours, will be your "crown of rejoicing in the presence of our Lord Jesus Christ at his coming."

MR. GRANT'S ADDRESS.

"O that they were wise, that they understood this, that they would consider their latter end!" (Deut. xxxii. 29.)

There is not a boy or girl here this afternoon, I am sure, who does not remember how that kind, loving Hebrew mother, took her little child, and with tender hands laid him in the ark of bulrushes. You remember how his little sister watched the basket as it floated among the flags by the river's brink; how afterwards it was discovered by Pharaoh's daughter; and how, when it was opened, the child wept and touched her royal heart with sympathy. You remember also how Miriam, at the bidding of the princess, called her mother, and how it was given back to her fond embrace, that she might nurse it without constant dread for the safety of its life.

You all know that this little child, when he became a man, was chosen by God to be the leader of the children of Israel from the land of Egypt.

It was he who stretched forth the rod when the Red Sea divided, allowing the people to pass through between its walls of water safe to the other side. It was by his hand the rock was smitten which sent forth water from its flinty sides. For forty years he was their faithful leader; but because of his rebellion at the waters of Meribah, he was not permitted to enter the promised land. He was to behold it from the top of Mount Nebo, but his feet were not to tread upon its sacred soil.

Before this solemn event, however, ere the old man was gathered to his unknown grave, he was commanded to teach the children of Israel a song, that after he was gone it might be a witness for the Lord whom they had forsaken; and as he looked upon the multitude gathered before him, and remembered God's countless mercies, their ingratitude, and the striking circumstances connected with his approaching death, he uttered the language which I have used, and said, "O that they were wise, that they understood this, that they would consider their latter end!"

That, dear children, is my most earnest desire at this time for each one of you; and I know well that could we bring back the beloved one who to-day is in the silent grave, he would express the same idea, and earnestly long that every child beneath this roof might be a possessor in early youth of that true wisdom which alone can comfort and sustain during life, and in the dying hour. Nothing can effectually do this but a firm resting upon the blood and righteousness of Jesus, that precious Redeemer on whom our dear friend trusted while he lived, and as he was passing across the dark river of death.

What a foolish thing it is to put off the salvation of the soul till you grow up! You may never be men or women. I suppose you have all sometimes looked with reverence upon an old man. You have seen his white hair, and furrowed cheeks, and trembling hands, and perhaps have said to yourselves he must be 60, or 70, or 80 years old, while I am but 6, or 7, or 14; and as you think of the long years between him and you, you resolve that you will wait till you are as old as he is before you prepare for death and eternity. Oh, dear children, this is not wise. It is wise to seek Christ early, and having found him, be prepared to die. You have all watched on a summer's day the beautiful butterfly winging its way in the sunshine; some of you may have cruelly chased it as it fluttered from place to place. You have also seen the busy humming-bee plying its weary task, "gathering honey all the day from every opening flower." Both seem alike to be enjoying themselves, but how differently are they occupied! the one lives for the present, the other for the future; and when the storms of winter are sweeping over the earth, the butterfly's beauty and its life are gone, while the careful bee is safely sheltered and provided for within its honied cells. The butterfly is a striking emblem of those who bestow all their thoughts and care upon the perishing body and the fleeting things of this world, while the bee illustrates well those who are anxious about the immortal soul and its eternal happiness.

Oh, dear children, hear the voice of God in this mysterious providence. It is very hard, indeed, to understand why he, so manly, so noble, so vigorous, so full of Christian earnestness and zeal, should thus be stricken down in early manhood; but, to use his own words, "It is all right." So far as he was concerned, he felt perfectly satisfied that *all was well.* The flower dies ere the fruit appears; the seed rots in the ground ere the root, the stem, the branches, the fruit is seen: even so may it be that in the death of him whose loss we mourn to-day the life of many may be traced.

In the early removal of one of our Sabbath school superintendents the Lord is teaching us the solemn lesson, that the day of labour and of grace is passing away. He would have the teachers to understand more fully the necessity of working while it lasts; and the children, that the tongue which tells them of a Saviour's love may soon be silent in death.

How often, dear children and Christian friends, do we forget our latter end! Whether we forget it or not, how swiftly is it approaching! In a very little we like him shall die. Oh, that when the hour of death comes, when the shadows of this life are departing and eternity stands before the mind as a great reality, when we feel that the cords which bind us to earth are being severed, we may, as he did, be able to say, "I know that my Redeemer liveth!"

What are earth's pleasures at this solemn hour?

> "Oh, pleasures past! what are ye now,
> But thorns about my bleeding brow;
> Spectres that hover round my brain,
> And aggravate and mock my pain?"

It is not so with the pleasure afforded by a life of labour in the Lord's vineyard. Oh, no! it plants no piercing thorn in the pillow of death.

But on Monday last, a few hours before his death, I said to him,

"Willie, I am sure you do not regret now that you have laboured for Christ." Gathering his remaining strength he exclaimed with remarkable emphasis, "Oh, no!—never!—never!"

A favourite illustration of his was this: In a certain European town there once lived a painter, who was observed by those who passed his little studio almost constantly seated at the canvas. Being asked why he laboured so earnestly and continually, he answered, "I am painting for eternity!" Mr. Stuart was the only one I ever heard relate this, and looking back from this point upon his short and useful life, one cannot but conclude he lived under the same impulse. I speak not this to pronounce an eulogy upon the dead; he needs no eulogy from my stammering tongue—his works praise him. Why is it that his memory is so precious? Why is it graven upon my heart as with "an iron pen, and lead in the rock for ever?" It is not because his prospects and position in society were bright and exalted, but because he was an active, earnest, vigorous, talented fellow-labourer in the cause of God.

Brethren! young men of this church! let me most earnestly call upon you, now that one of our number has fallen, now that that standard-bearer lies voiceless in the dust, to buckle on anew the Christian armour, and work for Jesus with energy while the day of labour lasts. Let us support our Sabbath schools, not with a feeble life, but vigorously; let us labour as those who are placed in this world not to live for ourselves, but for our race, and for God, and for eternity.

Not long since I met with a very beautiful incident conveyed in exquisitely poetical language. The writer of the lines represented himself as lingering near a wayside path, on a quiet summer's eve. The sun had just gone down, and all nature seemed retiring to rest. His attention was arrested by a little girl returning from a spring of water close by, with a well-filled pitcher upon her head. She was a lovely child: her hair hung in graceful ringlets around her neck; the pitcher was supported by her tiny hand; and as she lightly tripped along, her sweet voice filled the evening air with a joyous song. A little plant was blooming by the road-side—the hot sun had caused its tender flowers to droop; the dear child noticed it, and stepping aside, she lowered the pitcher from her head, poured a few refreshing drops upon the flower, and passed on to her cottage home.

It was a simple act, but it affords an admirable illustration.

We are travellers passing along life's highway. If we are God's children, we are filling our pitchers day by day with blessings at the never-failing spring of His boundless mercy and love: let us not pass on to our Father's house above bearing that pitcher erect upon our heads, never seeking to drop its refreshing waters upon our suffering and sin-stricken fellow-men; but let us lift the pitcher of salvation down and press it to the lips of the perishing, yea, even to the lips of the youngest, humblest, poorest child, and tell them of Jesus. As that little flower revived when the water fell upon it, so shall they revive. They will lift up their eyes towards you and bless you; and far more than even the blessing of them that are ready to perish shall be a glorious entrance into that peaceful, happy home,—

> "Where the labourers rest for ever
> 'Mid the white-robed angel band."

May it be ours, dear friends, to imitate the example of dear William Stuart. May God's grace fill our hearts as it filled his. May we be inspired with like earnest desires for the glory of God, and whether the sun of our life goes down while it is yet day, or after we have travelled along the dusty highway of time for a long course of years, it matters not; we will then gather our feet upon our bed and die, and enter upon the joys of eternity and the fellowship of beloved friends who are now parted from us by the hand of death.

May God's richest blessings rest upon our Sabbath schools, especially upon that one which Mr. Stuart loved so much. Oh that the children may be early sheltered beneath His wings who said of Jerusalem, "How often would I have gathered thy children together, even as a hen gathereth her chickens under her wings!"

www.ingramcontent.com/pod-product-compliance
Lightning Source LLC
LaVergne TN
LVHW010131110826
845151LV00002B/326

* 9 7 8 1 4 2 5 5 4 0 3 4 0 *